Write Powerful Rust Macros

Write Powerful Rust Macros

SAM VAN OVERMEIRE

MANNING
SHELTER ISLAND

For online information and ordering of this and other Manning books, please visit
www.manning.com. The publisher offers discounts on this book when ordered in quantity.
For more information, please contact

    Special Sales Department
    Manning Publications Co.
    20 Baldwin Road
    PO Box 761
    Shelter Island, NY 11964
    Email: orders@manning.com

Manning Publications Co. 20 Baldwin Road PO Box 761 Shelter Island, NY 11964	Development editor: Karen Miller Technical editor: Andrew Alexander Lilley Brinker Review editor: Kishor Rit Production editor: Andy Marinkovich Copy editor: Kari Lucke Proofreader: Katie Tennant Technical proofreader: Geert Van Laethem Typesetter and cover designer: Marija Tudor

ISBN 9781633437494
Printed and bound by CPI Group (UK) Ltd, Croydon, CR0 4YY

brief contents

1 ■ Going meta 1

2 ■ Declarative macros 12

3 ■ A "Hello, World" procedural macro 41

4 ■ Making fields public with attribute macros 57

5 ■ Hiding information and creating mini-DSLs with function-like macros 78

6 ■ Testing a builder macro 97

7 ■ From panic to result: Error handling 128

8 ■ Builder with attributes 163

9 ■ Writing an infrastructure DSL 203

10 ■ Macros and the outside world 235

contents

preface   xi
acknowledgments   xiii
about this book   xiv
about the author   xvii
about the cover illustration   xviii

1 Going meta   1

1.1   A day in the life of a Rust developer   2

1.2   What is metaprogramming?   3

1.3   Metaprogramming in Rust   4

> *Macro galore   5 ▪ Appropriate use cases   6 ▪ Unfit for purpose: When not to use macros   10*

1.4   Approach of this book   10

1.5   Exercise   11

2 Declarative macros   12

2.1   Creating vectors   13

> *Syntax basics   13 ▪ Declaring and exporting declarative macros   14 ▪ The first matcher explained   15 ▪ Nonemtpy matchers   15*

2.2   Use cases   19

> *Varargs and default arguments   19 ▪ More than one way to expand code   20 ▪ Newtypes   23 ▪ DSLs   28 ▪ Composing is*

easy 31 ▪ Currying, on the other hand . . . 34 ▪ Hygiene is
something to consider as well 35

2.3 From the real world 36

2.4 Exercises 38

3 A "Hello, World" procedural macro 41

3.1 Basic setup of a procedural macro project 42

3.2 Analyzing the procedural macro setup 45

3.3 Generating output 48

3.4 Experimenting with our code 50

3.5 cargo expand 51

3.6 The same macro—without syn and quote 52

3.7 From the real world 54

3.8 Exercises 55

4 Making fields public with attribute macros 57

4.1 Setup of an attribute macro project 58

4.2 Attribute macros vs. derive macros 59

4.3 First steps in public visibility 60

4.4 Getting and using fields 61

4.5 Possible extensions 66

4.6 More than one way to parse a stream 67

Delegating tasks to a custom struct 67 ▪ Implementing the Parse
trait 69 ▪ Going low, low, low with cursor 71

4.7 Even more ways to develop and debug 72

4.8 From the real world 73

4.9 Exercises 76

5 Hiding information and creating mini-DSLs with function-like macros 78

5.1 Hiding information 79

Setup of the information-hiding macro 79 ▪ Recreating the
struct 81 ▪ Generating the helper methods 83

5.2 Debugging by writing normal code 88

5.3 Composing 89

5.4   Anything you can do, I can do better   93

5.5   From the real world   94

5.6   Exercises   96

6 Testing a builder macro   97

6.1   Builder macro project setup   99

6.2   Fleshing out the structure of our setup   101

6.3   Adding white-box unit tests   103

6.4   Black-box unit tests   105

*A happy path test   105 ▪ A happy path test with an actual
property   107 ▪ Testing enables refactoring   112 ▪ Further
improvements and testing   116 ▪ An alternative approach   119
Unhappy path   122*

6.5   What kinds of unit tests do I need?   123

6.6   Beyond unit tests   124

6.7   From the real world   126

6.8   Exercises   127

7 From panic to result: Error handling   128

7.1   Errors and control flow   129

7.2   Pure and impure functions   130

7.3   Alternatives to exceptions   132

7.4   Rust's Result and panics   135

7.5   Setup of the panic project   137

7.6   Mutable or immutable returns   139

7.7   Getting results   140

7.8   Don't panic   145

*Changing the panic into a Result   145 ▪ Debugging
observations   148*

7.9   Error-handling flavors   149

*Using syn for error handling   150 ▪ Using proc_macro_error
for error handling   155 ▪ Deciding between syn and
proc_macro_error   159*

7.10   From the real world   159

7.11   Exercises   162

8 Builder with attributes   163

8.1   A rename attribute   164

    Testing the new attribute   164 ▪ Implementing the attribute's behavior   165 ▪ Parsing variations   168

8.2   Alternative naming for attributes   170

8.3   Sensible defaults   173

8.4   A better error message for defaults   177

8.5   Build back better   179

    Avoiding illegal states and the type state pattern   179 Combining the builder pattern with type state   182

8.6   Avoiding scattered conditionals   190

8.7   Attribute tokens and attributes   192

8.8   Other attributes   197

8.9   From the real world   199

8.10 Exercises   201

9 Writing an infrastructure DSL   203

9.1   What is IaC? What is AWS?   204

9.2   How our DSL works   205

9.3   Parsing our input   207

    Project setup and usage examples   207 ▪ Implementing the Parse trait for our structs   209

9.4   Two alternative parsing approaches   215

    Using Punctuated with a custom struct   215 ▪ Using Punctuated with a custom enum and builder   218

9.5   Actually creating the services   221

9.6   The two AWS clients   225

9.7   Errors and declarative macros   229

9.8   The right kind of testing   231

9.9   From the real world   231

9.10 Exercises   234

10 Macros and the outside world   235

10.1 A function-like configuration macro   236

    Macro project structure   236 ▪ Code overview   237 Using full paths   240

10.2   Adding another macro   242

10.3   Features   243

10.4   Documenting a macro   248

10.5   Publishing our macro   250

10.6   From the real world   253

10.7   Where to go from here   258

10.8   Exercises   258

appendix   *Exercise solutions*   *259*

index   *291*

preface

You are your own forerunner, and the towers you have builded are but the foundation of your giant-self. And that self too shall be a foundation.

— Kahlil Gibran

Like many developers, I have grown fond of the Rust language—not per se because of the language's great performance characteristics but because of its sound fundamentals, powerful type system, and excellent tooling. And while it may be a hard language to learn, there are a lot of guides available for getting started, including many books, tutorials, and videos. When it came to procedural macros, I felt a bit in the dark, though. Introductions and tutorials on that subject were short or partial. Peculiar, considering the vast number of libraries that were using macros for all kinds of amazing functionality!

So, after a lot of toying around with macros, I thought I could bring together what I had learned along the way, turning it into a book—a book that would take its reader on a journey from the simplest example of a procedural macro to things that could, almost, find a place in real applications. I started writing. After creating a raw draft of about a hundred pages, I contacted Manning to ask whether they were interested. They too thought that this subject was worthy of a book, and they wanted to give me a chance to write it for them. That meant more writing, the exploration of additional ideas and suggestions, and rewrites after feedback, all of which has led to the book you see before you now.

Macros have their challenges: they can be hard to write and hard to read, especially for a newcomer. They also add complexity, as well as dreaded compilation time. But time and time again, Rust developers have found ways in which macros prove their worth.

"It is divine for mortals to help each other," as (my imperfect paraphrase of) Pliny the Elder would have it. I hope that this book, and the journey contained within, will be of some help to you in the fearless utilization of Rust's macros.

acknowledgments

First, I thank my wife, Annelies, for your love and support, as well as my father, Marc, and mother, Marleen. I will love you until the end of my days. Second, I thank my two brothers, sister, grandmother Rafaella Otte, family, and friends, among them Joost Barclay, Thomas Wijnendaele, and Bernard Vanderhaeghen in particular. I have also been fortunate to encounter many talented, kind, fun colleagues at every company I have ever worked at. They have all proven to be very tolerant when it comes to my very annoying habit of pointing out the things "Rust does better" than other languages.

All the people from Manning that I interacted with have been welcoming, friendly, and helpful from day one. Specifically, I would like to thank my development editor Karen Miller, technical editor Andrew Lilley Brinker, review editor Kishor Rit, production manager Aleksandar Dragosavljević, production editor Andy Marinkovich, copyeditor Kari Lucke, and proofreader Katie Tennant.

Finally, thank you, my reviewers: Alessandro Campeis, David Jacobs, David Li, Etienne de Maricourt, Guillaume Schmid, Horaci Macias, Irach Ramos, Jakub Guzikowski, Jaume López, Jonathan Reeves, Lev Veyde, Mehmet Yilmaz, Nick Keers, Olivier Stas, Rui Liu, Sandeep Sandhu, Scott Ling, Simone Sguazza, Vojta Tuma, and William E. Wheeler. Your feedback was both kind and useful, and this book is better, more helpful, and more polished than it could ever have been without you.

about this book

The goal of this book is to teach the advantages, disadvantages, and common use cases of Rust macros. The reader will learn what makes `#[derive(Debug)]` work, how `tokio` transforms an asynchronous `main` function, or how `yew` checks HTML for errors. They will write macros to avoid boilerplate and duplication or Domain-Specific Languages that make everyone else's life easier and—this is Rust after all—safer. Tests will help you ensure the correct behavior of those macros, while precise error messages give users a great idea of what goes wrong when they leave the happy path. Debugging issues arise frequently, and it's an experience that teaches us to better handle issues with other people's macros. As a bonus, the reader will probably pick up some additional knowledge about a load of other programming topics.

Who should read this book?

> *If Hello, World! did print, congratulations! [...] That makes you a Rust programmer.*

That, at least, is what the Rust documentation states after the obligatory "Hello, World" example. This book, unfortunately, has a bit more stringent requirements. Its reader should at least be familiar with the syntax and building blocks of the language: structs, functions, modules, traits, control flow—basically, knowledge of the first 10 chapters of *The Rust Programming Language* (by Steve Klabnik and Carol Nichols; No Starch Press, 2018) will be taken for granted. The book also assumes some basic familiarity with declarative macros, sometimes called "macros by example" (the kind of macro you create with `macro_rules!`). If that is not you but you would still like to read this book, first, read an introductory Rust text. Right now! And maybe a couple more from Manning, for example, *Rust in Action* by Tim McNamara (2021) and *Learn Rust in a Month of Lunches* by David MacLeod (2024).

How this book is organized: A roadmap

This book contains 10 chapters:

- Chapter 1 introduces metaprogramming. It talks about when you should use macros but also when you should instead turn to Rust's more basic building blocks, like functions and structs.
- Chapter 2 talks about declarative macros, starting with the basics and then moving on to examples and use cases.
- Chapter 3 is when we turn to procedural macros. We write our first derive macro, which generates a simple "Hello, World" method.
- Chapter 4 teaches the reader to use attribute macros to change the fields of a struct.
- Chapter 5 shows the flexible and powerful function-like macros, the final type of procedural macro, in action.
- Chapter 6 talks about (unit) testing a macro, using a derive macro that generates a builder as its leading example.
- Chapter 7 will help you understand error handling and giving error feedback to users.
- Chapter 8 goes back to the builder example from chapter 6, using it to show how we can use attributes to make a macro more flexible.
- Chapter 9 lets the reader write a Domain-Specific Language that can create actual infrastructure in the cloud.
- Chapter 10 finishes up by telling the reader about feature flags, documenting, publishing, and possible next steps.

Readers are advised to go through the book linearly, though chapter 2 can be skipped by people who are only interested in learning about procedural macros. All other chapters build on the knowledge acquired in earlier ones. Doing the exercises is useful but not essential, as they are a recap of the chapter—meaning that if they touch on anything not discussed in the main text, the lessons learned will be repeated in one of the next chapters. You can find solutions in the appendix.

About the code

This book contains many examples of source code both in numbered listings and in line with normal text. In both cases, source code is formatted in a `fixed-width font like this` to separate it from ordinary text.

In some cases, the original source code has been reformatted; we've added line breaks and reworked indentation to accommodate the available page space in the book. Code annotations accompany many of the listings, highlighting important concepts.

You can get executable snippets of code from the liveBook (online) version of this book at https://livebook.manning.com/book/write-powerful-rust-macros. The complete code for the examples in the book is available for download from the Manning website at www.manning.com and from GitHub at https://github.com/VanOvermeire/rust-macros-book. In the toolchain of the repository, you will see that everything was written in stable Rust 1.75.0, 2021 edition. The most recent versions of libraries—at the time of writing—like `quote` and `syn` were used, and those versions are noted in the text.

liveBook discussion forum

Purchase of *Writing Powerful Rust Macros* includes free access to liveBook, Manning's online reading platform. Using liveBook's exclusive discussion features, you can attach comments to the book globally or to specific sections or paragraphs. It's a snap to make notes for yourself, ask and answer technical questions, and receive help from the author and other users. To access the forum, go to https://livebook.manning.com/book/write-powerful-rust-macros/discussion. You can also learn more about Manning's forums and the rules of conduct at https://livebook.manning.com/discussion.

Manning's commitment to our readers is to provide a venue where a meaningful dialogue between individual readers and between readers and the author can take place. It is not a commitment to any specific amount of participation on the part of the author, whose contribution to the forum remains voluntary (and unpaid). We suggest you try asking the author some challenging questions lest his interest stray! The forum and the archives of previous discussions will be accessible from the publisher's website as long as the book is in print.

about the author

 **SAM VAN OVERMEIRE** is a software developer with a background in history and archaeology. He has 10 years of experience working as a cloud engineer, writing code in languages such as Java, JavaScript, Python, Groovy, and Go. He is the author of multiple books, scientific articles, and blog posts about programming and other topics.

About the technical editor

ANDREW LILLEY BRINKER is a lead cyber security engineer at MITRE, where he works on software supply chain security. In his spare time, he develops in, writes about, and teaches Rust. He holds an MCS from Rice University.

about the cover illustration

The figure on the cover of *Write Powerful Rust Macros* is captioned "Devineresse de Krasnoyarsk," or "Soothsayer of Krasnoyarsk," taken from a collection by Jacques Grasset de Saint-Sauveur, published in 1797. The illustration is finely drawn and colored by hand.

In those days, it was easy to identify where people lived and what their trade or station in life was just by their dress. Manning celebrates the inventiveness and initiative of the computer business with book covers based on the rich diversity of regional culture centuries ago, brought back to life by pictures from collections such as this one.

Going meta

This chapter covers

- What metaprogramming is
- Metaprogramming in Rust
- When to use macros
- What this book will teach you

Macros are some of the most important and powerful tools Rust has to offer. Because they have powers that Rust's normal tooling (like functions) lacks, they can serve as "a light in dark places when all other lights go out." That of itself is enough to make macros a core topic of this book. They have another neat quality though: they can be a pathway to other abilities. When you want to write a macro, you need knowledge of testing and debugging. You have to know how to set up a library because you cannot write a *procedural macro* without creating a library. Some knowledge about Rust internals, compilation, types, code organization, pattern matching, and parsing also comes in handy. Thus, teaching about macros allows me to talk about a variety of other programming topics. We will be learning about Rust macros and using them to explore other subjects.

But we are getting ahead of ourselves. Let's take a step back and start from the beginning.

1.1   A day in the life of a Rust developer

You are a Rust developer, starting a new application that will accept JSON requests containing user data, like first and last names, and output useful information, say, the user's full name. You start by simply adding a function that generates a full name based on a combination of first and last names, using `format!`. To turn JSON into a `struct`, you annotate `Request` with `#[derive(Deserialize)]`. And you always write tests, so you add a function for testing, annotating it with the `#[test]` attribute. To make sure everything matches your expectations, you use `assert_eq!`. And when something goes wrong, you either turn to a debugger or add some logging with `dbg!`.

Listing 1.1   The program you just wrote

```rust
use serde::Deserialize;

#[derive(Deserialize)]          A procedural
struct Request {                macro
  given_name: String,
  last_name: String,
}

fn full_name(given: &str, last: &str) -> String {
  format!("{} {}", given, last)
}

fn main() {
  let r = Request {
    given_name: "Sam".to_string(),
    last_name: "Hall".to_string()
  };
  dbg!(full_name(&r.given_name, &r.last_name));
}

#[cfg(test)]
mod tests {
  use super::*;

  #[test]
  fn test_deserialize() {
    let actual: Request =
      serde_json::from_str("{ \"given_name\": \"Test\",
    \"last_name\": \"McTest\" }")
          .expect("deserialize to work");

    assert_eq!(actual.given_name, "Test".to_string());
    assert_eq!(actual.last_name, "McTest".to_string());
  }
}
```

This bit of code contains several declarative macros.

And suddenly it dawns on you. Even when writing the simplest of Rust code, you just cannot stop using macros. You are surrounded by the fruits of Rust's *metaprogramming*.

1.2   *What is metaprogramming?*

In brief, *metaprogramming* is when you write code that will use other code as a data input. That means you can manipulate existing code, generate additional code, or add new capabilities to an application. To enable metaprogramming, Rust has macros, which are a specific form of metaprogramming. Rust's macros run at compile time, expanding into "normal" code (structs, functions, and the like). When this process is complete, your code is ready for the next step, such as being linted, type-checked (`cargo check`), compiled into a linkable library, or transformed into a—runnable— binary by `rustc` (see figure 1.1).

```rust
#[derive(Deserialize)]
struct Request {
    given_name: String,
    last_name: String,
}
```

Expands to

```rust
struct Request {
    given_name: String,
    last_name: String,
}
#[doc(hidden)]
#[allow(non_upper_case_globals, unused_attributes, unused_qualifications)]
const _: () = {
    #[allow(unused_extern_crates, clippy::useless_attribute)]
    extern crate serde as _serde;
    #[automatically_derived]
    impl<'de> _serde::Deserialize<'de> for Request {
        fn deserialize<__D>(__deserializer: __D) -> _serde::__private::Result<Self, __D::Error>
        where __D: _serde::Deserializer<'de> {
            struct __FieldVisitor;
            impl<'de> _serde::de::Visitor<'de> for __FieldVisitor {
                type Value = __Field;
                fn expecting(
                    &self,
                    __formatter: &mut _serde::__private::Formatter,
                ) -> _serde::__private::fmt::Result {
                    _serde::__private::Formatter::write_str(__formatter, "field identifier")
                }
                fn visit_u64<__E>(self, __value: u64) -> _serde::__private::Result<Self::Value, __E>
                where
                    __E: _serde::de::Error,
                {
                    match __value {
                        0u64 => _serde::__private::Ok(__Field::__field0),
                        1u64 => _serde::__private::Ok(__Field::__field1),
                        _ => _serde::__private::Ok(__Field::__ignore),
                    }
                }
                fn visit_str<__E>(
                    self,
                    __value: &str,
                ) -> _serde::__private::Result<Self::Value, __E>
                where __E: _serde::de::Error {
                    match __value {
                        "given_name" => _serde::__private::Ok(__Field::__field0),
                        "last_name" => _serde::__private::Ok(__Field::__field1),
                        _ => _serde::__private::Ok(__Field::__ignore),
                    }
                }
                fn visit_bytes<__E>(
                    self,
                    __value: &[u8],
                ) -> _serde::__private::Result<Self::Value, __E>
                where __E: _serde::de::Error {
                    match __value {
                        b"given_name" => _serde::__private::Ok(__Field::__field0),
                        b"last_name" => _serde::__private::Ok(__Field::__field1),
                        _ => _serde::__private::Ok(__Field::__ignore),
                    }
                }
        // 170+ lines hidden!
            }
        }
};
```

Figure 1.1   I contain multitudes! How our simple example hides many more lines of code, generated by macros.

Rust is not the only language to offer metaprogramming capabilities. C and Clojure also have powerful macros, with C also offering templates. Java has reflection to manipulate classes, which famously allowed the Spring framework to develop some of its most impressive capabilities, including using annotations for dependency injection. JavaScript has `eval`, a function that takes in a string as data that will be evaluated as an instruction at run time. In Python, you get `eval` as well as better options like metaclasses and the very popular decorators, which can manipulate both classes and functions.

1.3 *Metaprogramming in Rust*

At some point in their career, most programmers will come into contact with a form of metaprogramming—often to do things that would be hard to do with normal coding tools. But unless you write a lot of Common Lisp or Clojure, where macros are very popular, on average such experiences are bound to be limited. So why on earth should we care about metaprogramming in Rust? Because Rust is *different*. This is something you have heard too many times before, but hear me out!

The first difference from many other languages is that, similar to Clojure, it is hard to imagine Rust code without macros. Macros are used extensively in both the standard library (think of the ubiquitous `dbg!` and `println!`) and custom crates. At the time of writing (mid-2024), among the top 10 downloaded packages on crates.io, three are for creating procedural macros (`syn`, `quote`, and `proc-macro2`). One of the others is `serde`, where procedural macros ease your serialization work. Or search for the keyword "derive," which often signifies that the package has a macro. You will get back over 10,661 results, about 7% of all packages! In brief, in Rust macros are not just some syntactic sugar but core functionality.

Why are so many people writing macros? Well, in Rust they offer a very powerful form of metaprogramming *that is also relatively easy and safe to use.* Part of that safety comes from being a compiled language. Compare that with Clojure, a difficult language (in my opinion) that makes macros easy to use but without the aid of any compile-time checking. The same can be said for JavaScript and Python. And for JavaScript, safety/security is an important reason for the "Never use direct `eval()`" advice in the Mozilla documentation (http://mng.bz/4JMv).

Meanwhile, all of Rust's macros are evaluated at compile time and have to withstand the *thorough* checks that the language employs to verify code. This means that what you generate is as safe as normal code, and you still get to enjoy the compiler telling you exactly why you are wrong! Especially for *declarative macros*, *hygiene* is part of that safety, avoiding clashes with names used elsewhere in your code. This means you get more safety than you would get with C macros, as these are unhygienic, allowing macros to unintentionally reference or capture symbols from other code. C macros are also less safe since they are expanded when type information is not available. Templates are safer, though the errors you get back can be cryptic.

Another advantage of doing everything at compile time is that the performance effect on your final binary is, in most cases, negligible. You are adding a bit of code.

Nothing to lose sleep over. (Meanwhile, there is an obvious effect on compile times, but those are annoyingly long with or without macros.) Compare that to Java, where the aforementioned Spring framework does *a lot* of reflection at startup for dependency injection. This means performance takes a hit, and metaprogramming becomes—I'm sounding like a broken record—less safe because you only find out if everything works at run time, perhaps only when you go to production.

Finally, for me, metaprogramming can sometimes be too "magical," with a Spring Bean in one part of your application altering behavior in an entirely different part. And while Rust macros may *seem* magical, there is less of Spring's, to paraphrase Einstein, "spooky action at run time." That is because macros in Rust are (a) more localized and (b) run at compile time, allowing for easier inspection and better verification.

1.3.1 *Macro galore*

To make the localized argument more concrete, let me introduce one of the main protagonists of this book, the procedural macro. Procedural macros *take a piece of your code as a stream of tokens and return another stream of tokens,* which will be processed together with the rest of your code by the compiler. This low-level manipulation stands in contrast to the approach of the better-known declarative macros (which feature in the next chapter). Those allow you to generate code using a higher ("declarative") level of abstraction. This makes declarative macros a safe and easy option to get started with—even if they lack the raw power of their procedural brothers.

> **NOTE** Streams of tokens, expanding macros: as you may have guessed, we will talk about all of this in more depth in the upcoming chapters.

There are three kinds of procedural macros (see figure 1.2). First are *derive macros.* You use them by adding a #[derive] attribute to a struct, enum, or union. When that is done, the code of that struct/enum/union will be passed as an input to your macro. This input is not modified. Instead, new code is generated as an output. These macros are for extending the capabilities of types by adding functions or implementing traits. So whenever you see #[derive] decorating a struct, you know it is adding some kind of additional functionality *to that specific struct.* No functionality is added to some random part of your application, and neither is the struct modified in any way. Despite (or maybe because of) these limits, these are probably the most widely used procedural macros.

Attribute macros, the second type, can be placed on structs, enums, and unions as well as trait definitions and functions. They get their name from the fact that they define a new, custom attribute (one well-known example is #[tokio::main]), whereas derive macros are required to use #[derive]. They are more powerful and thus more dangerous because they transform the item they are decorating: the output they produce replaces the input. Whereas derive macros are only additive, with an attribute macro, the definition of your type might change. But at least the annotation is telling you what struct it is transforming and is not changing other code and other files.

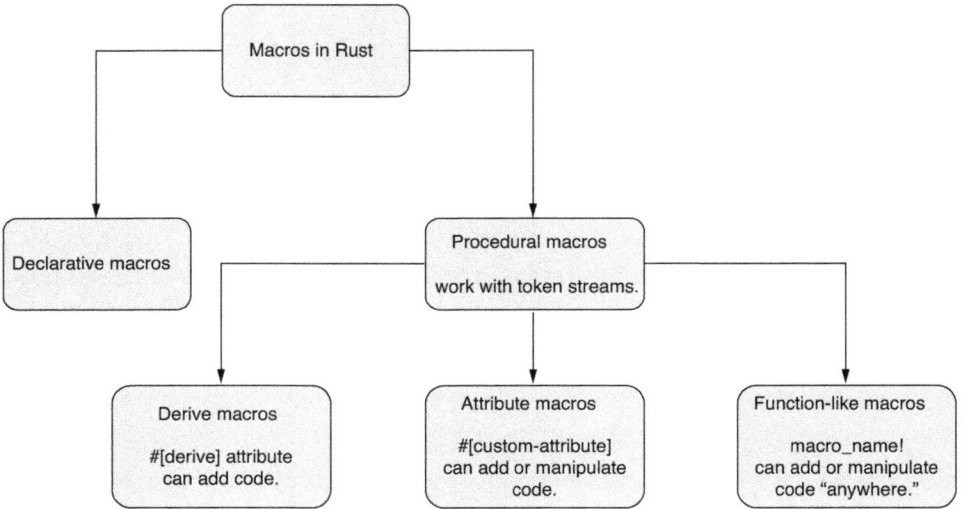

Figure 1.2   The types of macros in Rust

The third kind of procedural macro is called *function-like*. This one is invoked with the ! operator and works with any input you pass in. That input will disappear, replaced by what you generate as output, quite similar to attribute macros. But unlike the others, a function-like macro is not limited to annotating things like structs or functions. Instead, you can call it from almost anywhere within your code. As we shall see, this can produce some powerful magic. But—you probably already know where I am going with this—the input of that magic is whatever you decided to pass along. Rust, once again, seems to have found a way to take a known programming concept and make it safe(r) to work with.

1.3.2   *Appropriate use cases*

"Okay, so since macros are so great and safe, I should use them everywhere for everything." Wow, slow down there, straw man! Obviously, you should start any application without turning to *custom* macros. *Zero to Production in Rust* (https://www.zero2prod.com/index.html) built an entire deployable newsletter application without ever writing a macro. (The author uses a lot of those that are provided by the language and its libraries, though.) Structs, enums, and functions are just easier to understand and use, plain and simple. And while macros won't have a lot of effect on run-time performance, they still add to compile times and binary size. And the former is already the biggest pain point reported by Rust developers! For small macros, like the examples in this book, that compile-time cost is negligible. But for many "production-grade" macros, the tradeoff will be real—but hopefully worth it.

When and why would you use macros? In larger applications, they might be tempting to use for reducing boilerplate. But that might make the code harder to understand for people unfamiliar with the project because, compared to a function, the signature of a macro gives no insight into what is happening. In addition, your readers are bound to have more experience mentally parsing ordinary Rust code, so even if they have to "dive into" a function definition, it will take them less time to get the gist of it. And generic functions are a great tool for avoiding duplication, so they offer a valid alternative. Similarly, generic implementation blocks—or blanket implementations—are very powerful. Just look at the crazy piece of code in listing 1.2, an example of the "extension trait" pattern, combining a custom trait with a blanket implementation. We implement our trait for everything that implements `Copy`. Numbers, characters, Booleans, etc., suddenly have a new function available. We should probably be afraid of using blanket implementations as well as macros.

Listing 1.2   The powers and dangers of generics

```
trait Hello {
    fn hello(&self);
}

impl<T:Copy> Hello for T {
    fn hello(&self) {
        println!("Hello world");
    }
}

fn main() {
    2.hello();
    true.hello();
    'c'.hello();
}
```

So, the first takeaway: avoiding boilerplate, as well as duplication, is a good reason to use macros, but only if it doesn't make the code hard to understand. And if, in order to use the macro, developers often look at the implementation, that's bad. Consider the macros offered by the standard library: `Debug`, `Clone`, `Default`, etc. They all do the grunt work for one well-defined, repetitive task (e.g., `Clone` does only one thing: it makes your object cloneable). As a bonus, developers reading your code will immediately grasp your intent when they see the `#[derive(Clone)]` attribute. And they probably won't care about the actual details of how this is done. This is perfect, as it avoids the additional mental strain involved in diving into the code. This approach to avoiding duplication is far better than the automatic code generation offered by some languages. Yes, code generation might help with writing code by adding useful boilerplate to your application. But it adds noise and makes it *harder to read* the code. And writing is often not the difficult part of programming. Making things understandable for those who come after you is.

> **NOTE** I was reading about the `Decode` trait that `sqlx` offers and instinctively thought: "That trait probably has a derive macro, seems like a perfect use case." Lo and behold, there was indeed a derive macro available.

So look for repetitive tasks that are very easy to describe from a bird's-eye view ("clone this, copy that, print it") and whose output will be predictable (debug prints *every* property of your struct). These are often tasks with a universal appeal, useful in many applications and easy to understand. For example, making sure that something can be compared to others of the same kind (`PartialEq`) is a common task that most developers have been confronted with. Functions can help fight duplication as well, but they can't manipulate structs or add helper methods. (Blanket implementations can, but they are limited to working through traits.) Outside the standard library, you can find a lot of other examples that help you avoid duplication and boilerplate while being easy to describe and producing predictable results. Serde allows for easy serialization/deserialization of structs. Tokio manages the boilerplate involved in creating an `async main` for you.

Another reason to turn to macros, closely related to the previous category, would be ease of use. You want to take away the uninteresting technical details of a task that developers do not need to know about when they are writing an application. You could argue that Serde and Tokio belong to this category since they hide the details of serialization and asynchronous behavior. Only rarely will you have to look under the hood of these macros; most of the time they will "just work." How won't matter—once again, a win for both the reader and the writer. Also worth mentioning is Clap, which hides the details—and boilerplate—of parsing command-line arguments, and Rocket, which uses macros to hide REST application complexities.

One final use case is simulating capabilities that are not available in Rust. We will see an example of how declarative macros add varargs to the language in the next chapter. Outside the core language, Tokio is again worth mentioning as it enables you to have asynchronous main functions. But there are lots of other examples in this category. Static assertions also make guarantees about your code without ever running it, checking, for instance, whether a struct implements given traits. SQLx lets you write SQL strings, checks whether they are valid at compile time, and transforms the results into structs. Yew and Leptos allow you to write type-checked HTML within Rust. Shuttle sets up cloud infrastructure for you based on annotations. Obviously, a lot of these offer validation at compile time. After all, that is when your macro will run. But it is also the most interesting time to check and verify before you start doing more expensive, time-consuming things to verify your code, like unit testing, integration testing, end-to-end testing, or even testing in production (see figure 1.3). All of these have their place in modern application building. However, when a simple `cargo check` can point out errors before a single test has run, you are saving yourself a lot of time and effort. In addition, everything you do at compile time is a performance win for your users.

Besides verification, macros from this category add *Domain-Specific Language* (DSL) capabilities that allow you to write code in an easier, more elegant way than would be possible with native Rust. Using macros for DSLs is also interesting for application developers who want to enable easier expression of ideas in a way that is closer to the

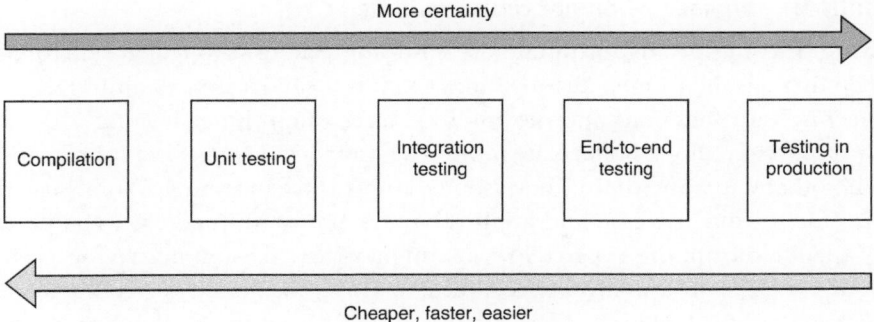

Figure 1.3 Spectrum of testing

language of the business experts. When done well, this type also belongs to the ease-of-use category.

> **DEFINITION**   What is a Domain-Specific Language (DSL)? The programming languages with which we programmers are most familiar are general-purpose languages, applicable to practically any domain. You can use JavaScript to write code regardless of the sector you are working in. But DSLs are written with a specific domain in mind. Think of SQL, which is designed specifically for interacting with databases. That means the creator can focus on making business concepts easier to express. If you were writing a language for use by banks, you might make it very easy for developers (or even end users) to write code that transfers money between accounts. A DSL can also allow you to optimize. If you were writing one for working with DNA, you could assume you would only need four letters (A, C, G, T) to represent your data, which could allow for better compression (and since A always pairs with T and G with C, maybe you would only need two options). DSLs come in two varieties: some are created entirely from the start, and others are created by using a general-purpose language like Rust as a base. In this book, we are interested in the latter.

To summarize, macros are a great fit when you are confronted with a task that has a predictable output, whose details are irrelevant to (most) developers, and that needs to be performed frequently. Additionally, macros are the best or only choice for extending the language and writing elegant or complex DSLs. In other cases, you probably want to turn to functions, structs, and enums. For example, avoiding the duplication of filtering and mapping incoming data in two or three places calls for a function, not a new macro.

> **NOTE**   If you do find a good use case for a procedural or declarative macro, do a (Google) search before you start coding. Someone may have beaten you to the punch.

1.3.3   *Unfit for purpose: When not to use macros*

When it comes to inappropriate use cases for macros, two categories come to mind. The first was mentioned already: things that you can easily accomplish with functions. Starting with functions and moving to macros when things become too complicated or require too much boilerplate is often a good idea. Don't try to overengineer things. The other category where I have some doubts is business logic. Your business code is specific to your use case and application. So almost all publicly available macros are disqualified from the get-go. Now you might write a custom macro for use inside your company. But in a microservice world, sharing business code between services and teams is often a bad idea. Your idea of a "user," "aircraft," "basket," or "factory" within a microservice will differ from that in the next microservice. It's a road paved with good intentions that leads to confusion and bugs or customization of an already custom macro. There are exceptions to this category, though. First, in larger codebases, macros could help you avoid some rare business boilerplate. Second, we already noted how DSLs can improve your quality of life as an application engineer—especially in a complex domain. And macros are a great tool for writing DSLs.

One final—but minor—point to keep in mind before we move to the next section: *integrated development environment* (IDE) support for macros will always be less advanced than that for "normal" programming. This is pretty much an unavoidable downside. With more powerful tools come more options. That makes it harder for your computer to guess what you can and cannot legally do. Imagine a programming language whose only valid statement is `2 + 2 = 4`. An IDE would be *incredibly* helpful in pointing out mistakes ("You typed b - @? !, did you mean 2 + 2 = 4?") and giving code completions. Now imagine a language where everything is allowed. Does `struvt Example {}` have a typo? Maybe, maybe not. Who knows? This is also why it is harder for an IDE to help you when you work with dynamic languages; that is, types are helpful for the machine too! A type system limits your options, and that can limit the power of your language. But it can offer things like more safety, performance, and ease of use in return.

In the case of procedural macros, one additional complexity is that your IDE has to expand the code in the same way that Rust would. Only that way can it tell you whether the fields or methods you *think* will be added by a macro are actually there. IntelliJ, RustRover, and Visual Studio Code (to a lesser extent) do this, as we will briefly discuss in a later chapter, but even so, their advice can still run into trouble when expansion fails, at which point they should report back to the user with details on what went wrong. But that is easier said than done. Where, for example, should they point to when it comes to that error?

1.4   *Approach of this book*

The approach of this book can be summarized as example driven and step by step. Most chapters will have one application as a central theme to explore a macro topic as well as other relevant themes from Rust. Starting with a simple "Hello, World," we will add layers of knowledge, piece by piece: how to parse, how to test, how to handle errors. We will also point out common errors that you might run into and give you some debugging hints. Finally, the chapters will briefly point out how popular crates (including those mentioned in this chapter) use the explained techniques or accomplish specific feats. This will give you insights into how you can apply what you have learned. Finally, while the next chapter will give a pretty thorough overview of declarative macros, the rest of the book will focus on the procedural ones, mainly because the latter are harder to use, and there is already a lot of useful content on the former.

Exercise

Think of a recent application that you worked on. Can you think of places where duplication and boilerplate were unavoidable? Did you have the feeling you were lacking a tool to make the application easier to use? Was there something that could not be done within the constraints of the language? Hopefully, by the end of this book, you will think of macros as one possible tool for fixing such problems.

Summary

- Metaprogramming allows you to write code that generates more code.
- Many languages offer some way to do metaprogramming, but these tools are often difficult to use and not well integrated into the language, which can lead to hard-to-understand or buggy code.
- Rust's macros are powerful and avoid many of these shortcomings, with a focus on safety and without real effect on run-time performance.
- Macros in Rust are "expanded" into code checked by the compiler.
- Rust has high-level declarative macros and three kinds of procedural macros (derive macros, attribute macros, and function-like macros) that process code as a stream of tokens.
- Metaprogramming should not be your first choice when solving problems, but it can help you avoid boilerplate and duplication, make your applications easier to use, or do things that are difficult to do with "normal" Rust.
- This book will explore macros, all the while using them to discuss other advanced subjects through an example-driven approach.

Declarative macros

2

This chapter covers

- Writing declarative macros
- Avoiding boilerplate and duplication, implementing newtypes, writing simple domain specific languages, and composing functions
- Understanding the `lazy_static` crate

We will start this book in easy mode with declarative macros. These macros have a syntax that will immediately remind you of pattern matching, with a combination of *matchers* and *transcribers*. The matchers contain what you want to match against; the transcriber has the code you will generate when you find that match. It's just that simple.

> **NOTE** This chapter's focus is a broad overview of declarative macros and their usage. This stands in contrast with the rest of this book, where we will focus on specific topics and a limited number of examples. The reason is that declarative macros are not the main focus of this book, and I expect the reader to know more about them than procedural macros. That means we can go through the subject of this chapter more quickly.

2.1 Creating vectors

But wait, this is an example-driven book! That means we should drag a first example into this. vec! is used in several beginner's explanations of declarative macros. We will go through a *simplified* implementation that shows how the aforementioned matchers and transcribers work together to generate the correct kind of code output for any given situation.

Listing 2.1 my_vec, our first declarative macro

```
macro_rules! my_vec {        ◁──┐  We declare a new           () is our first matcher. Since it
    () => [                       macro called my_vec.        is empty, it will match a macro
        Vec::new()                                            call without any arguments.
    ];                     ◁──
    (make an empty vec) => (                        Everything between the pair of square
        Vec::new()          ◁──                     brackets is the first transcriber. This is what
    );               ◁──                            we will generate for an empty invocation of
    {$x:expr} => {                                  our macro. Note the semicolon at the end.
        {
            let mut v = Vec::new();                 (make an empty vec) is our second
            v.push($x);                             matcher. It will match when our input
            v                                       literally matches "make an empty vec."
        }
    };                                              This is our second transcriber, this time
    [$($x:expr),+] => (                             between parentheses. We generate the same
        {                                           output as before, in the first transcriber.
            let mut v = Vec::new();
            $(                                      The next two matcher-transcriber pairs.
                v.push($x);                         The first accepts one expression (expr)
            )+                                      and will bind it to x. The second accepts
            v                                       multiple expressions separated by a
        }                                           comma. These will similarly be bound to x.
    )
}

fn main() {
    let empty: Vec<i32> = my_vec![];
    println!("{:?}", empty);
    let also_empty: Vec<i32> = my_vec!(make an empty vec);   These two print [ ].
    println!("{:?}", also_empty);
    let three_numbers = my_vec!(1, 2, 3);      This one
    println!("{:?}", three_numbers);    ◁──┘   prints [1, 2, 3].
}
```

2.1.1 Syntax basics

You start your declaration of a declarative macro with macro_rules!, followed by the name you would like to use for the macro, similar to how you would create a function by writing fn followed by a function name. Inside the curly braces, you put the desired matchers and transcribers. A matcher and its transcriber are (similar to the syntax of pattern matching) separated by an arrow: `(matcher) => (transcriber)`. In this case, we have four pairs of matchers and transcribers. Our first pair consists of an empty matcher, represented by some empty brackets, and a transcriber whose content is wrapped in square brackets. Square brackets are not a requirement though: for both matcher and transcriber, you have your choice of brackets: `()`, `{}`, and `[]` are all valid. You need to pick one of these three alternatives though, as removing them entirely (e.g. `() => Vec::new()`) will lead to Rust getting confused. It will start complaining about the double colons: `no rules expected the token ´::´`. If you remove those, it becomes more helpful, saying that the "macro's right-hand side must be delimited"— that is, by using brackets!

> **NOTE** The alert reader will notice that every pair in the example has a differ-
> ent syntax. This is only intended as a demonstration of your options regard-
> ing brackets. Your code will look cleaner if you settle for *one* of these options.
> Which one should you pick? Going for the curly braces can have the down-
> side of making your code a bit less clear if you have code blocks within your
> transcriber (see the second pair in listing 2.1). And square brackets seem to
> be the less popular choice, so parentheses are probably a good default.

Another important syntactic element is that the pairs are separated by a semicolon. If you forget to do this, Rust will complain:

```
5 |      {$x:expr} => {
  |      ^ no rules expected this token in macro call
```

This is its way of saying that there should not be any rules if you end a matcher-transcriber without a semicolon. So keep adding them as long as you have more matcher-transcriber pairs coming. When you get to your last pair, the semicolon is optional.

2.1.2 *Declaring and exporting declarative macros*

A limitation to consider is that declarative macros can only be used after they have been declared. If I had placed the macro below the main function, Rust would complain like this:

```
error: cannot find macro `my_vec` in this scope
 --> src/main.rs:5:25
  |
5 |      let three_numbers = my_vec!(1, 2, 3);
  |                          ^^^^^^
  |
  = help: have you added the `#[macro_use]` on the module/import?
```

Once you start exporting macros, this is no longer a problem, because `#[macro_use]` on top of a module or import (e.g., `#[macro_use] mod some_module;`) adds the macros to the "`macro_use` prelude." In programming, a *prelude* is used as a term for the collection of things from the language that are globally available for coding. For example, `Clone` (`#[derive(Clone)]`) does not require an import because it is in

Rust's prelude. When you add a #[macro_use], the same becomes true for macros from the chosen import: available everywhere, without an import. So the tip from the previous error message will solve the error, albeit by using a cannon to kill a mosquito. Also, this is *the "older way" of exporting macros, and it is no longer the recommended approach.* But we will get to that.

When you need to invoke your macro, you use its name followed by an exclamation mark and arguments between brackets. Similar to the macro itself, during invocation you can have any bracket you like, as long as it is normal, curly, or square. No doubt you have often seen vec![], but vec!() and vec!{} are also valid, though curly brackets do not seem to be very popular for brief invocations. In this book, you will see me use curly braces for multiline quote! calls throughout.

2.1.3 *The first matcher explained*

Now that we have covered the basic syntax, here is our first matcher again:

```
() => [
    Vec::new()
];
```

Since our matcher is empty, it will match any empty invocation of our macro. So when we called let empty: Vec<i32> = my_vec!(); in our main function, this is the matcher we ended up in, since (a) Rust goes through the matchers from top to bottom and (b) we did not pass anything in within the brackets. We said that the content of the transcriber is located between the (in this case, square) brackets, so that means Vec::new() is the code that Rust will generate when we have a match. So, in this case, we are telling it that we want to call the new method of the vector struct. This piece of code will be added to our application in the location where the macro was called.

That brings us back to the first call in main. Rust sees my_vec!() and thinks, "An exclamation mark! This must be a macro invocation." And since there are no imports in our file, this is either a macro from the standard library or a custom one. It turns out to be a custom one because Rust finds it in the same file. With the macro found, Rust starts with the first matcher, which turns out to be the correct one. Now it can replace my_vec!() with the content of the transcriber, Vec::new(). So by the time you do anything with your code (check, lint, run, etc.), let empty: Vec<i32> = my_vec!(); has already changed to let empty: Vec<i32> = Vec::new();. This is a minor but important detail: since only my_vec!() is being replaced, the semicolon at the end of the statement remains where it is. Because of this, we did not need to add one to our transcriber.

2.1.4 *Nonemtpy matchers*

Let's turn to the second matcher, which looks like this:

```
(make an empty vec) => (
    Vec::new()
);
```

In this case, the matcher contains *literal values*. This means that to match this particular "arm" of the macro, you would need to put that exact literal value between brackets when calling the macro, which is what we do in the second example from our main function: `let also_empty: Vec<i32> = my_vec!(make an empty vec);`. Our transcriber has not changed, so the output is still `Vec::new()` and the code becomes `let also_empty: Vec<i32> = Vec::new();`. In this case, the literals do not add anything interesting. But we will see some more useful sample cases later on.

The next pair is more interesting:

```
{$x:expr} => {
    {
        let mut v = Vec::new();
        v.push($x);
        v
    }
};
```

This time we are telling Rust that we want it to *match any single Rust expression* (`expr`) and *bind it* to a value called x. The dollar sign preceding x is significant, since it signifies that this is a *macro variable*. Without it, Rust thinks that this is just another literal, in which case there would be exactly one match (i.e., `my_vec![x:expr]`). Besides expressions, which are a common target for matching, you can also match identifiers, literals, types, and so on.

Metavariables

`expr` is called a *metavariable* in Rust lingo, or *fragment specifier*. The most powerful of these metavariables is `tt` (`TokenTree`), and it will accept almost anything you pass to it. That's a powerful option. But its comprehensiveness can also be a downside. For simpler types, Rust can catch mistakes, like when you pass in a `literal` while the macro only matches an `ident`. Plus, with `tt` your matchers become less fine-grained since this one is screaming "Give me anything you've got!" For the very same reason, `tt` can be overeager. There is really a lot that will match a token tree! This is somewhat similar to regexes. `\d+`, which will only capture one or more digits and is less powerful than `.*`, which will capture anyone and anything. But a limitation is also an advantage, making `\d` more predictable and easier to manage. In the case of metavariables, it is advisable to start with a more concrete type and only move up to things like `tt` when that proves necessary. And if you do need it, think and test carefully.

The following is a list of all the fragment specifiers. Don't worry; we will only use a limited subset of these to accomplish this chapter's goals:

- `block`—A block expression; that is, statements between curly braces.
- `expr`—An expression; a very wide variety of things within Rust.
- `ident`—An identifier or keyword. For example, the start of a function declaration (`fn hello`) has a keyword followed by an identifier, and we can capture them both by using `ident` twice.

- `item`—Things like structs, enums, imports ("use declarations").
- `lifetime`—A Rust lifetime (`'a`).
- `literal`—A literal, like a number or a character.
- `meta`—The content of an attribute, so `Clone` or `rename = "true"`. You get a good idea of what an attribute might contain in later chapters.
- `pat`—A pattern. `1 | 2 | 3` is one example.
- `pat_param`—Similar to `pat`, except it can have | as a separator. So the rule (`$first:pat_param | $second:ident`) will work, but (`$first:pat | $second:ident`) tells you that | is not allowed after `pat`. This also means you need to do some extra work to parse `1 | 2 | 3` with `pat_param` (as it sees three separate tokens instead of one).
- `path`—A path; things like `::A::B::C`, or `Self::method`.
- `stmt`—A statement; for example, an assignment (`let foo = "bar"`).
- `tt`—A `TokenTree`; see the previous explanation.
- `ty`—A type, for example, `String`.
- `vis`—A visibility modifier; `pub` comes to mind.

Within the transcriber, we are creating a new vector, adding the input expression, and returning the entire vector, which now contains the expression as its only element. This is basic Rust code with only two things worth mentioning. The first is that we have to use the dollar sign within the transcriber as well. Remember, with $ we have identified `x` as a macro variable. So what we are telling Rust is to push this variable, which was bound to the input, into the vector. Without the dollar sign, Rust will tell you that it `cannot find value x in this scope` because there is no `x`, only `$x`.

The second thing to note is the extra pair of curly braces. Without those, Rust gives you back an error saying `expected expression, found let statement`. The reason becomes clear once you try to mentally substitute the macro call with its output. Take this example, which should match our current rule: `let a_number_vec = my_vec!(1);`. We know that `my_vec!(1)` will be replaced with the content of the transcriber. So since `let a_number_vec =` will stay in place, we need something *that can be assigned to a* `let`— say, an expression. Instead, we are getting back two statements and an expression! How is Rust supposed to give that to `let`? Once again, the error sounded cryptic, but it makes perfect sense. And the solution is simply to turn our output into a single expression. The curly braces do just that. The following is the code after our macro has run:

```
let a_number_vec = {
    let mut v = Vec::new();
    v.push(1);
    v
}
```

Yes, writing macros does require some thinking and (a lot of) tinkering. But since you have chosen Rust, you know that thinking is definitely on the menu.

We are now almost past the basics! The final matcher-transcriber pair is
`$[($x:expr),+] => (:`

```
    {
        let mut v = Vec::new();
        $(
            v.push($x);
        )+
        v
    }
)
```

This is basically the same one as before, except with more dollar signs and some
pluses. Within our matcher, we can see that `$x:expr` is now wrapped with `$( )`,`+`. That
tells Rust to accept "one or more expressions, separated by a comma." As a program-
mer, it will not surprise you to hear that in addition to a `+`, you can use a `*` for zero or
more occurrences and `?` for zero or one. Like macros, regular expressions are everywhere. A slight gotcha is that this will not match an input with a trailing comma.
`my_vec![1,2,3]` will work, whereas `my_vec![1,2,3,]` will not. For that, you need an
extra rule (see the exercises at the end of this chapter).

Inside the transcriber, the only thing that has changed is that a similar dollar-
bracket-plus combo is surrounding our push statement, except, this time, without the
comma. Here, too, this indicates repetition. "For every expression from the matcher,
repeat what is inside these brackets." That is, write a push statement for every expression that you found. That means `my_vec![1,2,3]` will generate three push statements.

> **NOTE** By now it might be obvious that the third matcher-transcriber pair is
> covered by this pair. But that additional pair made it easier to explain things
> step by step.

There are a lot of alternatives that *won't* compile. For example, maybe you were hoping that Rust would be smart enough to figure out by itself that you want to push every
expression into the vector. So you remove the `$()+` from `$(v.push($x))+`—only to be
greeted by `variable x is still repeating at this depth`. With "repeating," the compiler is telling you that `x` contains more than one expression, which is a problem since
your code seems to assume you only have one expression to push into the `Vec`.

And if you like playing around with this code, like one of my reviewers, you will
eventually discover that you can use any repetition operator you want within the transcriber, regardless of the one in your matcher. You can do a push with `?` and `*` and
everything will work as expected, for now at least, since this is an open bug in Rust
(see https://github.com/rust-lang/rust/issues/61053 for some context). If you want
to make sure your code won't break because of this in a future version of the language, you can add the `#![deny(meta_variable_misuse)]` lint to your file, which
may, however, trigger false positives.

One final point before we end this section: what happens when you try to do illegal
things inside a macro? What if you try to mix integers and strings as input, something

a `Vec` cannot accept? Your integrated development environment might not realize that anything is amiss. After all, it's all valid expressions being passed in! But Rust is not fooled because it generates "normal" code from the "rules" of your macro. And that code has to obey Rust's compilation rules. This means that you will get an error `expecting x, found y` (with the names depending on what you passed in first) if you try to mix types.

Now that you have seen the basics, we can move on to more interesting stuff.

2.2 Use cases

In this section, we will show common ways declarative macros increase the power of applications. In some cases, their utility is straightforward: they help you avoid writing boilerplate code, as we will see in our *newtypes* example. But other examples show you how we can do things with macros that are hard or impossible to do in any other way, like creating DSLs and fluent composition of functions or adding additional functionality to functions. Let's get started.

2.2.1 Varargs and default arguments

First, how about when we bump into the limits of functions? For example, unlike Java or C#, Rust functions do not allow variadic arguments. One reason might be that variadic arguments make the compiler's life harder. Or it could be that it is not an important enough feature. Apparently, the discussion about adding them to the language is very old and extremely contentious (and the same goes for default arguments!). Be that as it may, if you do need varargs, there are always macros. In fact, our vector macro performs this exact trick. Pass in any number of arguments, and Rust will generate code to handle your needs.

If you are coming to Rust from one of the many, many languages that permit overloading or default arguments, macros have you covered as well. For example, I have a function for greeting, and I would like it to default to "Hello" while also allowing more creative, custom salutations. I could create two functions with slightly different names to cover these cases. But it's a bit annoying that the names would differ when they offer the same functionality. Instead, we will write a `greeting` macro.

Listing 2.2 Greeting people, with defaults, in `greeting.rs`

```
pub fn base_greeting_fn(name: &str, greeting: &str) -> String {
    format!("{}, {}!", greeting, name)
}

macro_rules! greeting {
    ($name:literal) => {
        base_greeting_fn($name,"Hello")
    };
    ($name:literal,$greeting:literal) => {
        base_greeting_fn($name,$greeting)
    }
}
```

For the first time in this chapter, our implementation is not located in the same file as our main function. Instead, it is placed in a separate file called `greeting.rs`. To use the macro outside the file with its definition, we have to put `#[macro_use]` above the module declaration that we add in `main`.

Listing 2.3   Example usage of our greeting macro in `main.rs`

```
use crate::greeting::base_greeting_fn;          ⊲──┐  Imports
                                                    base_greeting_fn
#[macro_use]
mod greeting;                    ⊲───────────────────  Imports the module that contains our macro. With
                                                        the annotation #[macro_use], we tell Rust that we
fn main() {                                             want to import macros that are defined in that file.
    let greet = greeting!("Sam", "Heya");
    println!("{}", greet);                       ⊲──┤  Prints "Heya, Sam!"
    let greet_with_default = greeting!("Sam");
    println!("{}", greet_with_default);          ⊲──┤  Prints "Hello, Sam!"
}
```

In a more complicated setup, with `mod.rs` importing and reexporting modules, you will need to put the annotation both in the "root" (your `main.rs` file) *and* any `mod.rs` files that do reexporting. But don't worry: Rust will keep complaining with `have you added the #[macro_use] on the module/import?` until you fix all of them. It can be tedious at times, but this focus on keeping things private unless they are explicitly made public does force you to think about information hiding. But, as we previously mentioned, this is the older way of exposing macros. Instead, you should prefer a "use declaration" for reexporting the macro—for example, `pub(crate) use greeting`. This is the approach you'll encounter in more recent Rust code.

Note that we had to make our `base_greeting_fn` function public (and import it into our `main.rs`). When you consider it, the reason is once again obvious: our declarative macro is *expanded in our main function*. In the previous section, we already learned that we can mentally take the content of our transcriber and replace the invocation with that content. In this case, `greeting!("Sam", "Heya")` is replaced by `base_greeting_fn`. And if `base_greeting_fn` is not public, you are trying to invoke an unknown function. This behavior might not be what you desire (because you might want the macro to be the entry point to all your holiday greetings), but it is a logical consequence of the way macros and visibility work in Rust.

2.2.2 *More than one way to expand code*

We interrupt this broadcast to talk a bit more about expanding, a more official term for "replacing with the content of the transcriber," because while replacing content in your mind is great, sometimes you want to see what is really going on. To help with that, Rust has a nice feature called *trace macros* (itself a declarative macro—turtles all the way down). They are still unstable in Rust 1.77.2, the most recent version of Rust at the time of writing, which means you have to activate them as a feature and run your code with the nightly build. You can do that with `rustup default nightly`, which sets nightly as your default. Or—if you would like to stay with a stable version of Rust—you can instruct Cargo to run a specific command with nightly using `cargo +nightly your-command`.

The following code shows how to activate and deactivate the trace macros feature.

Listing 2.4   Using the trace macros feature

```
#![feature(trace_macros)]                    ◄─┐  Adds the unstable trace
                                               │  macros feature
use crate::greeting::base_greeting_fn;

#[macro_use]
mod greeting;

fn main() {                            ┌─ Activates the
    trace_macros!(true);          ◄────┘  trace macros
    let _greet = greeting!("Sam", "Heya");
    let _greet_with_default = greeting!("Sam");  ┐  Deactivates the
    trace_macros!(false);         ◄──────────────┘  trace macros
}
```

This is our code from before with the `println!` statements removed and calls to `trace_macros!` added. With `true`, they are activated; with `false`, they are disabled. In our case, deactivation is not strictly necessary since we have reached the end of our program in any case. Running this code will print something like this:

```
--> ch2-trace-macros/src/main.rs:9:18
   |
9  |      let _greet = greeting!("Sam", "Heya");
   |                   ^^^^^^^^^^^^^^^^^^^^^^^^^
   |
   = note: expanding `greeting! { "Sam", "Heya" }`
   = note: to `greeting("Sam", "Heya")`

--> ch2-trace-macros/src/main.rs:10:31
   |
10 |      let _greet_with_default = greeting!("Sam");
   |                                ^^^^^^^^^^^^^^^^^
   |
   = note: expanding `greeting! { "Sam" }`
   = note: to `greeting("Sam", "Hello")`
```

The logs show our default at work! `greeting!("Sam");` is apparently transformed to `greeting("Sam", "Hello")`. How ingenious. The trace macros feature is now doing all the substitution work for us, which can save a lot of mental effort.

Another occasionally useful tool is the `log_syntax!` macro (also unstable in 1.77.2), which allows you to log at compile time. If you have never written macros before, you may not have considered why this might be important. As a minor demonstration, we can add a third option to our greeting macro. This third option uses log_syntax to tell the user what arguments were received, calls println! to inform them that the default greeting was returned, and calls the greeting function. All of this is wrapped in an additional pair of braces. That is because our macro has to return *a single expression* to bind to let. And by adding that second pair of braces, we create one expression by enclosing the two statements and the expression.

Listing 2.5 Using log syntax

```
macro_rules! greeting {
    ($name:literal) => {
        base_greeting_fn($name,"Hello")
    };
    ($name:literal,$greeting:literal) => {
        base_greeting_fn($name,$greeting)
    };
    (test $name:literal) => {{
        log_syntax!("The name passed to test is ", $name);
        println!("Returning default greeting");
        base_greeting_fn($name,"Hello")
    }}
}
```

We are using log_syntax! to log our input.

Double braces because we want to surround this generated code with { }, thereby creating just a single expression as our output

In our main file, nothing much has changed. We have added another feature and a macro invocation that will end up in our third matcher:

```
#![feature(trace_macros)]
#![feature(log_syntax)]

use crate::greeting::greetingu;
#[macro_use]
mod greeting;

fn main() {
    trace_macros!(true);
    let _greet = greeting!("Sam", "Heya");
    let _greet_with_default = greeting!("Sam");
    let _greet_with_default_test = greeting!(test "Sam");
    trace_macros!(false);
}
```

Log syntax is unstable, so we need to activate it with a feature.

We invoke the new branch of our greeting macro.

Now if you run this with cargo +nightly check, you will see the log_syntax! output (The name passed to test is Sam) because it is executed at compile time. Only when we invoke cargo +nightly run will we see both the log syntax output and the println! statements that we added inside the macro. This difference is important for anyone debugging things that happen at compile time. Using the former, you can debug declarative macros via print statements (objectively the best kind of debugging). Together, these tools allow you to trace the route from macro to expanded Rust code. It is not the power of a real debugger, but it is certainly better than nothing. It's a pity that you have to use nightly Rust. Later, we will see some tooling that works with stable Rust versions.

2.2.3 Newtypes

Another way declarative macros can help you is by avoiding boilerplate and duplication. To explore that theme, we will introduce *newtypes*. Newtypes are a concept from the world of functional programming. Essentially, they are a "wrapper" around an existing value that forces your type system to help you avoid bugs. Say I have a function that calculates pay raises. The problem with that function is that it not only requires four parameters, but the first and second parameters have the same type as the third and fourth. That means it is easy to make stupid mistakes.

Listing 2.6 Making mistakes

```
fn calculate_raise(first_name: String,
                   _last_name: String,
                   _age: i32,
                   current_pay: i32) -> i32 {
    if first_name == "Sam" {
        current_pay + 1000          Only people with first name
    } else {                        "Sam" will get a raise.
        current_pay
    }
}

fn main() {
    let first_raise = calculate_raise(
        "Smith".to_string(),
        "Sam".to_string(),         Whoops, I switched
        20,                        my first and last name.
        1000                       No raise for me!
    );
    println!("{}", first_raise);       Prints
                                       "1000"
    let second_raise = calculate_raise(
        "Sam".to_string(),
        "Smith".to_string(),       This time, at least the names are in the right
        1000,                      order and I will get a raise. But despite being a
        20                         thousand years old (!), my raise is only $20.
    );
    println!("{}", second_raise);      Prints
}                                      "1020"
```

By creating unique wrappers (`FirstName`, `LastName`, `Age`, `CurrentPay`) for our parameters, the type system can keep us from making such mistakes. In addition, our code becomes more readable because we are making everything a bit more explicit. All of this makes this pattern popular among *clean code* and *domain-driven design* (see section 2.2.4) advocates. And hiding the "real" value of our parameters and giving them types with more meaning within our domain also makes newtypes ideal for making public APIs easier to understand and easier to evolve.

> **NOTE** Rust also has type aliases that create an alternative name (alias) for a chosen type. If we wanted to do this for `FirstName`, we would write `type`

FirstName = String;. This can make your code more readable to other developers, who can now see that you desire one specific type of String, a first name. Type aliases are often used when you have a more complex type that you want to make easier to read and use. Crates often have one custom error that is used everywhere. The syn crate, for example, has syn::Error. Because of this, it is also convenient to offer a type alias for Result with the default crate error already filled in, for example, type Result<T> = std::result::Result<T, syn::Error>. Now code in the package can use Result<T> for its return type. But type aliases do not make your type system smarter: I can still pass in a String when my function requires a FirstName type alias.

You can see an example for the FirstName newtype in listing 2.7. I have kept the internal value of the wrapper private while presenting the rest of my application with a new method. In that method, I can do additional checks to make sure a valid value was passed in, giving back an error when this is not the case. Why would I do that? Because it will make using these types easier in other functions that can now rely on this validation to make additional assumptions. If there is only one way to create these wrappers, we *know that our newtype passed all its validations*. In the case of FirstName, I now know that it is not empty. For Age, functions can assume validation will check that we have, say, a positive number under 150. But even without safeguards, newtypes have their value because they make the type system more powerful and force you to think about the values you pass in. If a function requires a FirstName and you are required to manually wrap your String into one, maybe that will keep you from accidentally passing in a String called last_name.

NOTE An easy way to mitigate mistakes for our age versus pay problem without using newtypes would be to make the age parameter a u8. This would already guarantee a positive number below 256.

Besides the constructor, we are also exposing a get_value method that will give back an immutable reference to "my inner value" to be used, safely, by other parts of the code. We could also add some conveniences like AsRef and AsRefMut trait implementations, but that is beyond the scope of this example.

Listing 2.7 The FirstName newtype

```
struct FirstName {
    value: String,
}

impl FirstName {
    pub fn new(name: &str) -> Result<FirstName, String> {
        if name.len() < 2 {
            Err("Name should be at least two characters".to_string())
        } else {
            Ok(FirstName {
                value: name.to_string(),
            })
```

```
            }
        }

        pub fn get_value(&self) -> &String {
            &self.value
        }
    }
}

// code for the other three newtypes

fn calculate_raise(first_name: FirstName,
                   _last_name: LastName,
                   _age: Age,
                   current_pay: Pay) -> Pay {
    // ...
}
```

> Usage example: passes in the newtypes instead of the built-in types. If you accidentally switch arguments one and two or three and four, the compiler will throw an error.

Everything is a tradeoff in programming. Here, one downside to our approach is how bloated our code has become. Just to create a single newtype, we had to write 18 additional lines of code! We can turn to macros to reduce this overhead. Let's start with the get_value method for the FirstName struct.

Listing 2.8   A macro for the newtype `get_value` method

```
struct FirstName {
    value: String,
}

struct LastName {
    value: String,
}

macro_rules! generate_get_value {
    ($struct_type:ident) => {
        impl $struct_type {
            pub fn get_value(&self) -> &String {
                &self.value
            }
        }
    }
}

generate_get_value!(FirstName);
generate_get_value!(LastName);
```

> We want one input argument, an identifier.

> We use that argument to implement a get_value method for the given struct.

> Now our FirstName and LastName structs will get the new method implemented for them.

By now, you can read this code with ease. We declare a new macro with macro_rules! and write a single matcher-transcriber pair. The only thing that we need to receive is the name of our struct. ident (identifier) seems like the most suitable kind of input. Everything except this name is hardcoded in the transcriber. Note that you can have multiple `impl` blocks for a struct. If this was not the case, our macro would prevent users from implementing any methods of their own!

Are we done? Unfortunately, no. When we try this for the next two structs, `Age` and `Pay`, we are greeted by a compile error: `mismatched types: expected reference &String found reference &i32`. Rust is right! We were keeping things simple, assuming the return type would always be `String`. But that is not the case. One way to solve this problem is to make our macro accept an additional argument, a return type override. While `ident` would work, `ty`—which stands for "Type"—is more suitable. `String` will be the default when we only get one identifier. That way our existing code will keep working. With this override in place, we can use the macro for `Age` and `Pay` as well.

Listing 2.9 Making it work for types other than Strings

```
struct Age {
    value: i32,
}

struct Pay {
    value: i32,
}

macro_rules! generate_get_value {
    ($struct_type:ident) => {
        impl $struct_type {
            pub fn get_value(&self) -> &String {
                &self.value
            }
        }
    };
    ($struct_type:ident,$return_type:ty) => {
        impl $struct_type {
            pub fn get_value(&self) -> &$return_type {
                &self.value
            }
        }
    }
}

generate_get_value!(FirstName);
generate_get_value!(LastName);
generate_get_value!(Age,i32);
generate_get_value!(Pay,i32);
```

This pair is new. It takes an additional input, a type (ty), which is used to specify the correct return type in the signature of our get_value method.

And so we have exchanged some 18 lines of boilerplate code for 20? Okay, but we can do better than that. Another nice feature of macros, and one that we have avoided using for simplicity's sake, is that they can *call themselves*. You may have noticed that there is a lot of overlap between our two code paths. Why not have one of our cases use the other? Since the String pair is a special case of the other one (which can handle any type), it makes sense for our special case to use the generic internally. So we will call our macro and pass along the input, with `String` as a second argument. Rust sees the two identifiers and knows it has to move to the second matcher (see figure 2.1).

Listing 2.10 **Final version of the** `get_value` **macro**

```
macro_rules! generate_get_value {
    ($struct_type:ident) => {
        generate_get_value!($struct_type,String);
    };
    ($struct_type:ident,$return_type:ty) => {
        impl $struct_type {
            pub fn get_value(&self) -> &$return_type {
                &self.value
            }
        }
    }
}
```

Inside our first transcriber, we are now calling our own macro with two identifiers.

This means we end up in this matcher, which accepts two identifiers.

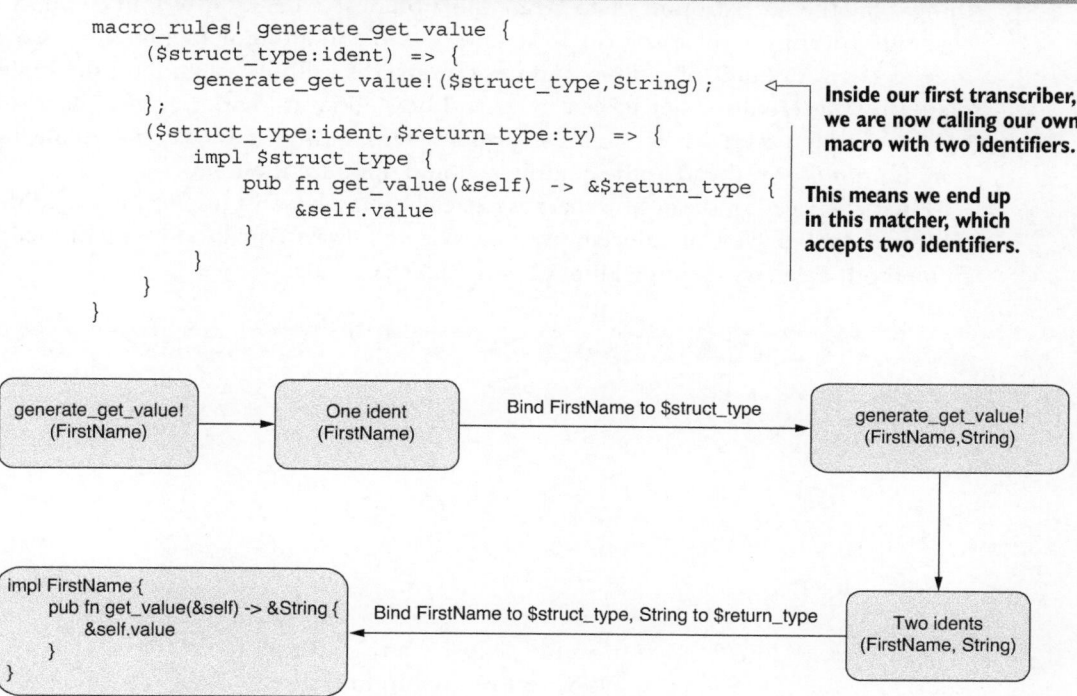

Figure 2.1 **What happens when we call** `generate_get_value` **with only one identifier**

We are now writing less boilerplate than before; all our logic for generating `get_value` methods is in one place; and the more newtypes we use, the more profit we gain from our macros. In a larger project, we could have additional macros for additional convenience methods and perhaps another one that calls all the others. But that is left as an exercise for the reader.

> **NOTE** The `derive_more` crate (https://docs.rs/derive_more/latest/derive _more/) is worth a mention before you start writing too much yourself. It can automatically implement some basic traits for wrappers like these. It uses procedural macros though, not declarative ones.

Before ending this section, I should mention that there is a Rust-specific reason for using newtypes: *orphan rules*. If you want to implement a given trait in Rust, either the trait, the type (e.g. a struct), or both should be local to your code. This avoids all kinds of problems. If I decide to reimplement `Clone` for `String`, what implementation should Rust prefer? In an application, maybe it would make sense to prefer the local implementation. But what if people write new implementations in libraries? Should Rust prefer the `Clone` implementation from the standard library? or the one from library A, B . . . X?

On the other hand, sometimes these rules keep you from doing cool—eh, useful—things. So the workaround is to wrap the nonlocal type (`String`) in a newtype (`MyString`). This newtype is local, so we are free to add an implementation of `Clone` to `MyString`. All kinds of built-in and custom macros will make handling the boilerplate that this entails easier to bear. Oh, and how about using declarative macros to ease the burden even further? Like we just did? Plus, newtypes are a zero-cost abstraction: no *runtime* overhead as the compiler should optimize them out.

Finally, since we just saw how macros can call themselves, it's important to add that the recursive behavior of a declarative macro is not always equal to that of a function or method. Take, for example, the following piece of code.

Listing 2.11   A recursive fumble

```
macro_rules! count {
    ($val: expr) => {
        if $val == 1 {
            1
        } else {
            count!($val - 1)
        }
    }
}
```

If this was a function, you would expect any invocation (e.g., `counter!(1)`, `counter!(5)`...) to return 1. Sadly, you will bump into a `recursion limit reached` error at compile time instead. Add trace macros, and the resulting output is revealing. Here are the first few lines:

```
= note: expanding `count! { 5 }`
= note: to `if 5 == 1 { 1 } else { count! (5 - 1) }`
= note: expanding `count! { 5 - 1 }`
= note: to `if 5 - 1 == 1 { 1 } else { count! (5 - 1 - 1) }`
= note: expanding `count! { 5 - 1 - 1 }`
= note: to `if 5 - 1 - 1 == 1 { 1 } else { count! (5 - 1 - 1 - 1) }`
```

`$val - 1` is not evaluated, and so we never reach our terminal condition. That is not to say that recursion with an unknown number of arguments is impossible. See section 2.2.5 for an example of how you can make this work.

2.2.4   *DSLs*

Declarative macros are also good for creating DSLs. As mentioned in the introduction, DSLs encapsulate knowledge about the domain—that the developers have learned from domain experts—into the application. This idea of capturing domain knowledge is related to that of a ubiquitous language, which comes from Domain-Driven Design and argues that communication between experts and developers is easier when they use the same words and concepts. This leads to better code.

The goal of a DSL is to create a specialized language that is suitable to the domain and hides irrelevant complexities. Among these complexities could be things like additional validation and taking care of certain subtleties. Some think that a DSL could make a codebase understandable to nonprogrammers, and one idea behind testing frameworks like Cucumber (https://github.com/cucumber-rs/cucumber) is to write tests in a language that the domain experts could understand. Another idea is that experts would even be able to add their own tests using these tools! Within the Rust ecosystem, mini-DSLs abound, and they are often created by using macros. Two simple examples from the standard library are `println!` and `format!`, which offer a special syntax using curly braces to determine how to print specified variables.

As an example, we will write a DSL for handling transfers between accounts. First, we create an `Account` struct that contains the amount of `money` in our account. It also has methods for adding and removing money from the account. We only want positive amounts (hence the use of `u32`), but handling accounts going into the negative is beyond scope. `Account` also derives `Debug`. This is a good idea in general, though our motivation here is simply to print some outcomes.

Listing 2.12   The `Account` structure

```
use std::ops::{Add, Sub};          ◁──   The Add and Sub traits allow us to use the
                                          add and sub methods on u32 inside the
#[derive(Debug)]                          Account implementation below.
struct Account {
    money: u32,
}

impl Account {
    fn add(&mut self, money: u32) {
        self.money = self.money.add(money)
    }

    fn subtract(&mut self, money: u32) {
        self.money = self.money.sub(money)
    }
}
```

Now check out the `exchange` macro in listing 2.13, which presents users with a mini-DSL. As you can see, this macro allows us to use natural language, understandable to outsiders, to describe actions. And when the macro does not understand a command, it will complain about this at compile time. Also, when transferring money between two accounts (third pair), we are hiding the complexity of a transaction from the DSL user.

Listing 2.13   Macro that presents a mini-DSL for exchanging money

```
macro_rules! exchange {
    (Give $amount:literal to $name:ident) => {
        $name.add($amount)
    };
    (Take $amount:literal from $name:ident) => {
        $name.subtract($amount)
    };
```

```
(Give $amount:literal from $giver:ident to $receiver:ident) => {
    $giver.subtract($amount);
    $receiver.add($amount)
};
}
```

> We have to end $giver.subtract($amount) with a semicolon because the transcriber has two statements instead of one, and the compiler would complain about expecting a ;.

```
fn main() {
    let mut the_poor = Account {
        money: 0,
    };
    let mut the_rich = Account {
        money: 200,
    };

    exchange!(Give 20 to the_poor);
    exchange!(Take 10 from the_rich);
    exchange!(Give 30 from the_rich to the_poor);

    println!("Poor: {the.poor?}, rich: {the.rich?}");
}
```

> This prints "Poor: Account { money: 50 }, rich: Account { money: 160 }".

> Uses natural language to specify transactions

And there is no need to stop here. You could add currency types and automatically convert them. Or you could have special rules for overdraft. Good testing is needed to make sure that your macro scenarios do not "collide" (which is when you think you will land in matcher X but you end up in Y) with each other, though. As a simple example, the following macro is meant for giving money to the poor and berates people who don't give anything. We call our macro and are complimented for giving nothing. That's because the first clause accepts any literal, *which includes zero*. And since the macro checks the matcher in order and always matches the first more general clause, the second one is never reached.

Listing 2.14   A faulty wealth-transfer macro

```
macro_rules! give_money_to_the_poor {
    (Give $example:literal) => {
        println!("How generous");
    };
    (Give 0) => {
        println!("Cheapskate");
    };
}

fn main() {
    give_money_to_the_poor!(Give 0);
}
```

> Prints "How generous"! That is not what we expected.

The solution—in this case—is simple. Just switch the order of the cases! The underlying rule is this: *write macro rules/matchers from most-specific to least-specific.* This rule also applies to pattern matching with match, though the order is not enforced by the compiler, which only produces a warning. (Try putting the catchall _ before other matches.) More worrisome is ignoring this rule still results in a valid macro implementation according to Rust, which won't even produce a warning. So static checks are insufficient to root out these bugs, and you should test all your "branches."

2.2.5   *Composing is easy*

Besides avoiding boilerplate, macros also help us do things that are inelegant, hard, or even impossible to do in plain old Rust. (And you could see DSLs as a specific example of this more general category.) Take *composition,* which is a common feature of functional programming and a design pattern in *object-oriented programming.* Composition allows you to combine simple functions into bigger ones, creating larger functionality from smaller building blocks. This is a very interesting way to build applications when you want to keep your functions simple, understandable, and easy to test. And it is useful as a way to combine components in a paradigm that avoids object interactions for application building. To make things more concrete: say we have functions to increment a number, to change a number to a string, and to prefix a string. These three are shown in the following listing.

Listing 2.15   Three simple functions

```
fn add_one(n: i32) -> i32 {
    n + 1
}

fn stringify(n: i32) -> String {
    n.to_string()
}

fn prefix_with(prefix: &str) -> impl Fn(String) -> String + '_ {
    move |x| format!("{}{}", prefix, x)
}
```

> The String + _ in the return type is needed because we are passing in a &str and that lifetime has to be made explicit.

The following pseudocode shows how we would like to compose these functions, similar to how it works in other languages. We pass our three functions to compose and get back a *new function that expects one input.* That input is the same type as the parameter of the first function we passed in. In our case, that function is add_one, which expects an i32. Internally, our composed will pass this argument to add_one, which will output an incremented number. That incremented number is given to the next function, stringify, which turns the number into a string. Finally, this string is passed to prefix_with. Since this last function needs two arguments, both a prefix and an input string, we already passed in a prefix. In functional lingo, the function has been *partially applied:*

```
fn main() {
    let composed = compose(
        add_one,
        stringify,
        prefix_with("Result: ")
    );
    println!("{}", composed(5));
}
```

> This should print "Result: 6".

And you are not limited to a few functions! You can keep adding more, as long as they accept a single parameter that matches the output of the previous function and return a value that the next one accepts.

> **NOTE**   In some implementations, the order in which compose calls the functions might be reversed (i.e., from the rightmost argument to the leftmost). In that case, you first give it the *last* function it should call and end with the first.

But how do we write this compose? We will start simply with two input functions. No macros are required to make this work—just a lot of generics. compose_two (see the code in listing 2.16) requires two functions as parameters, both of which take a single parameter and return a result. The second one has to take the first one's output as its single input:

```
Fn(FIRST) -> SECOND
Fn(SECOND) -> THIRD
```

For easier reading, we can put these in a where clause, binding to generics F and G: where F: Fn(FIRST) -> SECOND, G: Fn(SECOND) -> THIRD. We also return a function that takes the first function's input and has an output equal to the second one's output:

```
Fn(FIRST) -> THIRD
```

Compared to the signature, the implementation is simple: it's a closure that takes one argument (our generic FIRST), gives it to our first function, and gives that output (SECOND) to our second function, which will produce the final result (THIRD). Because of the closure, we add impl to our return type, since every closure is unique and won't match a normal generic function type.

Listing 2.16   A function to compose two functions

compose_two is a function that takes two generic parameters, called f and g, and returns a function (well, something that implements a function) that takes one generic argument and returns another generic argument.

In this part of the where clause, we determine that f is a function that takes a generic argument called FIRST and returns a generic result that we call SECOND. FIRST becomes the input of compose_two.

```
fn compose_two<FIRST, SECOND, THIRD, F, G>(f: F, g: G)
    -> impl Fn(FIRST) -> THIRD
    where F: Fn(FIRST) -> SECOND,
          G: Fn(SECOND) -> THIRD
{
    move |x| g(f(x))
}

fn main() {
    let two_composed_function = compose_two(
        compose_two(add_one, stringify),
        prefix_with("Result: ")
    );
}
```

Given an argument, passes it to the first function we received and passes that result to the second one we received

Also in the where clause, we decide that g takes SECOND and returns THIRD. THIRD is the output of our compose_two.

Repeatedly calls compose_two to compose our three functions from before

That is the first step. How would we go about making this work for multiple functions? One approach that I have occasionally seen in other languages is to just write an implementation for the most common number of arguments: `compose_three`, `compose_four`, etc. up to `compose_ten`. That should cover 90% of all cases. And if we need more, we could also start nesting the existing implementations (a `compose_ten` within a `compose_ten`). It is a decent workaround, and it is hard to do better with plain Rust tooling. Say we decided to write a `compose` with a vector of functions as a parameter. We would need some way to tell the compiler that each function in this vector takes the previous output as input if we want our code to compile. That's hard to express in Rust.

But expressing this idea in a declarative macro is trivial (see listing 2.17). Let's go through it step by step. If our `compose` macro receives a single expression, a function, it returns that expression—a simple base case. If the macro is invoked with two or more arguments (note the + after $tail, which is for when there is more than a single expression in our tail), we need recursive magic. What we do is call our `compose_two` and pass in the two required arguments. The first is the first function we receive, `head`. The second is the *result* of calling our `compose` macro again, this time on the remaining arguments. If this second `compose` invocation receives a single expression, we end up in the first matcher, and we only have to compose two functions with a simple `compose_two` call. In the other case, we end up in our second branch—again—and return a function that is the result of `compose_two`—again. This is, in fact, what we suggested doing manually with nesting, except now the macro takes care of everything in the background (see figure 2.2).

Listing 2.17 `compose` **macro**

```
macro_rules! compose {
    ($last:expr) => { $last };
    ($head:expr,$($tail:expr),+) => {
        compose_two($head, compose!($($tail),+))
    }
}

fn main() {
    let composed = compose!(
        add_one,
        stringify,
        prefix_with("Result: ")
    );                                       Prints
    println!("{}", composed(5));      ◁──┘  "Result: 6"
}
```

Commas are not the only way to separate the arguments that you pass to your macro. Similar to the brackets, you have some alternatives. In the case of `expr`, you can also go for a semicolon or an arrow. But if you're a Haskell fan and you would like to compose using periods, that won't do. You will get an error that says `$head:expr is followed`

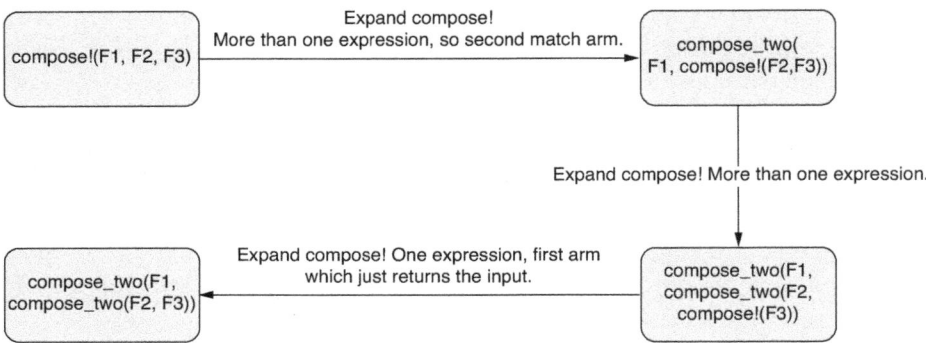

Figure 2.2 The `compose` macro with three functions, creatively called F1, F2, and F3

by '.', which is not allowed for `expr` fragments. Other macro input types, like `tt`, have more options, though.

Listing 2.18 Alternative with arrows separating the inputs to the macro

```
macro_rules! compose_alt {
    ($last:expr) => { $last };
    ($head:expr => $($tail:expr)=>+) => {
        compose_two($head, compose_alt!($($tail)=>+))
    }
}
```
← **Within the second matcher, we have replaced the commas with arrows.**

```
fn main() {
    let composed = compose_alt!(
        add_one => stringify => prefix_with("Result: ")
    );
    println!("{}", composed(5));
}
```
← **Now we use arrows in our invocation as well.**

2.2.6 *Currying, on the other hand . . .*

Suppose you are now hooked on a functional style of Rust, but you find the "one-input" requirement of `compose` an annoyance, because, in reality, you often have functions that require multiple parameters to be passed in at the same time. And composition can't handle that. Luckily, you find out that there is something called *currying*. Currying is when you have a function that requires more than one argument and gives back a "recursive" function that takes only one argument at a time. For example, currying turns

```
Fn(i32, i32) -> i32
```

into

```
Fn(i32) -> Fn(i32) -> i32
```

That makes *partial application* of functions—that is, supplying only a part of all the arguments that a function needs—easier, which in turn makes composing easier. You would like to make this possible in Rust. And after your positive experience with composing, you think declarative macros are the way to go.

You would soon discover that currying with declarative macros is harder, though. One problem is the lack of "visibility" of the function's signature: what does it require as parameters, and what does it return? Going back to our previous approach, we could start with the easiest case, a `curry2` function for changing a function with two arguments into a curried version. Now all we have to do is recursively call this function. But how many times should we (well, the macro) call it? Without access to the signature, we're in the dark, whereas with composing, we knew how many calls had to happen because the functions *were given to our macro* as arguments.

Whereas composing was trivial, currying is hard. And while explicitly passing in details would help, that is exactly the kind of busywork we are trying to avoid. Because they are explicit about their number of arguments, closures are easier. And so there's a crate for currying them (https://mng.bz/v8Pm). Take a look at the simplest rule in that crate:

```
macro_rules! curry {
    (|$first_arg:ident $(, $arg:ident )*| $function_body:expr) => {
        move |$first_arg| $(move |$arg|)* {
            $function_body
        }
    };
    // ...
}
```

This matcher expects one or more identifiers within pipes (| |), followed by an expression. Take the call `curry!(|a, b| a + b);` as an example. `a` and `b` are our two identifiers, and `a + b` is our expression. All the transcriber has to do is add a `move` for each of these identifiers and pass them to the function. In our example, this becomes `move |a| move |b| a + b;`. Suddenly, we have two closures, each of which takes one argument. But again, this works because everything we need to know is passed in as an argument. Normal functions have this information in their signature, making good solutions harder (though probably not impossible). Instead, as the blog post, "Auto-currying Rust Functions" (https://peppe.rs/posts/auto-currying_rust_functions) shows, procedural macros offer the right tools for the job. And while its result is more complicated and has more lines of code than the average declarative macro from this chapter, the actual solution is still decently short: under 100 lines.

2.2.7 Hygiene is something to consider as well

You should be aware that not everything you generate will be added as is to your code because declarative macros have a concept of hygiene for identifiers. Simply put, identifiers inside your macro will *always* be different from those in code outside the macro, even if their names overlap, which means a number of things are impossible. For example, I cannot let `generate_x!()` output `let x = 0` *and then increment that named variable* in my ordinary code. If I try that, Rust will complain that it `cannot find value x in this scope`. That's because the x I initialized in my macro is not the x I am trying to increment in my application.

The way I am presenting this, hygiene sounds like a bad thing. But it is useful as a safeguard against contamination. A difference in intent is something to consider. If I am getting an identifier via my input and writing an implementation block, I *want to affect code outside of the macro,* or else what would be the point of that implementation? But identifiers created within my macro can serve other goals. Maybe I want to perform a calculation or push things into a vector. That stuff is independent of what I am doing outside the macro. And since developers often go for variable names that are easy to understand, there is a chance that a user of my macro will have the same variable name(s) in their own code. So when you see compiler errors around "unresolved" and "unknown" identifiers that are somehow related to macro code, remember this behavior. And if you want to have an effect on an identifier, just pass it into the macro as an argument.

2.3 *From the real world*

Once upon a time, there was no good built-in way to create lazily initiated `static` values in Rust. But lazy statics are useful for several reasons. For one, maybe the value inside your `static` requires a lot of computation. If it turns out the value is never needed, you never pay its initialization price. Another advantage is that the initialization happens at run time, which has some additional options on top of those available at compile time. (Yes, this contradicts the preference for compile-time stuff that often bubbles up in this book. As always in software, it depends. Compile-time work makes things safer and faster. But at run time, you can do some things you could not do during compilation.) Seeing this lack, `lazy_static` (https://docs.rs/lazy_static/latest/lazy_static/) jumped in and filled a need. Nowadays, though, `once_cell` can be used for "initialization of global data." So `lazy_static` is no longer the recommended crate for this type of functionality. But that doesn't mean its code is not interesting anymore!

Listing 2.19 Lazy static example from the documentation

```
lazy_static! {
    static ref EXAMPLE: u8 = 42;
}
```

At the very root of the crate is the `lazy_static` macro. A `#[macro_export]` makes sure we can use it outside this file. The matchers can have `meta` (i.e., metadata) optionally (note the asterisk in the next listing) passed in, and the `static ref` is *literally* required as an input. A static also has an identifier, a type, and an initialization expression as well as some optional additional information (thrown together in `TokenTrees`). Most of the incoming variables are simply passed on to an internal macro called `__lazy_static_internal`. But to avoid parsing ambiguity, `()` is added as an indicator of the (default) visibility modifier. (In some other matchers of the macro, `(pub)` is passed along instead to indicate public visibility.)

Listing 2.20 `lazy_static` **macro entry point, simplified slightly**

```
#[macro_export]
macro_rules! lazy_static {
    ($(#[$attr:meta])* static ref $N:ident : $T:ty =
$e:expr; $($t:tt)*) => {
        __lazy_static_internal!($(#[$attr])* () static ref $N :
$T = $e; $($t)*);
    };
    // other arms...
}
```

Most of the implementation is hidden inside the internal macro, shown in listing 2.21. You could call the `@MAKE TY` and `@TAIL` a mini (nano?) DSL. It is used to make sure the other matcher-transcriber pairs within the macro are called, a pattern that appears in *The Little Book of Rust Macros* (https://veykril.github.io/tlborm/). The first of these two additional arms (`@MAKE TY`) is, as the name indicates, responsible for creating the type, which is just a struct with an empty internal field, decorated with the original metadata that was passed in (so it doesn't get lost). The second arm (`@TAIL`) creates a `Deref` and initialization. This is where the magic happens. If you need your lazily initialized static somewhere in your code, you will dereference it as soon as you start using it. It is at that point that the initialization expression that you provided will run. You can see that expression (`$e`) being passed to the `__static_ref_initialize` function within the `deref` method. Underneath it all, `Once`, from the `spin` library (https://docs.rs/spin/latest/spin), is used to make sure this initialization only happens one time. This is done in the `lazy_static_create` macro, which is called inside the generated `deref`.

Listing 2.21 `lazy_static` **internal, again simplified**

This is a declarative macro declaration for a macro called lazy_static_internal.

The first matcher expects optional attributes, optional visibility, a literal "static ref" value, an identifier, type, and expression. Finally, and again optionally, we capture everything else in a TokenTree.

```
macro_rules! __lazy_static_internal {

    ($(#[$attr:meta])* $($vis:tt)*) static ref
    $N:ident : $T:ty = $e:expr; $($t:tt)*) => {

        __lazy_static_internal!(@MAKE TY, $(#[$attr])*,
```

```
    ($($vis)*), $N);

            __lazy_static_internal!(@TAIL, $N : $T = $e);
    };
    (@TAIL, $N:ident : $T:ty = $e:expr) => {
        impl $crate::__Deref for $N {
            type Target = $T;
            fn deref(&self) -> &$T {
                fn __static_ref_initialize() -> $T { $e }

                fn __stability() -> &'static $T {
                    __lazy_static_create!(LAZY, $T);
                    LAZY.get(__static_ref_initialize)
                }
                __stability()
            }
        }
        impl $crate::LazyStatic for $N {
            fn initialize(lazy: &Self) {
                let _ = &**lazy;
            }
        }
    };
    (@MAKE TY, $(#[$attr:meta])*, ($($vis:tt)*),
  $N:ident) => {
        $(#[$attr])*
        $($vis)* struct $N {__private_field: ()}
        $($vis)* static $N: $N = $N {__private_field: ()};
    };
}

macro_rules! __lazy_static_create {
    ($NAME:ident, $T:ty) => {
        static $NAME: $crate::lazy::Lazy<$T> = $crate::lazy::Lazy::INIT;
    };
}
```

We call our own macro, and the @MAKE TY literal makes sure we end up in the last arm.

Similarly, here @TAIL makes sure we end up in the next arm.

This contains a lot of the magic of lazy static, using Deref to initialize our static.

Here, $crate is used to make sure that there is no collision with a LazyStatic defined anywhere else (i.e., we only want the LazyStatic defined in our crate).

Now you know like 80% (citation needed) of how the lazy_static crate works!

2.4   *Exercises*

See the appendix for solutions.

1 Fill in the question marks (???) and make the following declarative macro compile:

```
macro_rules! ??? {
    ??? => {
        impl $something {
            fn hello_world(&self) {
                println!("Hello world")
            }
        }
    };
```

```
}

struct Example {}
hello_world!(Example);

fn main() {
    let e = Example {};
    e.hello_world(); // prints "Hello world"
}
```

2 In our first declarative macro example, we use `expr` in some of our matches. But that was not our only option. Try to replace that with `literal`, `tt`, `ident`, or `ty`. Which ones work? Which don't? Do you understand why?

3 Allow trailing comments in the `my_vec` macro. You can do this by writing another matcher, but there's a simple solution with even less repetition. If you need help, take a look at the `vec` macro from the standard library for inspiration.

4 Another thing I like for newtypes is convenient `From` implementations. Write a macro that generates them for our four newtypes. Alternatively, you can go for `TryFrom` since that is a more suitable choice when input validation is required.

5 Now that we have two macros, we could make our lives even easier by creating a third macro, `generate_newtypes_methods`, that calls our existing two macros behind the scene.

6 Expand our `Account` example in listings 2.12 and 2.13 with dollar and euro currencies. You can use a hardcoded exchange rate of 2 dollars to 1 euro. All existing commands will require a currency type.

7 In the upcoming procedural chapters, ask yourself: Could I have done this with a declarative macro? Why not? What would be hard to do?

Summary

- Declarative macros are the first group of macros that Rust has to offer.
- They consist of one or more pairs of matchers and transcribers.
- The matcher has to match the content that was passed into the macro when it was invoked.
- If there is a match, the code inside the transcriber will be written to where the macro was invoked.
- Pieces of input can be captured in the matcher and used in the transcriber.
- Macros can call themselves to avoid duplication and to allow for more complex scenarios.
- To use macros outside the file where they were defined, you will need to export them.
- Declarative macros have hygiene, which means local identifiers do not collide with external ones.

- There are several use cases for declarative macros: avoiding duplication and boilerplate is a major one. Another is doing things that are hard—or impossible—to do otherwise, like default arguments, varargs, or DSLs.
- If declarative macros fall short, you still have procedural macros waiting in the corridor to assist you with even more powerful weapons.

3
A "Hello, World" procedural macro

This chapter covers

- Setting up a procedural macro
- Getting the name of a struct by parsing a stream of tokens
- Generating hardcoded output
- Using variables in generated code
- Inspecting generated code with `cargo expand`
- Writing a macro without help from `syn` and `quote`
- Understanding how Rust's internal macros are special

We now come to the meat of our book: procedural macros. As we explained earlier, both procedural and declarative macros are forms of metaprogramming and allow you to manipulate and extend code. But they go about it differently. Declarative macros offer a domain-specific language (DSL) that allows you to generate code based on a combination of matchers and transcribers. Procedural macros, on the other hand, deal with lower-level information. They receive a stream of tokens containing *every detail* of the code you want to work with.

In my mind, the difference between declarative and procedural macros—and when you should use them—is a bit like SQL and general-purpose programming languages when it comes to querying databases. SQL is powerful, expressive, and user friendly. It should be your first choice for querying. But at a certain level of complexity and for some kinds of tasks, it breaks down. It becomes complicated and difficult to read and extend. At that point, it can be worthwhile to replace SQL with a general-purpose language. Querying might require more effort and setup, but you will have more options and power. So the advice here is to start with declarative macros. They are simple and powerful, require only minimal setup, and have better IDE support to boot. If you want to do things that declarative macros can't (for example, manipulating existing structs), you should turn to procedural macros.

3.1   *Basic setup of a procedural macro project*

We start simple, with a macro that adds a "Hello, World" printing method to a struct or enum (see figure 3.1 for the project setup). Adding new functionality to a struct is a good use case for a *derive* macro. On the other hand, if we wanted to *modify* existing code, we would have to look elsewhere, since these macros are incapable of doing that. Derive macros are activated by adding the `#[derive]` annotation to your code, putting the name of the macro between brackets. No doubt you have encountered these annotations before when you wanted to add `Debug` (`#[derive(Debug)]`) or `Clone` (`#[derive(Clone)]`) functionality to your code.

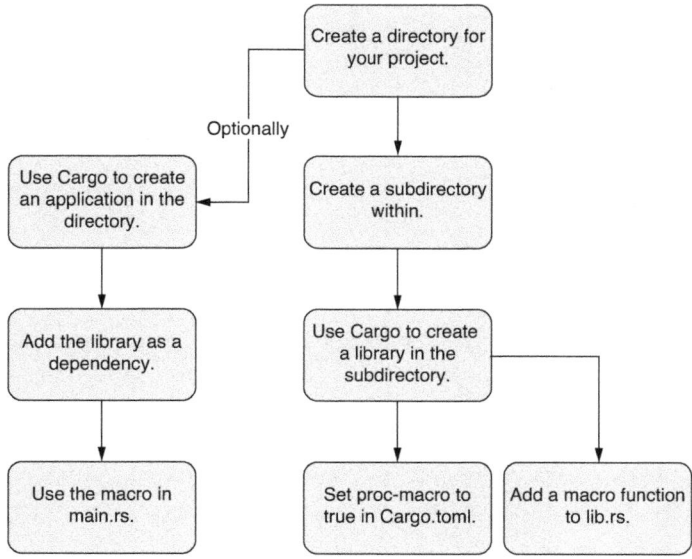

Figure 3.1   Basic setup of a procedural macro project

Creating a procedural macro takes some work, so bear with me while we go through the setup. First, we need a `hello-world` directory with another directory called `hello-world-macro` inside the former. In `hello-world-macro`, we will put the macro project; in the root, we will add an application (see figure 3.2).

You are probably used to creating new Rust projects with `cargo init`. However, for our macro, we do not need an application but a *library*. Developers who want to use our macro will import our library as a dependency. So run `cargo init --lib` in the `hello-world-macro` subdirectory of the project.

We have to modify the generated `Cargo.toml`. The most important change is adding a `lib` section, with the `proc-macro` property set to `true`. This tells Rust that this library will expose one or more procedural macros and will make some tooling available to us. We also want to add `quote` and `syn` as dependencies. These are not strictly required, but they will make our lives much easier.

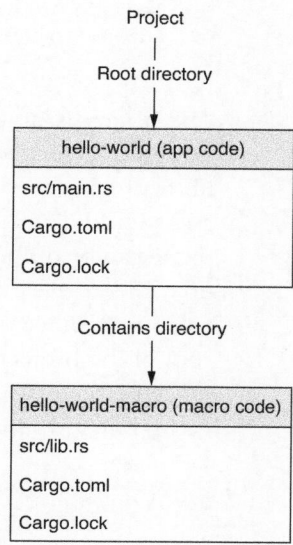

Figure 3.2 Our project structure

Listing 3.1   The `lib` section and dependencies of `hello-world-macro`

```
[package]
name = "hello-world-macro"
version = "0.1.0"
edition = "2021"

[dependencies]
quote = "1.0.33"
syn = "2.0.39"

[lib]
proc-macro = true
```

> **NOTE** We do not require Cargo workspaces to get this working, though we will see examples of such a setup later on.

Inside the automatically generated `lib.rs` file, we add a basic implementation that does not really do anything yet. We will discuss the code in the next section. For now, let us continue our setup.

Listing 3.2   The initial `lib.rs` file from our `hello-world-macro` library

```
use quote::quote;
use proc_macro::TokenStream;

#[proc_macro_derive(Hello)]
pub fn hello(_item: TokenStream) -> TokenStream {
```

```
    let add_hello_world = quote! {};
    add_hello_world.into()
}
```

The library is now ready. In the outer `hello-world` directory, we will set up a Rust example application with `cargo init`. This time, we add a dependency on the macro library we just created using a relative path. The name of the dependency is important and should match the name of the package you are importing (the path and directory name can be different, though). Try changing the dependency name to "foo-bar," and do a `cargo run`. You will get something like `error: no matching package named foo-bar found`. Since our application is located one level above the macro directory, in the root of the project, our path is `./hello-world-macro`. Some later chapters will have a nested directory for both the application and the library. In that case, we will have to go up one level (`path = "../fill-in-the-name-of-your-macro"`).

Listing 3.3   The `Cargo.toml` file from our outer Rust application

```
[package]
name = "hello-world"
version = "0.1.0"
edition = "2021"

[dependencies]
hello-world-macro = { path = "./hello-world-macro" }
```

Finally, modify the default `main.rs`. You should now be able to compile and run your application with `cargo run`. It currently prints nothing (except for a warning that `Example` is never constructed).

Listing 3.4   The initial `main.rs` file from the outer application

```
#[macro_use]
extern crate hello_world_macro;

#[derive(Hello)]
struct Example;

fn main() {}
```

> **NOTE** If you don't like this setup or all the manual work, you could use `cargo generate` (https://github.com/cargo-generate/cargo-generate), which has a template (https://github.com/waynr/proc-macro-template) for generating macro setups. For learning purposes, setting things up manually at least once is advisable. But once you've got the hang of it, you can use the `util/create_setup.sh` script in the code repository (https://github.com/VanOvermeire/rust-macros-book), which automatically sets up projects in the various styles used in this book.

3.2 Analyzing the procedural macro setup

Now let us analyze the setup. The nested directory with `lib.rs` is the only piece of code we really need:

```
use quote::quote;
use proc_macro::TokenStream;

#[proc_macro_derive(Hello)]        Declares this function
pub fn hello(_item: TokenStream)   to be a derive macro
    let add_hello_world = quote!    named "Hello"        Generates a new (currently
    add_hello_world.into()                               empty) TokenStream using
}                                                        the quote macro

                                   -> TokenStream {
                                   {};

                                   Uses the Into trait to change this
                                   TokenStream into the normal/
                                   standard library TokenStream
                                   with the same name
```

Below the import of dependencies, we have `#[proc_macro_derive(Hello)]`. This is an attribute, a piece of metadata that informs Rust that something should happen. In our case, it tells Rust that this function is an entry point to a derive macro (see figure 3.3). This annotation requires a name between parentheses—"Hello" in our example—which will be used when invoking the macro: `#[derive(Hello)]`. The name of the function, on the other hand, is not used externally. So pick anything you want.

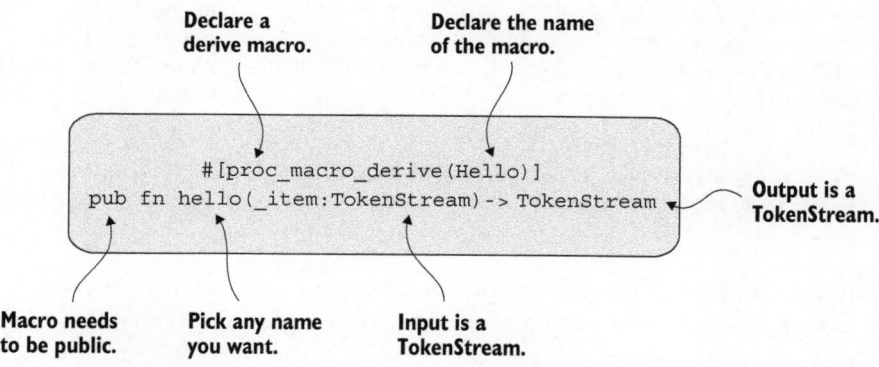

Figure 3.3 The signature of a derive macro

Moving on, we have the function signature. It has a single parameter of type `Token-Stream`, which we are not using yet. Therefore, it has been prefixed with an underscore. In earlier chapters, we already mentioned how procedural macros operate on a stream of tokens, a representation of the code that we want to modify—a struct, for example. Everything there is to know about that struct will be contained inside this `TokenStream`. Meanwhile, the `TokenStream` that we are returning will be used by Rust to generate additional code.

A high-level overview

Here is a high-level overview of what Rust does when you tell it to compile your application (and I am not an expert on the details). There are two steps involved: lexing and parsing. Lexing—also called tokenization—is the first step and is used to turn your code as a raw text stream into a stream of tokens. For example, pass the expression 1 + 11 to a macro, and the resulting stream will look like this (ignoring spans and suffixes for now):

```
TokenStream [Literal { kind: Integer, symbol: "1" }, Punct { ch: '+',
         spacing: Alone }, Literal { kind: Integer, symbol: "11" }]
```

Our raw text has been turned into three tokens (the two numbers and the + sign).

Parsing turns this information into an *Abstract Syntax Tree* (AST; http://mng.bz/5IKZ), a tree-like representation of all relevant data in your program. This AST makes it easier for the Rust compiler (as well as compilers in other languages) to do its work (i.e., creating an executable that computers can understand). In the previous example, an AST might interpret the plus sign as the root, with the two Literals (numbers) as its branches. Meanwhile, spans are used to link back to the original text, which is useful for things like error messages. Once the AST has been constructed, macros can be processed by the compiler.

While these are interesting little facts, you do not need to know the details of this process to write procedural macros. The most important takeaway is that Rust gives us code as parsed tokens. In return, we graciously give back information in the same format. Rust knows how to use these tokens. After all, all "normal" code is also turned into tokens, which means it is easy to turn your tokens into additional application code.

You can find more information in the Rust Compiler Development Guide (https://rustc-dev-guide.rust-lang.org/), *The Little Book of Rust Macros* (https://veykril.github.io/tlborm/), and The Rust Reference (https://doc.rust-lang.org/stable/reference/).

This brings us to the body of our function, where we are calling the quote macro from the dependency with the same name. We are not passing any parameters into quote, which means we are generating an empty TokenStream. Because quote is actually using the proc_macro2 TokenStream (a wrapper around the built-in type), we still have to use the Into trait to transform it into a "normal" proc_macro TokenStream: add_hello_world.into(). So the end result is a macro that generates nothing. Zero run-time overhead would be the marketeer's pitch for this version of our library. But there is no obligation for a macro to generate code, so this is acceptable in Rust.

Now take a look at main.rs:

```
#[macro_use]
extern crate hello_world_macro;       ◁──┐ Makes the macros inside the
                                          └ hello_world_macro directory available for use

#[derive(Hello)]          ◁─────────
struct Example;   ◁──┐              │ Adds the "Hello"
                     │              │ derive macro . . .
fn main() {}         │  . . .to our empty
                     │  Example struct
```

The first two lines tell Rust that we will want to use macros from this dependency, similar to how we import declarative macros. (This time we need to specify the dependency using underscores. In our `Cargo.toml` we used hyphens.) *This is the older style for importing procedural macros.* Nowadays, you should import them with a `use` one-liner (e.g., `use hello_world_macro::Hello;`). In this chapter, we primarily use the older style, which is still used in a lot of crates and therefore still worth knowing. But in subsequent chapters, we will switch to the newer (Rust 2018) style.

Next, the `#[derive(Hello)]` attribute tells Rust to run our derive macro named "Hello" for the `Example` struct, passing that struct along as an input of type `TokenStream`. The (currently empty) output code will be added to our `main.rs` file.

Earlier we said that the outer application was not strictly necessary. Instead, it is a convenience—a "consumer" that helps us verify that our code compiles. This is useful because Rust's compiler will not catch errors in code generated by our library. To make this more concrete, say we make a typo when adding the parameter for the derive macro function and write `TokenStrea`. If we run `cargo check`, Rust will point out that the `TokenStrea` does not exist. Failure prevented! But suppose we write invalid Rust *within* the `quote` macro invocation:

```
#[proc_macro_derive(Hello)]
pub fn hello(item: TokenStream) -> TokenStream {
    let add_hello_world = quote! {
        fn this should not work () {}
    };

    add_hello_world.into()
}
```

Running `cargo check` inside our macro library still succeeds! But when we do a `check` in the outer application, we get an error:

```
error: expected one of `(` or `<`, found `should`
 --> src/main.rs:4:10
  |
4 | #[derive(Hello)]
  |          ^^^^^ expected one of `(` or `<`
  |
  = note: this error originates in the derive macro `Hello`
```

Apparently, Rust thinks that `fn this` means we want to create a function called `this`. A function and its name are followed by either parentheses containing the parameters or generics (which are surrounded by `<` `>`). Instead, the word `should` appears. The lesson here is that `cargo check` inside your procedural macro library will only check for mistakes in your *library code,* not in the *code it generates.*

This makes sense because within the library we are not using the generated code. All Rust cares about is that we declared `TokenStream` to be the return type of our function. And as long as we return *any* stream of tokens, even an invalid one, it is happy. Even if it did care, the compiler has no way of knowing in what context your generated code will be used, which makes checking hard. So instead, we use a simple application with a basic usage example to generate code and force the compiler to stop being lazy and do some work. In later chapters, we will turn to tests for asserting the proper working of our macro.

3.3 Generating output

How about actually producing some code? Start by adding the following to `lib.rs`.

Listing 3.5 **Parsing the input and producing hardcoded output**

```
// earlier imports

#[proc_macro_derive(Hello)]
pub fn hello(_item: TokenStream) -> TokenStream {
    let add_hello_world = quote! {
        impl Example {
            fn hello_world(&self) {
                println!("Hello, World")     ⊲── Returns a hardcoded
            }                                     implementation block
        }
    };

    add_hello_world.into()
}
```

We are still not doing anything with the incoming tokens. But we are using `quote` to generate new code. Right now, that new code is a hardcoded implementation block for the `Example` struct we added to `main.rs`. This means we can now call this method and the following code should run. Do remember that the target for `cargo run` should be the application or else you will get `a bin target must be available for cargo run` since a library cannot be executed.

Listing 3.6 **Calling our generated function in our main file**

```
// the macro import

#[derive(Hello)]
struct Example;

fn main() {
    let e = Example {};          ⊲── Prints "Hello, World"
    e.hello_world();                  when executed
}
```

The only downside is that our code only works for structs named "Example." Rename the struct, and Rust will complain that it `cannot find type Example in this scope` as it can't match the implementation block to an existing type. The solution is to retrieve the name of the struct from the incoming tokens and use it for the `impl` that we are generating. In the terminology of macros, both declarative and procedural, this name is an *identifier*. And since our tokens represent the code that we decorated (a struct and its contents), we will need the topmost identifier. Once we have the name, we can combine it with `quote` to produce more interesting output.

Listing 3.7   Parsing the input and using it in our output

```
use quote::quote;
use proc_macro::TokenStream;
use syn::{parse_macro_input, DeriveInput};

#[proc_macro_derive(Hello)]
pub fn hello(item: TokenStream) -> TokenStream {
    let ast = parse_macro_input!(item as DeriveInput);    ◁─── Parses the incoming
    let name = ast.ident;                                      TokenStream into a
                                                               more user-friendly AST
                                         ◁─── Retrieves the top-level identifier. In our case, this
                                              will be the name of the annotated (Example) struct.
    let add_hello_world = quote! {
        impl #name {                     ◁─── Uses the special syntax that quote
            fn hello_world(&self) {           provides to add it to our output
                println!("Hello, World")
            }
        }
    };

    add_hello_world.into()
}
```

Everything else can remain hardcoded.

We start by parsing the input tokens into an AST by using `parse_macro_input`, provided by the `syn` crate. `syn` offers a lot of tools to help you parse Rust tokens, and this declarative macro is one tool in its arsenal. The `as DeriveInput` is a bit of custom syntactic sugar. Behind the scenes, the argument after `as` is used to determine the type that will be generated. We have gone for `DeriveInput`. As the name suggests, this is any kind of input that you might get when writing a derive macro. So it basically contains either an enum or a struct.

Once we have the `DeriveInput`, we can get the name of the struct by retrieving the topmost `ident`(ifier), which we save in a variable called `name`. If we want to use `name` in our output, we need a special syntax to tell `quote` that this is not a literal value but should be replaced with the content of a variable with a matching name. You can do that by prefixing the name of your variable with a hashtag (i.e., `#name`), which, in our case, will be replaced with the identifier `Example`. As you can see, generating output with `quote` is delightfully easy (see figure 3.4).

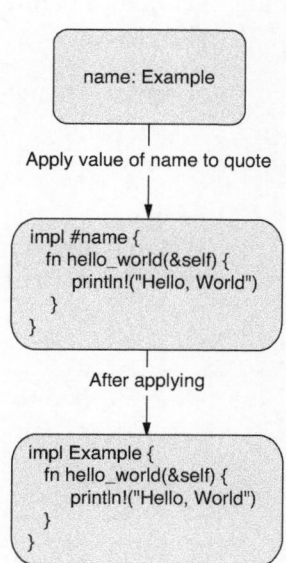

Figure 3.4   Using the `name` variable in `quote` for our `Example` struct

Run the code again, and it should produce the same output method as before, even if you change the name of your struct.

3.4   *Experimenting with our code*

Now let us run some experiments. Does our macro work with enums? Yes! Add the following to `main.rs`.

```
// previous code

#[derive(Hello)]
enum Pet {
    Cat,
}

fn main() {
    // previous code

    let p = Pet::Cat;
    p.hello_world();
}
```

How about functions? Unfortunately, this doesn't work, not only because `impl` cannot be used for functions but also because `derive` is not allowed for functions. The error brings this point across quite clearly: `derive may only be applied to structs, enums and unions`.

> **NOTE**   Though unions are a valid `derive` target, they do not feature in this book, mostly because they are much less ubiquitous than structs and enums, existing almost solely for compatibility with C over a foreign function interface (FFI).

Would our generated code overwrite existing implementation blocks? Thankfully, no. As we mentioned in an earlier chapter, Rust supports multiple `impl` blocks. So the following works.

```
// earlier code

impl Example {
    fn another_function(&self) {
        println!("Something else");
    }
}

fn main() {
    let e = Example {};
    e.hello_world();
```

```
        e.another_function();
        // other code
    }
```

Other things might still go wrong though. For example, if you were to define an additional `hello_world` function, you would get an error `duplicate definitions for hello_world`. You'd better hope no users of your macro will ever think to add a function with that name! Name overlap is a real risk—and something we will talk about later in this book.

3.5   cargo expand

In our previous chapter, we introduced a couple of ways to debug macros and to show what they expand to. But we skipped over one very useful tool: cargo expand (https://github.com/dtolnay/cargo-expand), which was unstable for some time but can now be used with stable Rust. You can install it with `cargo install cargo-expand`, after which you can run `cargo expand` in the root of the application directory or the `src` folder. This will print your application code after macro expansion. In listing 3.10, you can see that all macros, including `println!`, were expanded after running `cargo expand` in the root of our project. (Except, that `format_args!` was not expanded. That's a Rust problem [https://github.com/dtolnay/cargo-expand/issues/173], and fixing it is a work in progress.)

Listing 3.10 `cargo expand` **output (with changed formatting)**

```
#![feature(prelude_import)]
#[prelude_import]
use std::prelude::rust_2021::*;
```
As we saw earlier, a prelude contains globally available functions, traits, etc. Rust is adding annotations and an import to make them available. This is why, for example, Clone works without import.

```
// imports

struct Example;
```
The derive annotation has disappeared.

```
impl Example {
    fn hello_world(&self) {
        {
            ::std::io::_print(
                format_args!("Hello, World\n")
            );
        }
    }
}
```
The code from expanding #[derive(Hello)]

An expanded println!

```
// Pet enum and its expanded code

// main function
```

Our derive annotation has disappeared since it is not needed anymore, now that macro expansion is done. In its place, the macro-generated code has been added.

cargo expand is a useful tool for a visual inspection of our code, and it runs even when our output is invalid, making it useful for debugging compilation problems. Say I had mistyped self in our quote macro invocation. I would get a compilation error and the following output, showing that something was very wrong with the function parameter. If the error still wasn't clear, I could pipe the output to a file (cargo expand > somefile.rs) and have my IDE help me track down the problem. Or I could temporarily replace my main.rs and get pointed to the incorrect lines by cargo check:

```
impl ExampleStruct {
    fn hello_world(sel: ()) {
        {
            ::std::io::_print(format_args!("Hello, World\n"));
        }
    }
}
```

You can also use expand within the hello-world-macro library, but that will only show you how the macros you use—not the ones you create for others—are expanded, similar to how check will only point out errors in your code and not in generated code. So, most of the time, you want to use the expand command in applications that utilize your library and its macro.

3.6 *The same macro—without syn and quote*

The quote and syn libraries are very useful but not strictly necessary for writing macros. Listing 3.11 is the same application without them. To retrieve the name, we iterate over the incoming stream and take the second element with nth(1). That item is a TokenTree containing the name of the struct or enum. The first element, contained in nth(0), has the type (i.e., struct or enum) and is not relevant in this situation—so we skip it. With the ident_name function, we take the tree and return the name identifier or throw an error if we cannot find it.

> **DEFINITION** A TokenTree sits somewhere between a TokenStream and simple tokens. Basically, a TokenStream is a sequence of TokenTrees, which are themselves (recursively) composed of more trees and/or tokens. This is why we can iterate over our stream, pick an element, and assure Rust that the type is TokenTree. The tt fragment specifier for declarative macros, which we encountered in the previous chapter, is also a TokenTree.

To generate output, we use the format macro to inject our name variable in a string. For the transformation from string to TokenStream, we can use parse. We expect this to work, so we just use an unwrap on the Result that our parsing returns. This approach might seem very doable. We have removed two dependencies at the cost of a little bit of extra code. But even with such a basic example, we had to put in work to get the identifier and to output the new code. And with more complete examples, the complexity and additional burden of work would only grow.

Listing 3.11 Without `syn` and `quote`

```
use proc_macro::{TokenStream, TokenTree};

#[proc_macro_derive(Hello)]
pub fn hello_alt(item: TokenStream) -> TokenStream {
    fn ident_name(item: TokenTree) -> String {
        match item {
            TokenTree::Ident(i) => i.to_string(),
            _ => panic!("no ident")
        }
    }
    let name = ident_name(item.into_iter().nth(1).unwrap());

    format!("impl {} {{ fn hello_world(&self) \
    {{ println!(\"Hello, World\") }} }} ", name
        ).parse()
        .unwrap()
}
```

If we have a TokenTree containing an identifier, we return it as a string.

As an input for the previous function, we provide the second element of the TokenStream, which should be the name.

We use format! to add the retrieved name to a string representation of our impl block. Then we parse to turn it into a TokenStream. This will only fail if we made a mistake, in which case unwrap panicking is fine.

Even so, compilation speed is a reason why you might want to opt out of using `syn`. While it is a very powerful library, it is also big and slow to compile. So if our example was a real macro, and we only needed the name of the struct/enum, our naive example would compile a lot faster. Several libraries try to offer a lightweight alternative to `syn`—venial (https://github.com/PoignardAzur/venial), for example.

Listing 3.12 is what our macro looks like with that library. Don't forget to add `venial = "0.5.0"` to the dependencies if you are following along. The code looks very similar to what we had before. We use `parse_declaration`, which gives back an enum `Declaration`. With pattern matching, we retrieve the name from that enum.

Listing 3.12 Using a lightweight parser like venial

```
use quote::quote;
use proc_macro::TokenStream;
use venial::{parse_declaration, Declaration, Struct, Enum};

#[proc_macro_derive(Hello)]
pub fn hello(item: TokenStream) -> TokenStream {
    let declaration = parse_declaration(item.into()).unwrap();

    let name = match declaration {
        Declaration::Struct(Struct { name, .. }) => name,
        Declaration::Enum(Enum { name, .. }) => name,
        _ => panic!("only implemented for struct and enum")
    };

    let add_hello_world = quote! {
        impl #name {
            fn hello_world(&self) {
```

Retrieves the name if we receive an enum or a struct; panics in all other cases

```
                println!("Hello, World")
            }
        }
    };

    add_hello_world.into()
}
```

Even in this simple example, build times measured with `cargo build --timings` drop from 3.1 seconds to 1.8 on my machine. Still, in this book, we will use `syn` because it is well known, widely used, and very powerful. Plus, once you are familiar with how it handles the `TokenStream` parsing, switching to a lightweight alternative should not be too hard: many of the parsing concepts are always the same.

3.7   *From the real world*

We will save further library explorations for subsequent chapters and limit ourselves to a few observations for now. First, the developers of Rocket (https://rocket.rs/) are actually kind enough to teach you that macros can be imported in two ways (the ones we described in this chapter):

```
//! And to import all macros, attributes, and derives via `#[macro_use]`
//! in the crate root:
//!
//! ```rust
//! #[macro_use] extern crate rocket;
//! # #[get("/")] fn hello() { }
//! # fn main() { rocket::build().mount("/", routes![hello]); }
//! ```
//!
//! Or, alternatively, selectively import from the top-level scope:
//!
//! ```rust
//! # extern crate rocket;
//!
//! use rocket::{get, routes};
//! # #[get("/")] fn hello() { }
//! # fn main() { rocket::build().mount("/", routes![hello]); }
//! ```
```

Second, you may also be wondering how the standard library parses and outputs macros, since it cannot use external libraries like `syn` and `quote`. Instead, the standard library uses built-ins with similar concepts and names. For example, `rustc_ast`, the Rust abstract syntax tree, is used for parsing input. Outputting code is done with `rustc_expand`. And `rustc_span` contains utilities like `Ident` and `Span`. It is both familiar and alien when you are used to working with `syn` and `quote`. But it is not meant for external usage.

Finally, since procedural macros have to be placed in a library, in the root of the crate (or else you will get `functions tagged with #[proc_macro_derive] must currently reside in the root of the crate`), `lib.rs` is a great starting point for exploring other people's procedural macro code. You will see what macros they have and can dig in when needed.

Exercises

See the appendix for solutions.

1 Fill in the question marks (`???`) and make the following derive macro compile:

```
#[proc_macro_derive(???)]
pub fn uppercase(item: TokenStream) -> ??? {
    let ast = parse_macro_input!(item as ???);
    let name = ast.ident;
    let uppercase_name = name.to_string().to_uppercase();

    let add_uppercase = quote! {
        impl ??? {
            fn uppercase(&self) {
                println!("{}", #uppercase_name);
            }
        }
    };
    add_uppercase.into()
}
```

The following code fragment shows a usage example:

```
#[derive(UpperCaseName)]
struct Example;

fn main() {
    let e = Example {};
    e.uppercase(); // this prints 'EXAMPLE'
}
```

2 Try changing the name of the macro inside `lib.rs` and running the application. What error do you get? What do you have to do to fix things?

3 Add a function called `testing_testing` to the output of our macro. This is an *associated* function, one that takes no `&self` parameter. It should write `"One two three"` to the console.

4 See if you can output a greeting followed by the name of the input (e.g., "Hello Example"). Fair warning: passing `#name` to print will not be enough, because that's an identifier, and you need a string. So either call `to_string` on the identifier and save the result in a variable or use the `stringify` macro to change the `#name` into a string for you.

Summary

- Derive macros, the first kind of procedural macro, allow us to add functionality to structs and enums.
- To write procedural macros, we need to create a library with a function that accepts a `TokenStream` input and outputs another `TokenStream`.

- That output is the code that will be generated and added to our application.
- To verify our macro, we cannot rely solely on `cargo check` within the library, because that will only check the code within the library itself, not the code we generate. Therefore, it is useful to have an application that uses and tests our macro. At the very least, this way we can verify that the generated code compiles.
- You can write procedural macros with standard Rust tooling, but `syn` is of great help parsing input, and `quote` has a macro to generate output.
- You can retrieve values from your input and pass them into your output.
- `cargo expand` is a great tool that allows you to see the code generated by macros in your code.

Making fields public
with attribute macros

4

This chapter covers

- Understanding the differences between derive macros and attribute macros
- Finding field information in the abstract syntax tree
- Retrieving fields by using matching
- Retrieving fields with a custom struct
- Retrieving fields with a custom struct and a `Parse` implementation
- Adding multiple outputs in `quote`
- Debugging macros with log statements
- Understanding the `no-panic` crate

Rust likes to hide information. A function, struct, or enum is private by default, and the same goes for the fields of a struct. This is very sensible, though occasionally slightly annoying when you have a struct that has a lot of fields that are better off being public. *Data Transfer Objects* (DTOs) are a classic example of this and a common pattern in many programming languages, used for transferring information between systems or different parts of a single system. Because they are a simple wrapper for information, they should not contain any business logic. And "information hiding," a primary reason for keeping fields in a struct/class private, is not applicable when your only value is exposing the information contained in fields.

For the purpose of experimentation, we will show how we can change the default behavior with a few lines of code. We will create a macro that, once added to a struct, will make it and all of its fields public. This is a very different challenge than the one we faced in the previous chapter. Back then, we were adding things to existing code. Now we have to modify what is already there. So derive macros are out, and *attribute macros* are in.

Attribute macros get their name from the fact that they define a new attribute. When you annotate a struct or enum with that new custom attribute, the macro will be triggered. Otherwise, writing the library and code for an attribute macro is quite similar to creating a derive macro. But there are differences as well: an attribute macro also receives a `TokenStream` containing additional attributes (if any). And—more importantly for this chapter—its output tokens will *replace* the input. That sounds like something that could do the trick.

4.1 Setup of an attribute macro project

Let's go through this chapter's setup, which is very similar to the previous one:

- Create a new directory (`make-public`) with another directory (`make-public-macro`) inside it.
- Inside the nested `make-public-macro` directory, run `cargo init --lib` to initialize our macro.
- Add the `syn` and `quote` dependencies (with `cargo add syn quote`) and set `lib` to `proc-macro = true`.
- Run `cargo init` in the outer `make-public` directory and add our library as a dependency.

Listing 4.1 Part of the `Cargo.toml` file from `make-public-macro`

```
[dependencies]
quote = "1.0.33"
syn = "2.0.39"

[lib]
proc-macro = true
```

Listing 4.2 Part of the `Cargo.toml` from `make-public`

```
[dependencies]
make-public-macro = { path = "./make-public-macro" }
```

4.2 Attribute macros vs. derive macros

With the setup out of the way, we start simple by adding a bit of code to `lib.rs` in the nested directory. We define a public function that produces a `TokenStream`. It takes an `item` parameter and parses it into an abstract syntax tree (AST). That way we will once again be able to retrieve whatever we need from the original code. Just like before, the output is created using the `quote!` macro.

Listing 4.3   Initial setup

```
extern crate core;

use quote::quote;
use proc_macro::TokenStream;
use syn::{parse_macro_input, DeriveInput};

#[proc_macro_attribute]
pub fn public(_attr: TokenStream, item: TokenStream)
    -> TokenStream {
    let _ast = parse_macro_input!(item as DeriveInput);

    let public_version = quote! {};

    public_version.into()
}
```

The annotation tells Rust that this is an attribute macro.

The name of an attribute macro is determined by the name of the function ("public"). It takes two streams as parameters.

A leading underscore here because we are not using the AST yet

As before, our initial implementation takes the input and produces no output.

While the code should look familiar, there are some differences when you compare it to the previous chapter. First, we have a different attribute: `#[proc_macro_attribute]` instead of `#[proc_macro_derive]`. And, unlike before, we do not specify the name of the macro between parentheses (`#[proc_macro_derive(Hello)]`). Instead, the name of the function determines the attribute name. So, in our case, this macro creates a custom attribute `#[public]`. You can also see that we receive an additional `Token-Stream`—which we will ignore for the time being—that contains information about our attribute (see figure 4.1).

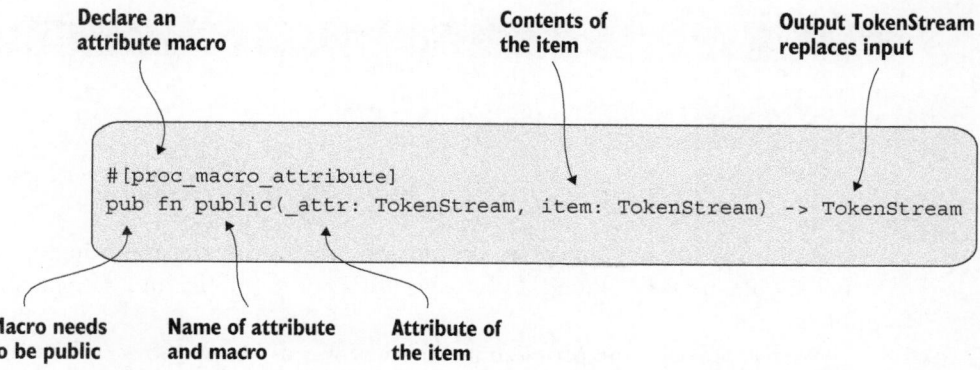

Declare an attribute macro

Contents of the item

Output TokenStream replaces input

```
#[proc_macro_attribute]
pub fn public(_attr: TokenStream, item: TokenStream) -> TokenStream
```

Macro needs to be public

Name of attribute and macro

Attribute of the item

Figure 4.1   The signature of an attribute macro

The starting point of our code is the same as that of the previous chapter: a macro that does not produce any output. But this time we do have an effect on our existing code by not returning anything. Try adding the code in the following listing to your application `main.rs` and running `cargo expand`.

Listing 4.4   **Running** `cargo expand` **with this** `main.rs`

```
use make_public_macro::public;

#[public]
struct Example {}

fn main() {}
```

The `Example` struct is now gone! Spooky.

Listing 4.5   **Our struct pulling a disappearing act**

```
#![feature(prelude_import)]
#[prelude_import]
use std::prelude::rust_2021::*;
#[macro_use]
extern crate std;

use make_public_macro::public;

fn main() {}
```

As we said earlier, Rust expects an attribute macro output to replace the input, which does make things slightly more complex than they were before.

4.3   *First steps in public visibility*

Back to the task at hand: we can now add properties to our struct to make things more concrete.

Listing 4.6   **Our example struct**

```
#[public]
struct Example {
    first: String,
    pub second: u32,
}
```

We would like for our macro to output this struct with the following changes: the struct should become public, `first` should become public, and `second` should stay public.

We can approach the problem in the same way as before. So we start with the easiest implementation, one that only works for this specific struct.

Listing 4.7   A hardcoded implementation

```
extern crate core;

use quote::quote;
use proc_macro::TokenStream;
use syn::{parse_macro_input, DeriveInput};

#[proc_macro_attribute]
pub fn public(_attr: TokenStream, item: TokenStream) -> TokenStream {
    let _ast = parse_macro_input!(item as DeriveInput);

    let public_version = quote! {
        pub struct Example {
            pub first: String,
            pub second: u32,
        }
    };

    public_version.into()
}
```

> **Still not using the AST!**

> We are returning our Example struct as we defined it earlier, as a hardcoded response.

That obviously works. Now, as a next step, we previously learned how we can retrieve the name of the input struct. By applying that knowledge here, we will be able to accept any kind of struct that has the same fields as our example.

Listing 4.8   Hardcoded properties with the struct name retrieved from the input

```
#[proc_macro_attribute]
pub fn public(_attr: TokenStream, item: TokenStream) -> TokenStream {
    let ast = parse_macro_input!(item as DeriveInput);
    let name = ast.ident;

    let public_version = quote! {
        pub struct #name {
            pub first: String,
            pub second: u32,
        }
    };

    public_version.into()
}
```

Applying what we already know, we retrieve the name of our struct and pass it to `quote`. We are finally using our AST, and we have taken another small step in making our struct more generally usable. Nice. What we would like to do next is to retrieve and use the incoming fields. They come from the same place as the name: our AST.

4.4   Getting and using fields

As noted before, the parameter `item` contains all relevant code, meaning the entire struct can be accessed via the `ast` variable. That variable is of type `DeriveInput`, which is a representation of the kind of input we might receive from a derive macro. And yes, we are writing an attribute macro. But the type works because these two share some important input targets: structs, enums, and unions. And while attribute macros can also target traits and functions, that's not currently important to us. If you prefer a more fitting type, `syn::ItemStruct` should be a drop-in replacement, but it does have the downside that it is hidden behind the "full" feature flag. So we would need to change our `syn` import to use it.

What does `DeriveInput` contain? This is the source code (https://docs.rs/syn/latest/src/syn/derive.rs.html#4-14):

```
pub struct DeriveInput {          ◁──   DeriveInput is a struct
    pub attrs: Vec<Attribute>,           to represent derive
    pub vis: Visibility,                 macro input.                    It has the
    pub ident: Ident,      ◁──┤ The identifier       ◁────────────       item's attributes.
    pub generics: Generics,       ◁──┤ Any generics    Its visibility
    pub data: Data,        ◁──┐                         modifier
}                              └ Other information
                                 (content)
```

You know Rust, so you can guess the meaning of most of these properties:

- `attrs` contains any attributes defined on the struct; for example, `#[derive(Debug)]`.
- `vis` has the `Visibility` of our struct (public, visible in crate, or just private, i.e., "inherited").
- `ident` has the name (identifier) of our struct.
- `generics` contains information if our struct is generic (`Example<T>`). But that's not the case here.
- `data` is where we can find details about the data within our struct.

`data` sounds the most useful to us; what does `data` contain? Go down the `syn` rabbit hole, and you will find that `Data` is an enum with three options: `Struct`, `Enum`, and `Union`. That makes sense, since `DeriveInput` was created specifically for derive macros, which, unlike attribute macros, can only be used for these three targets:

```
pub enum Data {
    Struct(DataStruct),
    Enum(DataEnum),          Data is an enum with
    Union(DataUnion),        three variants.
}
```

`Struct` is the variant we need. What does the `DataStruct` nested inside contain? Dig just a little deeper. You will see that it has a `struct_token`, which contains the `struct` keyword (not useful); `semi_token`, which is an optionally present semicolon (not interesting); and the `fields` of the struct (see figure 4.2):

```
pub struct DataStruct {
    pub struct_token: Token![struct],
```

```
    pub fields: Fields,
    pub semi_token: Option<Token![;]>,
}
```

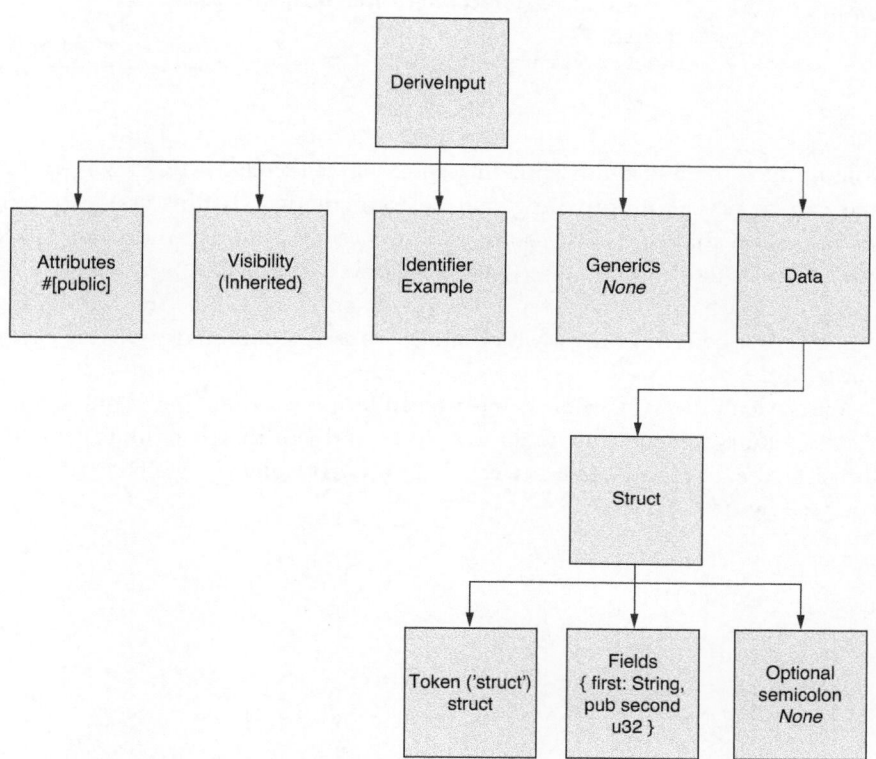

Figure 4.2   Finding the roots of the world tree: from `DeriveInput` to `Fields` for our `Example` struct

Now that we know where to find our fields, let's extract them from the data. For now, we just want this working for structs, so we will ignore enums and unions during matching. We will also use matching to drill down to the named fields—fields that have both a name and a type, `first: String`, for example. The "`..`" in the following code helps us ignore properties inside `DataStruct` and `FieldsNamed` that do not interest us, including the unnamed fields, which we will discuss later. If you forget to add those two dots, you will get back an error similar to `struct pattern does not mention fields someField and anotherField`. That is Rust telling you that a couple of fields are missing from your `match`:

```
let fields = match ast.data {
    Struct(
        DataStruct {
            fields: Named(
```

```
            FieldsNamed {
                ref named, ..
            }), ..
        }
    ) => named,
    _ => unimplemented!(
        "only works for structs with named fields"
    ),
};
```

> Matching makes it easy to only extract named fields from our input.

> When we do not receive a struct with named fields, we panic.

Now we have named fields with this type: `Punctuated<Field, Token![,]>`. Punctuated can be just about anything that has punctuation. In this case, the punctuation generics show that `Fields` are separated by a comma `Token`. And fields in a struct are indeed separated by a comma. Useful to know is that `Punctuated` implements `IntoIterator`, so we can iterate over it. Dig down, and you will see that we will be iterating over the first generic, `Field`, which makes sense. A comma is not very interesting to iterate over.

We have all the struct fields, and we can loop over them. Next question: what is in `Field`? Again, we turn to the source code and see that it contains lots of familiar things: `attrs`, `vis`, and `ident`, as well as a property called `ty`, which contains the field's type (see figure 4.3).

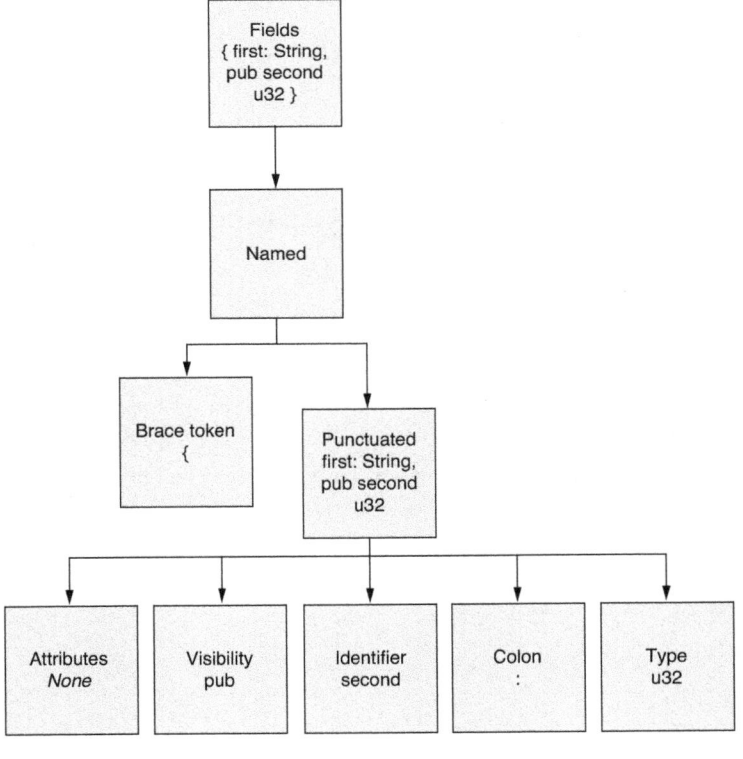

Figure 4.3
From `Fields` to `Punctuated` for the second **field** of `Example` (**simplified view**)

Now what? What is our goal? Well, we want to refill the struct with its properties, except now prefaced with a public visibility indicator. For our `Example` struct, we want to add the `pub first: String` using `quote`. Once that is done, we want to add `pub second: u32`. So all we need to do is retrieve the name and type. Any other information—including visibility, since we always set `pub`—is irrelevant.

> **NOTE** We are ignoring the other attributes that the struct might have, which means other macros might not work as expected for our struct. We will see how we can fix that later.

You can see the implementation of this idea in the following code. We iterate over the fields and use `map` to extract the identifier and type. With `quote`, we generate a `Token-Stream` with the public prefix, the name, and the type of the given field:

```
let builder_fields = fields.iter().map(|f| {
    let name = &f.ident;                    Now that we have an individual field
    let ty = &f.ty;                         within map, we can retrieve the name.
    quote! { pub #name: #ty }         With quote, we give back a TokenStream containing
});                                   the input plus a pub prefix for every field.
```

By now we know that anything that is not a literal should be prefixed by a hashtag in our output. That way, `quote` knows it needs to replace the given value with the value inside the identically named variable. Note that `quote` cannot access a variable's properties, so doing something like `quote! { pub #f.ident: #f.ty }` will only result in confusing errors, as `#f` will be "resolved" and a literal value `.ident` will be added to the output. Also interesting is that we don't need to `collect` the output of the map—because `quote` knows how to handle maps that produce `TokenStreams`. If you want to simplify a function signature, you can still call `collect` to get a `Vec<TokenStream>` output, though. We will see examples of that later.

Now all we have to do is add the map of streams to the struct that we are returning. And we need to tell Rust that these streams will be separated by a comma, or Rust will complain about syntax. `quote` offers a convenience for this, which looks quite similar to how you would handle multiple elements in a declarative macro: `#(#name-of-your-variable,)*` (i.e., take this variable, which contains zero or more values, and after every retrieved element, add a comma). Do note that you need two hashtags for repetition in `quote`. Forget the outer one, and you will be greeted by this error: "the trait ToTokens is not implemented for Map..."

Listing 4.9 **Our public fields macro**

```
use quote::quote;
use proc_macro::TokenStream;
use syn::{parse_macro_input, DeriveInput, DataStruct, FieldsNamed};
use syn::Data::Struct;
use syn::Fields::Named;

#[proc_macro_attribute]
pub fn public(_attr: TokenStream, item: TokenStream) -> TokenStream {
```

```
let ast = parse_macro_input!(item as DeriveInput);
let name = ast.ident;

let fields = match ast.data {
    Struct(
        DataStruct {
            fields: Named(
                FieldsNamed {
                    ref named, ..
                }), ..
        }
    ) => named,
    _ => unimplemented!(
        "only works for structs with named fields"
    ),
};

let builder_fields = fields.iter().map(|f| {
    let name = &f.ident;
    let ty = &f.ty;
    quote! { pub #name: #ty }
});

let public_version = quote! {
    pub struct #name {
        #(#builder_fields,)*
    }
};

public_version.into()
}
```

If we have a struct with named fields, we retrieve the fields.

From these fields, we get the name and type, and return a TokenStream containing pub, the name, and the type for each element.

In our output, we tell quote that builder_fields is a list of elements that should be added to the struct, separated by commas.

As you can see, `quote` is as versatile as you need it to be. We can add a single, simple `TokenStream` with #name, or we can add multiple elements in one go. In more complex macros, the output is often composed of a whole range of variables brought together in one final output. And those variables might also be the result of a composition of `quote` of undetermined complexity. In any case, thanks to the previous code, simple structs like `Example` now have all their fields set to public. Privacy is officially dead!

4.5   Possible extensions

There are lots of ways we could now expand our macro to make it more useful. For example, instead of panicking when we receive an enum, we could write code to handle it. Do remember that the variants of an enum are automatically public when the enum itself is public, meaning it is probably easier to just add `pub` to an enum rather than using a custom macro.

We have also been ignoring unnamed fields, which do appear in structs like, for example, `struct Example(u32, String);`. If we wrote our struct like this, we would have reached our `unimplemented` match. So how would we handle these structures? The first step would be to dig out the unnamed fields, which would be very similar to how we retrieved the named fields. We could do that in an additional match arm.

Once we have the fields, we can output them in the correct style—for example, `pub struct Example(pub u32, pub String);`. Finally, you would have to differentiate between a named and unnamed struct and decide on the kind of output to return. Luckily, this is a simple binary choice: a struct is either named or unnamed.

Somewhat surprisingly, our code will correctly handle empty structs but only when they are followed by brackets or curly braces. A struct without them like `struct Empty;` would not have anything in the way of fields at all, so it would end up in our `unimplemented` arm.

There are a few more potential problems (besides not handling `Unions`). For example, our macro won't make fields of nested structs public. As luck would have it, just adding `#[public]` to the nested items is an easy fix.

A much bigger problem is that when we have other macros annotating our struct, they are deleted by ours. Try adding a `#[derive(Debug)]` below our annotation and running `cargo expand`. Do you see how the additional annotation vanishes into thin air? We are simply superb at making things disappear. As macros are executed in order, from top to bottom, the simple workaround is adding the derive *above* our `#[public]`. Now everything will work as expected. Except—please do not do this. Instead, do things the proper way and retrieve and reattach all the available attributes.

Moreover, while we are keeping the generics of our named fields, we are recreating the struct's signature, meaning that its generics disappear. Fixing that would require using and re-adding the `generics` field from `DeriveInput`. You can try out several of these extensions in the exercises later.

4.6 *More than one way to parse a stream*

The previously described approach shows one way to create procedural macros. It uses `syn` for parsing your tokens, `quote` for creating new ones, and matching plus functions for everything in between. However, if gluing things together with functions is not your thing, there are alternatives, like a more "struct-focused" approach. As an example, we will revisit our public macro and show some options.

4.6.1 *Delegating tasks to a custom struct*

First, we could delegate getting and outputting the fields to a `StructField`. Start by adding a dependency to `proc-macro2`, which we will need shortly.

> **Listing 4.10 Two familiar dependencies in our library `toml` file and a new one**

```
[dependencies]
quote = "1.0.33"
syn = "2.0.39"
proc-macro2 = "1.0.69"
```

Now take a look at the new implementation. There are two big changes. Instead of using the primitives from `syn` directly, we have our struct gather/organize all required information (i.e., name and type). By convention, a method called `new` should be used for creating a struct, so we create one and call it when iterating over our fields. `map(StructField::new)` is a convenient shorthand—also known as point-free style—for `map(|f| StructField::new(f))`.

Listing 4.11   An implementation that uses structs to do most of the gluing

```
use proc_macro::TokenStream;
use quote::{quote, ToTokens};
// previous imports

struct StructField {
    name: Ident,                        This struct contains the data we
    ty: Type,                           need for every field of the struct.
}

impl StructField {
    fn new(field: &Field) -> Self {
        Self {
            name: field.ident.as_ref().unwrap().clone(),    Our new contains code
            ty: field.ty.clone(),                           for retrieving name and
        }                                                   type from a field.
    }
}

impl ToTokens for StructField {
    fn to_tokens(&self, tokens: &mut proc_macro2::TokenStream) {
        let n = &self.name;                     ToTokens outputs a token stream
        let t = &self.ty;                       with the field set to public. Because
        quote!(pub #n: #t).to_tokens(tokens)    it is part of the quote library, it uses
    }                                           proc_macro2::TokenStream.
}

#[proc_macro_attribute]
pub fn public(_attr: TokenStream, item: TokenStream) -> TokenStream {
    // unchanged: get fields
    let builder_fields = fields.iter().map(StructField::new);   ◄──────
    // unchanged: quote for output
}                                              During iteration, we map
                                               every Field to StructField
                                               by calling new.
```

`builder_fields` contains our custom structs. How can `quote` transform this into a `TokenStream`? It can't, because it has no idea how to change a random struct to a bunch of tokens. One solution would be to write a second method that turns the struct into a `TokenStream` and call it during iteration. But there's a trait for that! `ToTokens`, from `quote`, turns the implementor into `TokenStream`, so we will use that trait instead.

The code inside `to_tokens` is similar to what we were doing before in our mapping, except `to_tokens` requires us to give all our new tokens to a mutable parameter of type `proc_macro2::TokenStream`, which, as we briefly mentioned, is a community-built token stream that wraps around the built-in stream and adds additional features. It is used internally by `quote`, which is why we always have to add `into` to the result of quote when returning our tokens. Now that we use it explicitly in the signature of an impl block, we have to add it to our project's dependencies. What also would have worked is using quote::__private::TokenStream, but let's go with the cleaner approach. And with that, our builder_fields is automatically turned into a Token-Stream, and our final quote code does not need to change.

This is more code—and complexity—than we had before, but there are positives as well. There is a separation of concerns: we have made a struct responsible for the retrieval and outputting of a field. This can enable reuse and could prove to be more readable and structured. In this basic example, it is probably overengineering, but some structuring of data into structs might prove useful in a bigger procedural macro.

4.6.2   Implementing the Parse trait

We could go one step further and incorporate an additional built-in from syn, the Parse trait, which is used for changing a TokenStream into a struct or enum. In the next code listing, we add an implementation of this trait and its method parse, which receives syn::parse::ParseStream as input. Just think of that as a sort of TokenStream.

Listing 4.12   Parsing instead of using new

```
// imports

struct StructField {          Instead of Type, ty is now an
    name: Ident,              Ident, because that is what we
    ty: Ident,           ◁──┘ are receiving from our Parse.
}

// ToTokens implementation remains unchanged
                                                          We try to parse the
                                                          visibility into a variable of
                                                          type Result<Visibility, _>
                                                          to get rid of it, moving the
impl Parse for StructField {                              pointer to the next token.
    fn parse(input: ParseStream) -> Result<Self, syn::Error> {
        let _vis: Result<Visibility, _> = input.parse();   ◁──
        let list = Punctuated::<Ident, Colon>::parse_terminated(input)
            .unwrap();        ◁──┐ A field without visibility is a kind of Punctuated, so we
                                   call parse_terminated to parse the rest of the field.
        Ok(StructField {
            name: list.first().unwrap().clone(),
            ty: list.last().unwrap().clone(),          The first element should be the
        })                                             name and the type should be
    }                                                  last. Because we parsed the
}                                                      field as identifiers separated by
                                                       a colon, ty is now Ident.
#[proc_macro_attribute]
pub fn public(_attr: TokenStream, item: TokenStream) -> TokenStream {
    // unchanged
    let builder_fields = fields.iter()                   Iterates over the fields and
        .map(|f| {                                       uses parse2. The Result
            syn::parse2::<StructField>(f.to_token_stream())  might be any number of
                .unwrap()                                things, so we have to say
        });                                              that we want a StructField.
    // unchanged
}
```

The new method has been made redundant by parse.

We expect to receive a `ParseStream` representation of a single field in our `parse` implementation. That means the first thing we will receive is a token indicating the field's visibility. We are not interested in that value, but handling it now will make the rest of our parsing easier. So we call `parse` on the input and tell it that we want to bind this `Visibility` to a variable `_vis`. `parse` might fail, so `Visibility` is wrapped in a `Result`, which we won't even unwrap because this was just to get rid of the value. Now our `ParseStream` no longer contains the field's visibility modifier, and we can continue (see figure 4.4).

> **NOTE** Perhaps you thought visibility was an optional part of the field definition, which is certainly what I used to think. But look back at the AST diagrams and source code: `Parse-Stream` always has a `Visibility`. By default, it's just `Inherited`, which—according to the documentation—"usually means private."

In our next step, `Punctuated::<Ident, Colon>` tells Rust that we expect something that consists of identifiers separated by a colon (`:`). That, after all, is what a field declaration looks like without its visibility: `field_name: FieldType`. And, as our example shows, the first element should be the name and the last element the type. So we can add those to our struct. Note that because of `Punctuated`, `ty` is now parsed as an `Ident`, which is perfectly valid.

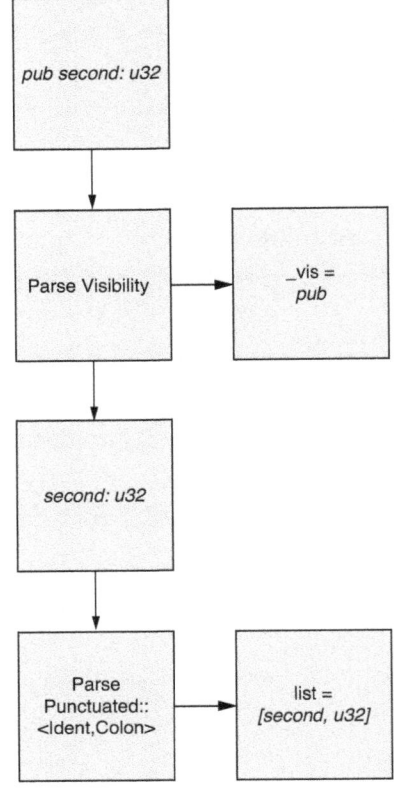

Figure 4.4   Parsing the `second` field

If visibility was still part of our stream at this stage, Rust would complain with `Error("expected identifier")`, because it expected a list of identifiers and got a `Visibility` type. But even though we avoid that error, this is still not a production-ready macro. We are expecting simple, unannotated, named fields. Nothing else. And that is only part of the range of content that a struct might have, albeit an important part. But this will do for now.

All that remains is to pass in the field tokens for parsing. We can use `syn::parse2` to accomplish that task. It accepts a `TokenStream` and can return any type that implements `Parse`. But since a lot of things implement `Parse`, we have to tell the function what return type we would like. In our case, that is a `StructField`. `parse2::<Struct-Field>` is probably the most elegant way to relay this info. One clumsy alternative is `map(|f| { let field: StructField = parse2(f.to_token_stream()).unwrap(); field })`.

> **NOTE** Why parse2? parse also exists and is very similar, but it accepts an ordinary `TokenStream`, whereas parse2 takes the `proc_macro2` variant (hence the names). By the way, `parse_macro_input!` is just syntactic sugar for parse.

`.map(|f| parse2::<StructField>(f.to_token_stream())` is not great, though. We have some nicely parsed data from `syn`, and we are turning it back into a `TokenStream`. You could avoid this ugliness by, for example, parsing all the fields (or the entire input) into custom structs instead of parsing every individual field.

4.6.3 *Going low, low, low with cursor*

As a final example, we could also have chosen `cursor` for low-level control over our parsing:

```
impl Parse for StructField {
    fn parse(input: ParseStream) -> Result<Self, syn::Error> {
        let first = input.cursor().ident().unwrap();

        let res = if first.0.to_string().contains("pub") {
            let second = first.1.ident().unwrap();
            let third = second.1.punct().unwrap().1.ident().unwrap();
            Ok(StructField {
                name: second.0,
                ty: third.0,
            })
        } else {
            let second = first.1.punct().unwrap().1.ident().unwrap();
            Ok(StructField {
                name: first.0,
                ty: second.0,
            })
        };

        let _: Result<proc_macro2::TokenStream, _> = input.parse();
        res
    }
}
```

We call `cursor` on our input parameter and tell it the first thing it will encounter is an identifier. `cursor` does not differentiate between names, types, visibility, etc., so this will capture either the visibility or the name of the field. If the name contains the string "pub," we probably have the visibility, which means the next identifier is the name, which we get by calling `first.1.ident()` and unwrapping the result. Our variable `second` should have the name and the rest of our data. Our type is behind a colon, so we expect to find punctuation (`punct()`) followed by the identifier. Now that we have both name and type, we give them to `StructField`. The other conditional branch is similar. When we do not have an explicit visibility modifier, we already have the name and only need to retrieve the type.

The final `let _: Result<proc_macro2::TokenStream, _> = input.parse();` is icky, though. `cursor` is giving us immutable access to the existing stream. This is great—except that after calling your parsing method, `parse2` does a check to make sure there's nothing left unhandled inside your stream. And, in our case, we did not—could not, even—change anything, so we will get a confusing `Error("unexpected token")` error. So we just call `parse` and make it give back a `Result`, which we ignore. This is a bit similar to ignoring the visibility in our previous example (listing 4.12).

What style should you prefer? It depends. Functions and matching are relatively easy and seem ideal for smaller macros or writing a proof of concept. Structs can give additional structure to your solution and offer a nice way to delegate responsibility: every struct does a bit of the parsing and outputting. They are also very useful when you are passing things into macros that do not count as proper Rust code, like DSLs. Default parsers are obviously not well equipped to deal with seemingly random input that only has meaning within your particular domain. So instead, you write your own structs and capture relevant information. `cursor`, meanwhile, gives low-level control and a lot of power, but it is verbose and less easy to use. It should probably not be your first choice.

In this book, many chapters focus on functions as the glue for building macros, because this style is convenient for brief examples. But because structs are often used "in the wild," we will also have examples using that style.

4.7   *Even more ways to develop and debug*

In previous chapters, we talked about development and debugging tools like `cargo expand`. In this chapter, we also did a lot of digging through source code, which helped us understand more of what data is available when `syn` has parsed your input. Another useful tool worth mentioning is—please don't slam this book shut—printing to the console, because seeing the structure of your AST via types is useful, but printing it tells you what is actually in there, which is very useful when you are uncertain about what you are receiving.

Two things to note: first, to debug–print `DeriveInput` and other types from `syn`, you will need to activate the `extra-traits` feature of `syn`:

```
syn = { version = "2.0.39", features=["extra-traits"]}
```

Second, there is a good chance that standard output will get captured and won't show up in your console. The easy workaround is to use error printing, which should always find its way back to you:

```
let ast = parse_macro_input!(item as DeriveInput);
eprintln!("{:#?}", &ast);
```

Next, you can see an abbreviated output from this command when we add the `eprintln` command to our macro. There is a lot of information in there, and learning to read it takes some time. But you should recognize many types that we discussed in this chapter—Ident, Struct, DataStruct, FieldsNamed, etc.:

```
DeriveInput {
    vis: Inherited,
```

```
            ident: Ident {
                ident: "Example",
                span: #0 bytes(67..74),
            },
            ...
        data: Struct(
            DataStruct {
                struct_token: Struct,
                fields: Named(
                    FieldsNamed {
                        named: [
                            Field {
                                attrs: [],
                                vis: Inherited,
                                ident: Some(
                                    Ident {
                                        ident: "first",
                                        span: #0 bytes(81..86),
                                    },
                                ),
                                colon_token: Some(
                                    Colon,
                                ),
                                ...
            },
        ),
    }
```

4.8 *From the real world*

Lots of libraries use attribute macros to do cool things. For example, Tokio, a widely used asynchronous runtime for Rust, uses its #[tokio::main] macro to transform your main into something that can handle asynchronous calls. This is the source code entry point:

```
#[proc_macro_attribute]
pub fn main(args: TokenStream, item: TokenStream) -> TokenStream {
    entry::main(args, item, true)
}
```

Wait, just main? Then why do all code examples show #[tokio::main]? Well, probably to make it clear to the reader that this is Tokio's main macro. But since the bit before :: only signifies from which crate we are getting the macro, use tokio::main; plus #[main] is also perfectly valid (the more you know ...).

There are also lots of examples of libraries using the Parse and ToTokens traits. Here are some examples from Rocket, a web framework that uses a lot of macros for generating endpoints, among other things. Want to respond to a GET call? Just add the custom #[get("/add/endpoint")] annotation:

```
impl Parse for Invocation {
  fn parse(input: ParseStream<'_>) -> syn::Result<Self> {
    Ok(Invocation {
      ty_stream_ty: (input.parse()?, input.parse::<syn::Token![,]>()?).0,
```

```
        stream_mac: (input.parse()?, input.parse::<syn::Token![,]>()?).0,
        stream_trait: (input.parse()?, input.parse::<syn::Token![,]>()?).0,
        input: input.parse()?,
      })
    }
}

impl ToTokens for UriExpr {
    fn to_tokens(&self, t: &mut TokenStream) {
        match self {
            UriExpr::Uri(uri) => uri.to_tokens(t),
            UriExpr::Expr(e) => e.to_tokens(t),
        }
    }
}
```

As you can see, the `Parse` implementation has better error handling than our code (it uses ? instead of unwrapping). Good error handling is advisable for a production-grade macro, so we will get back to that in a later chapter. Even so, occasionally you see panics appearing in the wild. Yew, a web framework that has a cool macro for writing and verifying HTML, has `unimplemented!("only structs are supported")` appearing in two places.

As a final example, take a look at `no-panic` (https://github.com/dtolnay/no-panic), a macro that makes your compiler prove that a given function never panics—which is pretty amazing. How could that possibly work? Consider the following code:

```
struct Dropper {}
impl Drop for Dropper {
    fn drop(&mut self) {                    Implements Drop for
        println!("Dropping!")               our Dropper struct
    }
}

fn some_fun() {
    let d = Dropper {};                     After creating a Dropper
    panic!("panic");                ◄───┐   instance, panic!
    core::mem::forget(d);           ◄─┐  core::mem::forget(d) causes Rust
}                                       to forget about d. So if it runs,
fn main() {                             the drop will not be executed.
    some_fun();
}
```

We have a struct called `Dropper` that implements `Drop`, the trait that you can use in Rust when custom cleanup of a resource is required. When you run the code, `some_fun` will trigger a panic, followed by an unwinding of the stack. At that point, `Drop` from Dropper is invoked to clean up our struct.

But if we comment out the panic, we reach `forget` on the next line. That will make Rust forget about the `Dropper` struct and its `Drop` implementation. In that case, `Drop` will not be called. (Remember, we stop executing when a panic is encountered. So, in the first case, we never reach `forget`. But—by default at least—Rust does do a cleanup of resources on panic.) This has an interesting implication. If the compiler can "prove" that there is no chance that some_fun will panic, the logical conclusion is that Drop *will never be called* because of the forget call! As a consequence, Rust can safely optimize away the Drop implementation, since it is never used.

This library and others similar to it do a neat trick: they create a struct, implement Drop and call a nonexisting C function within the implementation, and add a forget call. That means we will get a linking error if the code is not optimized away. And the code is not removed when a panic is possible before the forget call, because, in that case, Rust might have to call Drop after all. Neat, huh?

```
struct __NoPanic;
extern "C" {
    #[link_name = "does_not_exist"]
    fn trigger() -> !;
}
impl Drop for __NoPanic {
    fn drop(&mut self) {
        unsafe {
            trigger();
        }
    }
}
```

The code from the library itself is fairly brief (some 150 lines of code). The following is a selection with some annotations. Among other things, I removed some error handling because we haven't discussed that yet. And for now, all you need to know about parse_quote is that it is similar to the regular quote macro:

```
#[proc_macro_attribute]
pub fn no_panic(args: TokenStream, input: TokenStream) -> TokenStream {
    let expanded = match parse(args, input.clone()) {
        Ok(function) => expand_no_panic(function),
        // error handling
    };
    TokenStream::from(expanded)
}
```

The macro entry point. Calls a custom parse function and forwards an Ok result to expand_no_panic.

```
fn parse(args: TokenStream2, input: TokenStream2) -> Result<ItemFn> {
    let function: ItemFn = syn::parse2(input)?;
    let _: Nothing = syn::parse2::<Nothing>(args)?;
    Ok(function)
}
```

ItemFn is a syn built-in for parsing functions, similar to how DeriveInput helps us with enums and structs.

```
fn expand_no_panic(mut function: ItemFn) -> TokenStream2 {
    // ...
    let stmts = function.block.stmts;
    let message = format!(
        "\n\nERROR[no-panic]: detected panic in function `{}`\n",
        function.sig.ident,
    );
    function.block = Box::new(parse_quote!({
        struct __NoPanic;
```

This function is doing the heavy lifting. In the ItemFn type, function.block has the body of the function. The __NoPanic stuff is added to that body.

```
        extern "C" {
            #[link_name = #message]
            fn trigger() -> !;
        }
        impl core::ops::Drop for __NoPanic {
            // ...
        }
        let __guard = __NoPanic;
        let __result = (move || #ret {
            #move_self
            #(
                let #arg_pat = #arg_val;
            ) *
            #(#stmts) *
        }) ();
        core::mem::forget(__guard);
        __result
    }));

    quote!(#function)
}
```

> **This function is doing the heavy lifting. In the ItemFn type, function.block has the body of the function. The __NoPanic stuff is added to that body.**

You should recognize a lot of familiar elements in this code. We start with the declaration of our macro using the attribute macro. Because the function name determines the name of the macro, we know that we need to write #[no_panic] when using this macro. We receive two token streams as parameters and use parse2 to parse the input into ItemFn, a syn built-in for parsing functions that we will study in more detail in an upcoming chapter. The args are not used and so are parsed into an ignored variable of type Nothing. If there is anything inside this TokenStream, parsing into Nothing will fail (hence the name). By the way, the double specification of types (Nothing and syn::parse2::<Nothing>) is redundant. Either will do.

expand_no_panic contains the bulk of what we discussed previously. It adds the fake linked C function and tries to forget it. As a bonus, the link_name of the fake C function is used as a message to report the detected panic when Drop is not optimized away. The implementation, contained within function.block.stmts (stmts stands for "statements"), is added to our new implementation, which overwrites the existing one. With our new code in place, the final expression (quote!(#function)) returns the partially overwritten function as a TokenStream.

Exercises

See the appendix for solutions.

1 Fill in the question marks (???) and make the following macro compile:

```
#[???]
pub fn ???(_attr: TokenStream, _item: TokenStream) -> TokenStream {
    let public_version = quote! {};
    public_version.into()
}
```

The following code fragment shows a usage example:

```
#[delete]
struct EmptyStruct {}
```

2   Handle structs with unnamed fields. If you use matching, your new match arm will probably look a bit like this: `Struct(DataStruct { fields: Unnamed (FieldsUnnamed { ref unnamed, .. }), .. })`…. Note that you will need to decide whether to output a "normal" struct or an unnamed one.

3   Make our macro handle enums. Two things to keep in mind: First, you do not need to add `pub` to the fields (only to the enum), but you do have to retrieve and re-add them (they are called `variants` under `Enum`, `DataEnum`). Second, your code will now also have to decide whether it has to return an enum or a struct.

4   Keep the existing attributes of the struct instead of letting them disappear. This requires little more than getting the `attrs` (attributes) of our `item` and adding them above the struct. You might have to play around with the `quote` syntax a bit. Just remember that—unlike before—we do not need a comma to mark the end of an attribute.

5   Combine all of these exercises into a single solution.

6   Using `Punctuated::<Ident, Colon>` is one way to parse the field, but in the case of our public fields macro, there is an even simpler solution. Just put everything in variables, as we did with `Visibility`, and pass the useful things to `StructField`. Change our `Parse` implementation to use this simpler parsing.

Summary

- Like derive macros, attribute macros can be used on enums, structs, and unions. Additionally, they can be added to traits and functions.
- Unlike derive macros, attribute macros overwrite their input, making it possible to change existing code.
- Attribute macros get their name from defining a new custom attribute.
- We can use the `syn` parsing result (our AST) to retrieve all kinds of information, like the fields of a struct.
- `quote` allows us to combine multiple token streams into a single output.
- We can use matching and functions to glue together our parsing and outputting.
- For more structure and larger macros, you might consider creating custom structs and delegating the parsing and outputting to them.

Hiding information and creating mini-DSLs with function-like macros

The third and final type of procedural macro is the *function-like macro*, which—unlike the other two—is not limited to annotating structs, enums, and the like. Here, two examples will demonstrate its power. In our first example, we will stay close to familiar grounds by sticking to manipulating structs. Wilder experiments can wait until later in this chapter when we take another look at composing functions.

5.1   Hiding information

Like a professional skateboarder or a sophist trying to impress an Athenian audience, we will do a cool 180 flip: instead of telling you to expose fields, this time we will argue that you need a macro to hide them. This is not as strange as it sounds, since the answer to every question in programming is, "It depends." Yes, as we mentioned in the previous chapter, structs with public fields are great when you just want to transfer information between systems. But in many other cases, structs and classes are more at ease with hiding information. This makes code easier to understand and reason about. If, for example, a module exposes only a single function to accomplish a task, you may never need to learn anything about the potentially hundreds of methods, structs, and variables that it needs to accomplish its work. Not having to take into account all the implementation details makes your life easier.

Another related reason for hiding fields is safety. Granted, this is less of a problem in Rust, because the compiler is very good at detecting dangerous (mutating) actions. But in languages like Java, C#, or JavaScript, you'd be wise to hide fields and methods so nobody can change them and mess things up. This becomes even more important in an environment where multiple threads could access the same objects and mutate them, causing all kinds of weird problems—hence the reason for functional programming's focus on immutability. If your objects cannot be manipulated by others, your code is safer and easier to understand.

Even in Rust, these practices have their place, at the very least from the perspective of easier reasoning about code. In fact, the language provides programmers with very good tooling for hiding information in structs, files, modules, etc. Information hiding is clearly dear to the creators' hearts. Thus, our first example will focus on writing a macro that adds methods for allowing immutable access to fields via references. This is useful when structs contain fields that should be consulted or used but not manipulated.

5.1.1   Setup of the information-hiding macro

The `Cargo.toml` and project structure remain the same as before, except this time the name of the nested directory (the macro) is `private-macro`. That means the outer directory (the application) will have to import this dependency with `private-macro = { path = "./private-macro" }`. `lib.rs` and `main.rs` require more changes. `main.rs` is shown in the following listing.

> **Listing 5.1   Our application code**

```
use private_macro::private;        ◁─────┐  An import activates our macro.

private!(              ◁─────────────┐    We call the macro by writing its name
    struct Example {                      followed by an exclamation mark. We
        string_value: String,             pass along any relevant data.
```

```
            number_value: i32,
        }
    );

fn main() {
    let e = Example {
        string_value: "value".to_string(),
        number_value: 2,
    };
```

> Once we have an instance, we can use the generated methods to get references to our fields (a &String and a &i32).

```
    e.get_string_value();
    e.get_number_value();
}
```

Instead of decorating a struct with the derive annotation, we call a function-like macro by writing its name followed by an exclamation mark and passing on useful data between parentheses. This is similar to how a declarative macro is used, which also means it can be hard to see the difference between these two. And to make the two even more indistinguishable, Rust also allows you to choose between parentheses, square brackets, and curly braces for arguments. Since we want to add a method to a struct, we simply pass in the entire struct as an argument. Next, inside the main function, we expect that we can build the Example struct and call its generated methods.

On to lib.rs: the following listing shows the first version of our code. Can you spot the essential differences from derive/attribute macros?

Listing 5.2   First version of our macro implementation

```
use quote::quote;
use proc_macro::TokenStream;
use syn::{parse_macro_input, DeriveInput};
```

> A function-like macro requires #[proc_macro]. The macro name is determined by the name of the decorated function.

```
#[proc_macro]
pub fn private(item: TokenStream) -> TokenStream {
    let ast = parse_macro_input!(item as DeriveInput);
    let name = ast.ident;

    quote!(
        struct #name {}
        impl #name {}
    ).into()
}
```

> The output replaces the input, so we recreate the struct in our output.

> The "getter" methods that we will generate will be added to this impl.

First, we have #[proc_macro] instead of #[proc_macro_derive(Hello)] or #[proc_macro_attribute]. And since we cannot define the name explicitly, the function name (i.e., private) will do.

Next, unlike attribute macros—but like derive macros—we only receive one parameter. That is because the additional TokenStream contained information about the attribute you were creating, and function-like macros do not create a custom attribute.

Finally, function-like macros are similar to their attribute brothers—and different from derives—in that their output tokens replace the input (see figure 5.1). And it makes perfect sense for the input of a function-like macro to replace the output. With other macros, we receive structured data (a struct, an enum), but a function-like macro allows you to pass in *anything*, even stuff that is not valid Rust. If that input were to remain in your source code, the compiler would complain loudly about invalid syntax, which is probably not what you want.

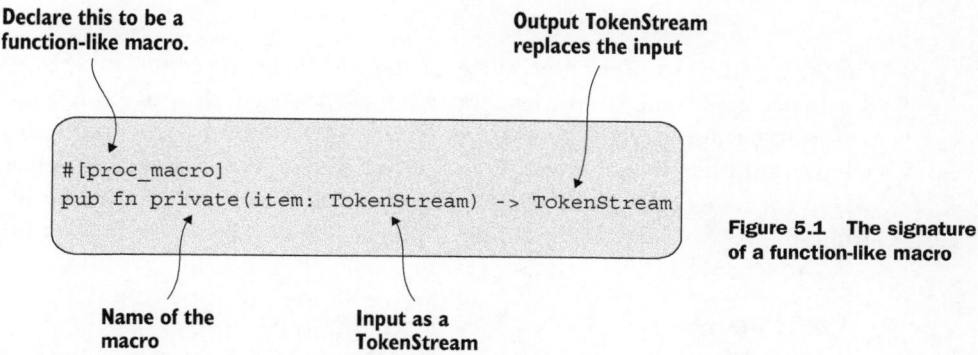

Figure 5.1 The signature of a function-like macro

That means we have to recreate the struct we gave to the macro. In our current version, we take the name and use it to create an empty struct and empty implementation.

5.1.2 *Recreating the struct*

As it stands, our application will not compile, even if we comment out the method calls—because the fields are gone! That's a major déjà vu: we are once again deleting things that were already there. Bad, macro, bad! So let's improve our code by fixing the struct recreation. This is pretty easy to fix: just give back what you receive when you create your output. There are at least two ways to do this: we either return the incoming TokenStream in our output or we give back the AST.

In the code in listing 5.3, we choose the first approach. Because the incoming stream is *moved* by parse_macro_input, we clone the stream and use the Into trait to change the built-in TokenStream into a type that implements the ToTokens trait required by the quote macro. Once we have our transformed clone, all that remains is to pass it to the output.

Listing 5.3 Second version of our macro implementation

```
// imports

#[proc_macro]
pub fn private(item: TokenStream) -> TokenStream {
```

```
let item_as_stream: quote::__private::TokenStream = item
    .clone()
    .into();
let ast = parse_macro_input!(item as DeriveInput);
let name = ast.ident;

quote!(
    #item_as_stream

    impl #name {}
).into()
}
```

> Clones the incoming (standard) TokenStream and turns it into a private TokenStream that implements ToTokens

> Passes this clone to the output

The AST path is even simpler, since (a) `DeriveInput` implements `ToTokens` and (b) we can use a reference to retrieve the name of the struct, thus avoiding a partial move. So the latter approach is actually preferable. Alternatively, you could also solve the deletion problem by not having it in the first place. As it currently stands, there is no reason for us to pass in the entire struct—so we could just pass in the name of the struct. But in this particular example, that will not work, as we will soon find out.

Partial moves

A partial move is one of those tricky Rust topics, right up there with—well—macros. In essence, this is an example of Rust being conservative with ownership and forcing you to think carefully about what you do with it. Say we have a struct and a function that steals things:

```
#[derive(Debug)]
struct Car {
    wheels: u8,
    gps: String,
    infotainment: String,
}

fn steal(item: String) {
    println!("I am stealing {item}");
}

fn main() {
    let car = Car {
        wheels: 4,
        gps: "Garmin".to_string(),
        infotainment: "Android".to_string(),
    };
    println!("My car before the theft: {car:?}");
    steal(car.gps);
    // println!("My car after the theft: {car:?}"); // does not compile
}
```

This code runs. But add the final `println`, and Rust starts complaining about a partial move. What is happening? Well, `steal` takes a property, the `gps`, from the car. By taking that string as an argument, it is "moved" into the function, thereby making the function the sole owner of that string. So the GPS is now the property of `steal` (and will be dropped after the `println` statement inside that function finishes executing).

When we get to the final commented-out print, the compiler complains: "You are asking me to print this car and all its properties. But how can I print the GPS when someone already stole—and dropped—it?" Regretfully, the compiler is right: *ownership of a part of the struct has been moved*—meaning the struct can no longer be used, though we can still retrieve (and, for example, print) any values that haven't moved yet, like `infotainment`. A simple solution for avoiding partial moves is to clone. If we create a clone of `car` and steal the GPS from there, our original is still fine and printable. Cloning has performance implications, but sometimes it might be the only solution. A better solution is to use references whenever possible. At the very least, that will minimize the number of times you need a clone. Other times, you can pull a clever trick, like using `take` on an `Option`:

```
#[derive(Debug)]
struct Car {
    wheels: u8,
    gps: Option<String>,
    infotainment: String,
}

// steal function unchanged

fn main() {
    let mut car = Car {
        wheels: 4,
        gps: Some("Garmin".to_string()),
        infotainment: "Android".to_string()
    };
    println!("My car before the theft: {car:?}");
    steal(car.gps.take().unwrap());
    // works, though the gps is now missing (None)
    println!("My car after theft: {car:?}");
}
```

But for us mortals, using references where possible and only cloning when needed are a great start!

5.1.3 Generating the helper methods

Now we can focus on generating methods, and the code in listing 5.4 shows a mix of mostly familiar building blocks. Since the methods return references to the fields and their names are based on those fields, we need to extract field information to generate these new methods. This is the reason why only passing in the name, as suggested earlier, will not work: our macro needs more detailed knowledge of the struct. So we will iterate over the fields and map each one to a stream of tokens containing code for one method. In the solution to an exercise from the previous chapter (you've solved all

those, right?), we had an ugly return type (`Map<Iter<'a, Field>, fn(&'a Field) ->`
`quote::__private::TokenStream>`). That is why we use a `collect` this time, which
allows us to return a nice, clean `Vec`.

That's the overview. Now focus on the code inside `map`. Besides the field name and
type, we want to create a method name that consists of the field name prefixed with
`get` (e.g., `get_string_value`). You might think that the solution is simply to generate
a `String` with that exact value. Sadly, passing a string to `quote` will generate an error—
for example: `expected identifier, found "get_string_value"`.

In retrospect, the reason is obvious. We are outputting a stream of tokens and asking Rust to add it to our code. Rust starts checking the code, including the parts we
generated, and finds the keyword `fn`. That can only mean that the next token is a
function name, which is always of type `identifier`. Instead it finds a string
(`get_string_value`).

For the same reason, we need `field_name` to be an identifier, since we will use it to
get a reference (`&self.field_name`), and Rust would complain if we tried to get a
field from `self` using a string.

So we need an identifier. We can create one with a constructor (the `new` method),
which requires two arguments: a string reference—which we have—and a span. In an
earlier chapter, we mentioned that spans are a way to link back to the original code,
which is useful for reporting errors to the user. When you create a new identifier, Rust
wants to know what it should reference in the original code if something goes wrong.
There are several ways to create a suitable span for our method name:

- One simple and valid option is to take the `field_name` span and reuse it for our
  method name. Reusing spans is also useful when you want to "link" an existing
  piece of code with generated code.
- `call_site()` is one of the associated functions of `Span`. This span "will be
  resolved as if . . . written directly at the macro call location," meaning it resolves
  at the place where you invoke the macro—the application code.
- `mixed_site()` is another associated function. The difference is that it obeys the
  same hygiene rules as a declarative macro. Depending on the role of the identifier, the span will resolve at either the place of invocation (call site) or the location where the macro was defined. The pull request author (https://
  github.com/rust-lang/rust/pull/64690) thought it was a sensible default since
  it provides some additional safety. Still, it does not really match our *intent* here.
  We actually want our generated methods to be used within the application.

More on call_site and mixed_site

Okay, so maybe the difference between `call_site()` and `mixed_site()` is not clear yet. Some code will help. Say we had a macro that generated a local variable and decided to use `mixed_site` for the span of the variable's identifier:

```
#[proc_macro]
pub fn local(_: TokenStream) -> TokenStream {
    let greeting = Ident::new("greeting", Span::mixed_site());
    quote!(
        let #greeting = "Heya! It's me, Imoen!";
    ).into()
}
```

We can now call the macro and try to print the variable. Note that this particular macro is invoked inside a function, not outside, as local variables can only exist within functions:

```
fn main() {
    local!();
    println!("{}", greeting);
}
```

This will cause an error telling you that `greeting` was `not found in this scope`. What went wrong? As you probably suspect, it's because of hygiene. As stated, `mixed_site` has the same hygiene rules as declarative macros. And in declarative macros, local variables are not exposed to the outside world. In the parlance of the documentation: a local variable's span only exists "at the definition site" of the macro but not at the call site, which is, in our case, the `main` function. Change the `greeting` span to `call_site`, and the application compiles and runs. Now the span exists at the place of invocation, `main`, where we are trying to print it.

I can almost hear some curious reader wondering what `quote` is doing. After all, we could have used it to generate the right span for us:

```
#[proc_macro]
pub fn private(item: TokenStream) -> TokenStream {
    quote!(
        let greeting = "Heya! It's me, Imoen!";
    ).into()
}
```

And this works automatically, meaning `quote` probably uses `call_site`, which it does. From the source code:

```
pub fn push_ident(tokens: &mut TokenStream, s: &str) {
    let span = Span::call_site();
    push_ident_spanned(tokens, span, s);
}
```

Back on topic: while all three options could work, we have gone with `call_site()` for our example. Besides creating a name, we also retrieve the field identifier and field type. These three variables are then used to generate the method (see figure 5.2).

Listing 5.4   A method for generating methods

```
// other imports
use syn::{DataStruct, FieldsNamed, Ident, Field};
use syn::__private::{Span, TokenStream2};
use syn::Data::Struct;
use syn::Fields::Named;

fn generated_methods(ast: &DeriveInput) -> Vec<TokenStream2> {
    let named_fields = match ast.data {
        Struct(
            DataStruct {
                fields: Named(
                    FieldsNamed {
                        ref named, ..
                    }), ..
            }
        ) => named,
        _ => unimplemented!(
            "only works for structs with named fields"
        ),
    };
    named_fields.iter()
        .map(|f| {
            let field_name = f.ident.as_ref().take().unwrap();
            let type_name = &f.ty;
            let method_name =
                Ident::new(
                    &format!("get_{field_name}"),
                    Span::call_site(),
                );

            quote!(
                fn #method_name(&self) -> &#type_name {
                    &self.#field_name
                }
            )
        })
        .collect()
}
```

This is code from an earlier chapter, where we had to retrieve fields to make them public. (pointing to `};`)

We need the name and type of the field to generate the method. (pointing to `let type_name = &f.ty;`)

We generate the method name as an identifier using format and new. (pointing to `let method_name = Ident::new(...)`)

We use method_name, field_name and type_name to generate the method. (pointing to the `quote!` block)

This is optional: to get a simple Vec return type, we collect the results. (pointing to `.collect()`)

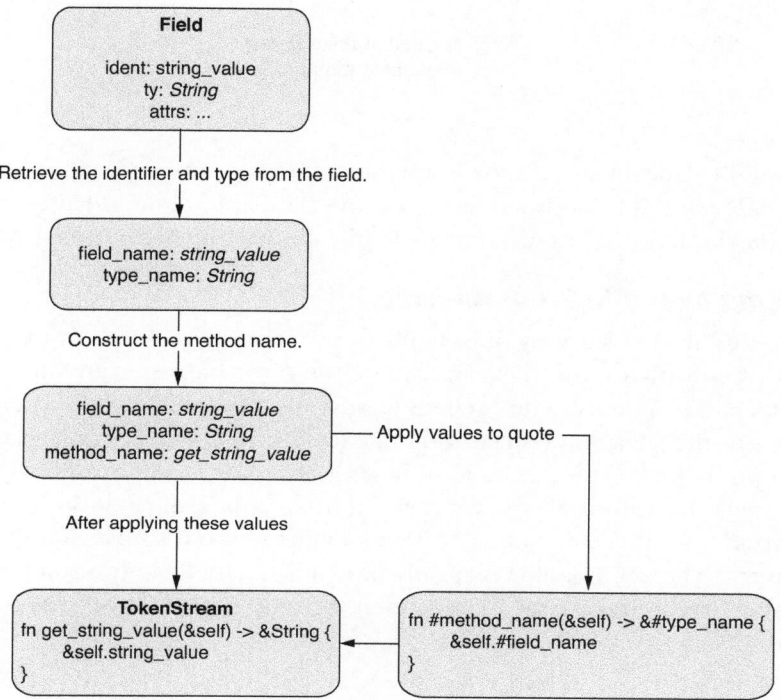

Figure 5.2   Mapping our first field from the `Example` struct

Now all we have to do is call the function and pass the result to the generated `impl` block. Remember, we have a vector of token streams to add, so we need to use the correct notation to tell this to `quote`: `#(#name_of_variable)*`. Previously, we had a comma in there because fields are separated by commas. That is not the case for method declarations. With our macro fully up to date, the code should compile.

Listing 5.5   Using our new method in our macro

```
// imports

#[proc_macro]
pub fn private(item: TokenStream) -> TokenStream {
    let item_as_stream: quote::__private::TokenStream = item
        .clone()
        .into();
    let ast = parse_macro_input!(item as DeriveInput);
    let name = &ast.ident;
    let methods = generated_methods(&ast);        <-- Generates the method
                                                       token streams
    quote!(
        #item_as_stream
```

```
        impl #name {
            #(#methods)*
        }
    ).into()
}
```

Adds all of them to our implementation block

There are still some loose ends to tie up: the methods we are generating are not public, the fields can still be accessed directly (not safe!), and we should also have a (new) method for creating a struct with private fields. We leave all that for the exercises.

5.2 Debugging by writing normal code

At times, you can get confusing or unfamiliar error messages from your macro without having a clue of what to do next. Rereading the error message carefully might help (yes, this section contains some "well, duh" advice), but if that does not help, another option is to write what you want to generate as normal code. That's because most of what you put between the quote parentheses is accepted as the truth of God by IDEs and compilers (at least until you try to use it in an application)—a serious downside for everyone who, like me, counts on IDE support to avoid stupid mistakes. Luckily, once you try to create the same piece of code in ordinary Rust, your tooling has your back again. As an example, say I had written the following piece of code for our "private" macro:

```
quote!(
    fn #method_name(&self) -> #type_name {
        self.#field_name
    }
)
```

This is the (abbreviated) error that I would get:

```
error[E0507]: cannot move out of `self.string_value` which is behind
  a shared reference
  |
3 | / private!(
4 | |     struct Example {
5 | |         string_value: String,
6 | |         number_value: i32,
7 | |     }
8 | | );
  | |_^ move occurs because `self.string_value` has type `String`,
      which does not implement the `Copy` trait
```

If that error message does not "click" for me, I might be stuck. Somewhere in my generated code, something is going wrong. But what? Instead of staring at my macro or the message, what if I just wrote the method I wanted to generate for a dummy struct, based on the piece of code that I am passing to quote?

```
struct Test {
    value: String
}
```

```
impl Test {
    fn get_value(&self) -> String {
        self.value
    }
}
```

Well, if I did that, my IDE would start pointing me to `self.value` as the source of my problems. After adding an ampersand, it would point out that there is a mismatch with the returned type. Step by step, the errors melt away, putting us in a better place to continue work on the macro.

A final piece of obvious but still valuable advice is to work step by step, as we have done in these last few chapters. If there is a problem right after adding a single piece of functionality, the source of the error is obvious. And the satisfaction of already having something up and running is a nice bonus.

5.3 Composing

We saw how to use a function-like macro as a stand-in for a derive (or attribute) macro. Now let's turn to an example where function-like is the *only* good fit. In an earlier chapter, we talked about composition and how to write a declarative macro for composing functions. We also talked about limitations in the symbols we could use for chaining expressions together in declarative macros (i.e., we could not mimic Haskell, which allows for composing functions by using .., though we also explained that the tt type does not suffer from the same limitations). The second example of this chapter is composition. But this time *we will have our dots*.

Again, we won't go over the entire setup. You've seen it all before. Instead, take a look at the application code in `main.rs`, where we see two of the example functions from chapter 2, "Declarative macros." Inside `main` we combine these functions with dots (.) using the `compose` macro that we are going to write. Note that it would not be possible to pass this info to a derive or attribute macro, because those two expect a struct, enum, function (i.e., a bit of valid Rust code).

Listing 5.6 Our application, featuring some familiar functions

```
use function_like_compose_macro::compose;

fn add_one(n: i32) -> i32 {
    n + 1
}

fn stringify(n: i32) -> String {
    n.to_string()
}

fn main() {
    let composed = compose!(
        add_one . add_one . stringify
    );
```

We use compose, our function-like macro, to combine three functions.

```
        println!("{:?}", composed#E);
}
```

How does this work? Turn to `lib.rs`. (Because there is a bit more code than usual—about 60 lines—we will first look at the macro entry point in isolation.) First, we parse the input into a custom struct of type `ComposeInput`. `DeriveInput` is ill equipped to deal with our current input, since we are definitely not receiving a struct or enum as input. More generally, this kind of composing is not natively supported by Rust, so there is no reason to assume that a prebuild parser would be able to handle it for us.

Listing 5.7   Our compose macro entry point

```
#[proc_macro]
pub fn compose(item: TokenStream) -> TokenStream {
    let ci: ComposeInput = parse_macro_input!(item);   ◁——— Parses our input into
                                                             a custom struct
    quote!(
        {
            fn compose_two<FIRST, SECOND, THIRD, F, G>(first: F, second: G)
            -> impl Fn(FIRST) -> THIRD
            where
                F: Fn(FIRST) -> SECOND,
                G: Fn(SECOND) -> THIRD,
            {
                move |x| second(first(x))
            }             ◁——— Adds the compose_two function from
            #ci                chapter 2 to our output, followed by
        }                      the output created by the ci variable
    ).into()
}
```

Next, we produce output. Our application code did not contain the `compose_two` function from our declarative macro example, so we generate it. The custom struct is responsible for input *and* output, so we just pass it along behind the `compose_two` declaration. The additional pair of curly braces is essential. Whatever we return has to be bound to a variable (`let composed = ...`). And without the curly braces, we are returning two things: a function *plus* a call to it. With the curly braces, we create one block scope and only return that.

Generating compose_two

Putting the `compose_two` function inside the block scope has an additional advantage in that it hides the function declaration from other parts of our code. Remember, we are creating this output for every invocation of our macro. So if we call `compose!` four times, we have four `compose_two` functions in their own, limited scopes, hidden from each other.

But always generating the same function is a bit inefficient. Can't we just export `compose_two` and reference it in our generated code? Well, no: a `proc-macro` library can only export procedural macros. One way to work around this limitation would be to put the `proc-macro` library in another library. That outer library has our `proc-macro` as a dependency and simply exports `compose_two` and reexports the macro (e.g., `pub use function_like_compose_macro::compose;`). If your code takes a dependency on this new library, you can import both the function and the macro and avoid generating the same code all the time.

Perhaps you are now thinking of *monomorphization*. Monomorphization is Rust compilation creating a copy of a generic function for every concrete type that needs it. So, when you write a generic function with signature `foo<T>(t: T) -> T` and call it once with an `i32` and once with `u8` as a type for `T`, Rust will replace that generic function with two versions: one in which `foo` accepts and returns an `i32` and another where it takes and gives back a `u8`. This transformation generally leads to faster code but also large binary sizes, especially when generic functions are invoked with a lot of different types.

In any case, monomorphization does lessen the usefulness of our reexport technique, as a function will be generated for every type regardless. Even so, in the current setup, a `compose_two` is generated even when we have multiple invocations with the same types. And that, at least, does not happen with monomorphization.

A minor detail: this time we did not create a temporary variable for our output to call `into()` on. Instead, we did all that in one go. And because IDEs are not fond of curly braces followed by method calls (plus, we would have two pairs of curly braces wrapping), I used parentheses.

Now all that is left is to take a look at the custom struct that is doing all the heavy lifting. The `Parse` input is simple enough: we expect to get function names separated by dots. That sounds like `Punctuated`! Identifiers will suffice for the function names (see figure 5.3). And to get the dot, we can use the `Token` macro, which can handle around 100 different symbols. Behind the scenes, `Token!(.)` will generate `Dot`, so we could also import that type. Or we could even mix and match these two if we are so inclined.

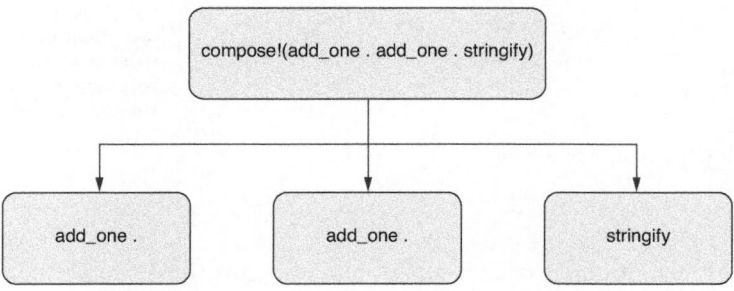

Find identifiers separated by periods.

Figure 5.3   Parsing our application example with `Punctuated::<Ident,` `Token!(.)>::parse_terminated`

Listing 5.8 Our custom struct

```
use proc_macro::TokenStream;
use proc_macro2::Ident;
use quote::{quote, ToTokens};
use syn::{parse_macro_input, Token};
use syn::parse::{Parse, ParseStream};
use syn::punctuated::Punctuated;

struct ComposeInput {
    expressions: Punctuated::<Ident, Token!(.)>,
}

impl Parse for ComposeInput {
    fn parse(input: ParseStream) -> Result<Self, syn::Error> {
        Ok(
            ComposeInput {
                expressions: Punctuated::<Ident, Token!(.)>::
                    parse_terminated(input).unwrap(),
            }
        )
    }
}

impl ToTokens for ComposeInput {
    fn to_tokens(&self, tokens: &mut proc_macro2::TokenStream) {
        let mut total = None;
        let mut as_idents: Vec<&Ident> = self.expressions
            .iter()
            .collect();
        let last_ident = as_idents
            .pop()
            .unwrap();

        as_idents.iter()
            .rev()
            .for_each(|i| {
                if let Some(current_total) = &total {
                    total = Some(quote!(
                        compose_two(#i, #current_total)
                    ));
                } else {
                    total = Some(quote!(
                        compose_two(#i, #last_ident)
                    ));
                }
            });
        total.to_tokens(tokens);
    }
}
```

> We turn to **Punctuated** again since our composition input is a repetition.

> We need a mutable version of the identifiers to pop the last element.

> For each remaining element, if we did not compose anything yet, we place compose_two with the current plus last_ident in total. Otherwise, we add compose_two with the current element and total.

The ToTokens implementation is a bit more complex (and there are definitely other ways of writing this). Because we want to retrieve the last identifier (function) in the list, we iterate over the expressions, create a mutable variable, and pop the final identifier.

Next, we iterate over our functions in reverse order with `for_each`. If `total`, which contains our output, is empty, we are at our first element and should combine it with `last_ident` using `compose_two`, putting that entire `TokenStream` into `total`. This is why we popped the last element: so we would know when we need to combine the first two elements of the *reversed* vector. Once past this first composition, things become simpler: we keep taking the current element and putting it into a `compose_two` with the current total. The resulting `TokenStream` becomes our new `total` (see figure 5.4). Finally, we pass all our gathered tokens along using `to_tokens`. As before, we need `proc_macro2` identifiers and token streams because `quote` uses the `proc_macro2` variants instead of the built-in versions.

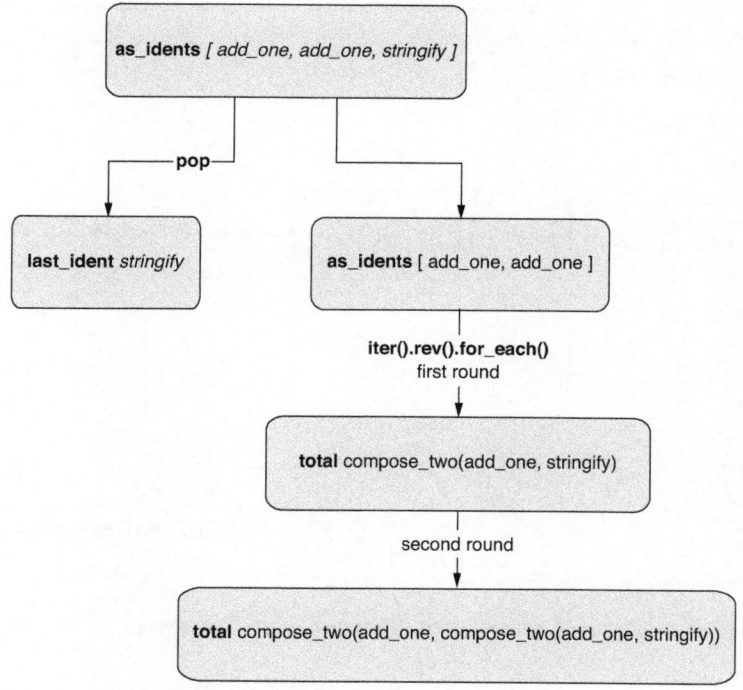

Figure 5.4 Going through the identifiers in `to_tokens`

We are now able to use periods in our composing macro. Once again, `syn` made it easy to parse our input, even though it was not valid Rust, and `quote` helped us elegantly combine outputs.

5.4 Anything you can do, I can do better

Because they are the most powerful macro, you might decide to just use function-like macros for every purpose. That would be unwise. Surely it means something that derive macros, the most limited of the three, are perhaps the most popular of the three: a limitation can also be a strength. For instance, derive macros are predictable in their effects, both for users and creators, since they only add without changing or deleting. So if you only want to add functionality to a struct or enum, and the problem is too complex for a declarative macro, you have already found the right tool for the job.

Derive macros have the limitation and advantage of only working for structs, enums, and unions, while attribute macros work on these plus traits and functions. Again, this makes them more predictable. As a user, I know not to use derive macros on functions. As a creator, the "input token space"—if you will—is much more narrow than that of a function-like macro. That is, I am reasonably sure that I will get a struct or an enum, and I know what those look like.

So if you only want to add functionality to a struct or enum, go with the derive macro. If you need to alter them, default to an attribute macro. And when you want to change functionality *and* need the macro to apply to other categories as well, go for function-like (see figure 5.5).

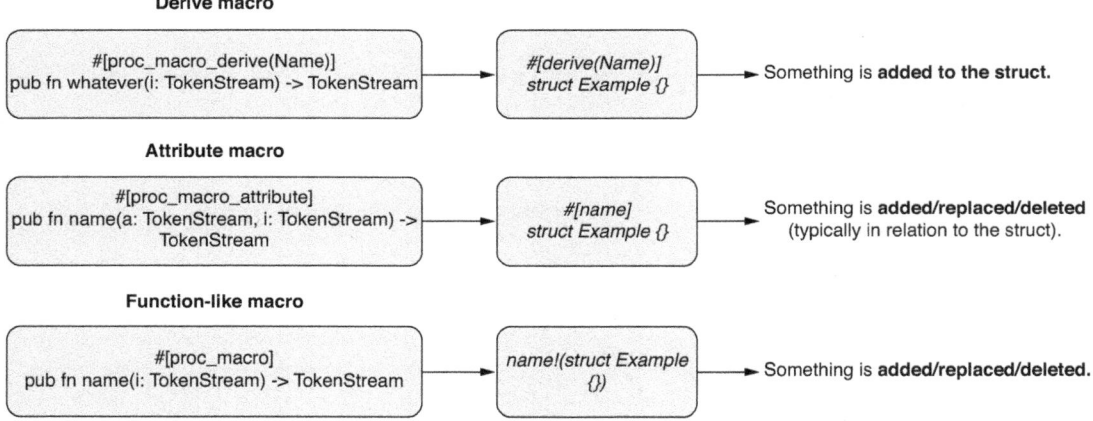

Figure 5.5   An overview of our procedural macro signatures, usage, and effects

5.5   *From the real world*

Without going into detail, here are a few examples of crates that put macros to creative use. SQLx (https://github.com/launchbadge/sqlx) is a "Rust SQL crate featuring compile-time checked queries," a common choice for interacting with relational databases when you do not want to add the complexity of an object-relational mapping. You can write SQL queries by calling the `query` method. But to get the advertised compile-time checks, you should look for a macro with the same name:

```
let countries = sqlx::query!(
    "SELECT country, COUNT(*) as count
    FROM users
```

```
      GROUP BY country
      WHERE organization = ?",
      organization
)
.fetch_all(&pool)
.await?;
```

Yew (htps://yew.rs) is a "framework for creating reliable and efficient web applications." Among its features is the `html` macro, which allows you to write HTML that is checked at compile time. For example, if you forget to close the nested div, you will get an error telling you `this opening tag has no corresponding closing tag`:

```
use yew::prelude::*;

html! {
    <div id="my_div">
        <div id="nested"/>
    </div>
};
```

Taking a bit of a side tour, here is a Yew example where the library authors decide to create a span by calling `mixed_site()`. (It also contains an example of the `format_ident` macro, which we will use in our next chapter.) The choice makes sense in this context since the authors do not want this builder to conflict with anything in the client application:

```
impl ToTokens for DerivePropsInput {
    fn to_tokens(&self, tokens: &mut proc_macro2::TokenStream) {
        // ...
        let builder_name = format_ident!(
            "{}Builder", props_name, span = Span::mixed_site()
        );
        let check_all_props_name = format_ident!(
            "Check{}All", props_name, span = Span::mixed_site()
        );
        // ...
    }
}
```

Meanwhile, Leptos (https://leptos.dev/) has a `view` macro that allows you to mix HTML and Rust. As an example, the following code creates an incrementing button. Here too you will get warnings about mismatches in tags or problems with Rust code *inside* the macro:

```
#[component]
fn App(cx: Scope) -> impl IntoView {
    let (count, set_count) = create_signal(cx, 0);

    view! { cx,
        <button
            on:click=move |_| {
                set_count.update(|n| *n += 1);
```

```
            }
        >
            "Click me: "
            {count}
        </button>
    }
}
```

Exercises

See the appendix for solutions.

1 Write a function-like macro to generate a struct method that prints `"Hello, World"`. It should only take the struct name as an input. Remember to declare a struct with the correct name in your application code.

2 Our `private` macro creates convenience methods, but the fields can still be public and directly accessible *and* our newly generated methods are not public. Change the macro so that it sets all fields to private and generates public methods. You can ignore the complexity of re-adding the struct attributes and hard-code a `new` method for your example struct.

3 Go look at the `Token!` source code, and see what other tokens are available. Try a different one for our composing macro, and fix the application code.

Summary

- Function-like macros replace their input.
- Just like declarative macros, you use them by writing their name followed by an exclamation mark.
- Their input is placed in the parentheses that follow.
- They are not limited to structs and the like, instead taking anything you want to pass along as input.
- Writing a function-like macro is very much like writing other procedural macros. But since their inputs are more varied, they may require more parsing effort.
- One way to deal with the input is creating a custom struct for gathering all information. The `syn` library has a lot of useful goodies to help you on your way with this.
- When you're stuck thanks to a compile error in your generated code, try writing out the code you want to generate and see if the compiler or IDE gives you any useful advice.
- You should think about requirements when deciding on the kind of macro you need: Where will you use it? Does it have to change existing code?
- Whenever possible, go for the simplest option.

Testing a builder macro

6

This chapter covers

- Writing a derive macro that will generate a builder for structs
- Creating white-box tests to verify the behavior of functions within your macro
- Using black-box tests that take an outside view of your code
- Deciding what types of tests are most useful for your macro

The builder pattern is a very convenient, fluent way of constructing structs. Because of that, it is omnipresent in Rust code. Often, though, the code required to write a builder is boilerplate—boilerplate that we can automate away! In this chapter, we will write a macro to do just that. Because we are not touching the original struct, we can use a derive macro (remember, go for the simplest option). In an implementation block, we create a temporary `Builder` struct that stores information and offers a `build` method for creating the original struct (see figure 6.1).

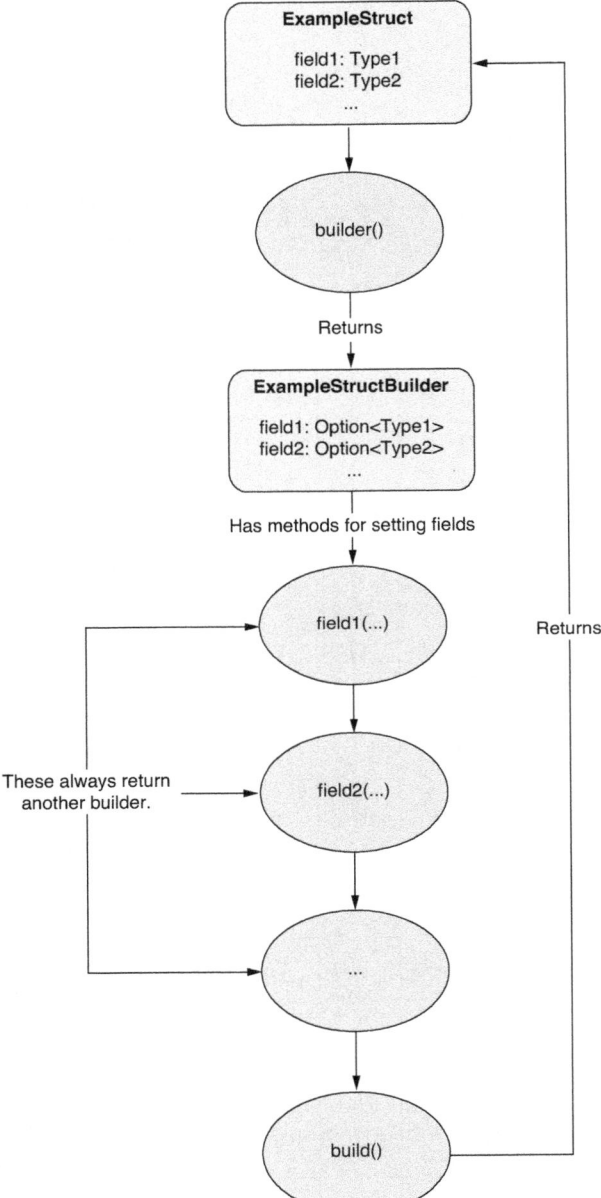

Figure 6.1   The builder from this chapter is used for an example struct

This is not an original idea, sprung wholly from my head in all its glory. There is, for example, a procedural macro workshop where you create this kind of macro on Git-Hub (https://github.com/dtolnay/proc-macro-workshop), and Jon Gjengset's *Crust of Rust* (https://www.youtube.com/watch?v=geovSK3wMB8) walks you through one possible implementation. Being original is thus not the point of this chapter. Instead, while implementing this builder, we will discuss how we can *test* procedural macros. And ideally, such a chapter would be written using test-driven development (TDD).

> **NOTE**   *Test-driven development* (TDD) is a way of coding that puts tests in the center of things. Rather than testing being an afterthought, every piece of code that we write is preceded by a test verifying the behavior we would like to see. The test starts out red (failing) because there is no implementation yet. After we write code and the test turns green (succeeds), we write another test for the next bit of behavior. This approach has the obvious advantage of creating applications with excellent test coverage; proponents feel that TDD also drives developers into writing better-designed code.

For us, one option would be to start with a high-level test, which we ultimately try to turn green. To get there, we would define smaller unit tests for pieces of the desired behavior. Unfortunately, because TDD relies on small incremental steps, this makes for unpleasant reading (and writing!) and would make this chapter even longer than it already is. So instead, we start with a basic setup and explore tests while further fleshing out the macro. Afterward, we will also talk about which type of unit test (*black-box* or *white-box*) seems the most useful when writing macros.

6.1   Builder macro project setup

For this chapter, we will use a slightly more complex project setup. Instead of having one directory for our application and one for our macro, we will split up the latter into a simple library exposing the macro itself and one containing its implementation. This kind of setup is said to be a good practice, creating a separation between the macro function, which uses built-in macro utilities, and the underlying code, which will use the `proc_macro2` wrapper (which we have encountered before and is used by libraries like `quote`). While this is true, there are other ways to separate and isolate code—which we will talk about in this and subsequent chapters—and I do think this approach is often overkill. But a demonstration is not a bad idea. Afterward, you can decide whether the isolation is worth the additional setup (see figure 6.2).

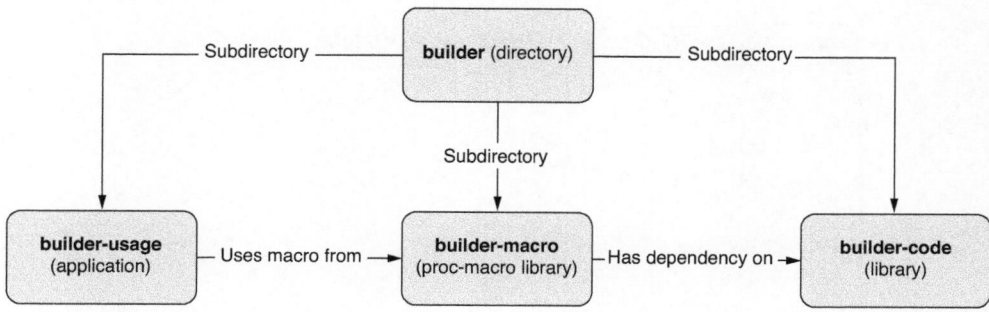

Figure 6.2   Our setup for the builder project

Here's what we have to do:

1   We need a root directory, which we will call `builder`.
2   Inside this directory, we add three more: `builder-code`, `builder-macro`, and `builder-usage`.
3   The first two are libraries, so create them with `cargo init --lib`. The last one is a normal (executable) Rust project and needs `cargo init`.
4   Now make the root directory a Cargo workspace with another `cargo init`.
5   Finally, change the contents of the `toml` files to match the code in the following listing.

Listing 6.1   Our `Cargo.toml` files

```
[package]
name = "builder-code"
version = "0.1.0"
edition = "2021"                                          builder-code

[dependencies]
quote = "1.0.33"
syn = { version = "2.0.39", features = ["extra-traits"]}
proc-macro2 = "1.0.69"


[package]
name = "builder-macro"
version = "0.1.0"
edition = "2021"
                                                         builder-macro
[dependencies]
builder-code = { path = "../builder-code" }

[lib]
proc-macro = true


[package]
name = "builder-usage"
version = "0.1.0"
edition = "2021"                                         builder-usage

[dependencies]
builder-macro = { path = "../builder-macro" }

[workspace]
members = [
    "builder-macro",          builder
    "builder-code",
    "builder-usage"
]
```

Thanks to the Cargo workspace, we can combine our three subprojects into one greater whole. This is not strictly necessary, but it does allow us to run checks and tests for all our subdirectories in one go.

NOTE Someone wrote some additional tooling (https://crates.io/crates/cargo-workspaces) to help you with creating and managing workspaces.

6.2 Fleshing out the structure of our setup

We can now add some code to `lib.rs` in `builder-code` to create the builder (helper) struct.

> **Listing 6.2 The `lib.rs` file in `builder-code`**

```
use proc_macro2::{TokenStream};
use quote::{format_ident, quote, ToTokens};
use syn::DeriveInput;

pub fn create_builder(item: TokenStream) -> TokenStream {
    let ast: DeriveInput = syn::parse2(item).unwrap();          ◄─── Uses parse2 to get a proc_macro2::TokenStream
    let name = ast.ident;
    let builder = format_ident!("{}Builder", name);             ◄─── Creates an identifier for the name of our builder, reusing the span of the received struct

    quote! {
        struct #builder {}     ◄─── Creates the builder struct in our output
    }
}
```

Readers with a keen eye may have noticed that our `builder-code` has not been marked as a procedural macro. This is because we are exposing the macro from another directory (`builder-macro`). This does mean that we no longer have access to `proc_macro` types since these are only available inside a library that has been marked as a procedural macro. Instead, we use the `proc_macro2` wrapper. And because we use this wrapper, we turn to `parse2` for parsing, unwrapping the `Result`.

As usual, we retrieve the name of the struct after parsing. In this case, we do that because we want to have a helper struct for temporarily storing field values. And as we will be injecting this builder in user code, we cannot simply name it "Builder" because the chance of the name clashing with the user's code is too great. Furthermore, you would only be able to use this macro once per module, lest it generates two structs named "Builder." So, instead, we use the name of the annotated struct as a prefix. This should be relatively safe, but if you want even more certainty, the Rust Reference (http://mng.bz/v84r) advises adding underscore prefixes (__) as well, which makes a clash with code that follows standard naming very unlikely.

This is, in fact, a convention that you encounter in lots of macro code, and we have seen it in several of our real-world examples already. Flip back to previous chapters if you don't believe me. But it should only be used when you do not want the struct to be used directly by the macro users. If we want them to pass around builders in the application code, we want the naming both to be predictable and to follow Rust naming conventions. And while double prefixes do not generate a warning, few people use them for naming structs in application code.

To create an identifier for our helper, we need to generate the right string and pass it into the identifier constructor together with a span. Instead of writing those two lines of code, we can offload work to `format_ident`, which will take care of everything. For a span, it selects that of the final identifier it received, falling back to `call_site` ("current location"—this is the one we used in the previous chapter); if there is none, the builder will get the span of the struct it will help "build." That's perfect.

Once we have our name, we return an empty struct as placeholder code. As our code now returns a `proc_macro2::TokenStream`, we no longer have to turn the result from `quote` into the standard `TokenStream` expected by a proc macro—or at least not in this part of our code.

Now let's turn to the `builder-macro` code.

Listing 6.3   The actual macro (in `builder-macro`)

```
use proc_macro::TokenStream;
use builder_code::create_builder;

#[proc_macro_derive(Builder)]
pub fn builder(item: TokenStream) -> TokenStream {      Turns a normal TokenStream into
    create_builder(item.into())                         a proc_macro2::TokenStream
        .into()              Changes the result proc_macro2::TokenStream
}                            into the normal one, so we can return it
```

The macro definition is very similar to the one we had before, except that it is now in a separate package. We have defined a derive macro called `Builder` that accepts a normal `TokenStream` as a parameter and returns another. Because our `builder-code` is *only* using the `proc_macro2`, we are forced into a "translation" when we pass this data to `builder-code`. And when we get back results, we do the same because procedural macros don't know or care about the wrapper; they expect a "normal" stream. In both cases, we can turn to the `Into` trait to take care of transformations for us.

Finally, we will fill in our main file in `builder-usage`. Right now, it just adds the macro to an empty struct called `Gleipnir`.

Listing 6.4   Our `builder-usage` `main.rs` file with an empty example struct

```
use builder_macro::Builder;

#[derive(Builder)]
struct Gleipnir {}

fn main() {}
```

This is merely a simple way to verify that everything compiles. That task is better left to tests that not only verify compilation but actual behavior. That's the subject we now turn to.

6.3 Adding white-box unit tests

There are two ways we can unit-test our procedural macros. The first is using "internal" or white-box testing, where we have access to the internals of the code. The other way is black-box testing, where we adopt an outsider's perspective. We will start with the first.

Testing internals in Rust is easier than it is in most programming languages because we can—and should—add tests to the files containing our implementation. This allows us to verify any behavior, including that which is hidden in private structs, fields, and functions. Our first tests will be added to lib.rs in our builder-code. And if we had a large macro, we would add tests to other files as well.

The first test, seen in listing 6.5, is a very basic assertion. Since we already wrote code to generate a struct, we can assert that we get back something with the expected builder name. For example, when we pass in a struct called StructWithNoFields, we expect that the returned token stream contains StructWithNoFieldsBuilder.

Listing 6.5 Our `builder-code` with a first, basic test

```
// imports

pub fn create_builder(item: TokenStream) -> TokenStream {
    let ast: DeriveInput = syn::parse2(item).unwrap();
    let name = ast.ident;
    let builder = format_ident!("{}Builder", name);    ⟵ Remember, here we are
                                                          creating the builder
    quote! {                                              name (identifier).
        struct #builder {}
    }
}

#[cfg(test)]                  Our test module is located in the
mod tests {        ⟵         same file as our production code.
    use super::*;

    #[test]
    fn builder_struct_name_should_be_present_in_output() {
        let input = quote! {
            struct StructWithNoFields {}        Uses quote to
        };                                      generate an input

        let actual = create_builder(input);     We change the output into a String
                                                and run one simple assertion: does
        assert!(actual.to_string()                    it have the expected name?
            .contains("StructWithNoFieldsBuilder"));   ⟵
    }
}
```

This is very basic, but it already gives us some assurance about our code. For example, we now know that the code is returning the builder name somewhere in its output. But would it not be better to check that the *entire* output matches our expectations?

We can do that by comparing the output with a `TokenStream` of our own. That does mean we need to somehow manually build that expected output, and there are several ways to do this. For example, we could create a new `TokenStream` and use `to_tokens` to add all the expected output to that stream. While that would work, it requires way more effort than the alternative: just use `quote` to generate the expected output.

Listing 6.6   Adding a second test

```
#[test]
fn builder_struct_with_expected_methods_should_be_present_in_output() {
    let input = quote! {
        struct StructWithNoFields {}
    };                                          Uses quote to create the
    let expected = quote! {                     input and expected output
        struct StructWithNoFieldsBuilder {}
    };

    let actual = create_builder(input);

    assert_eq!(
        actual.to_string(),        Asserts that the expected and
        expected.to_string()       actual produce the same string
    );
}
```

Since `TokenStream` does not implement `PartialEq`, we cannot directly compare both. Changing them to strings and comparing the result is an easy enough workaround.

Instead of making sure our expected value is of the same type as our output, we can also transform our output to make verifying it easier. So a third option is to use `parse2`. If the parse fails, the test correctly panics thanks to the `unwrap` call. If it succeeds, we have an AST that we can easily extract information from—and verify that it matches expectations.

Listing 6.7   Adding a third test

```
#[test]
fn assert_with_parsing() {
    let input = quote! {
        struct StructWithNoFields {}
    };
                                                    We parse our result into
    let actual = create_builder(input);             DeriveInput, panicking if
                                                    this does not work.
    let derived: DeriveInput = syn::parse2(actual).unwrap();   ◁────────────┘
    let name = derived.ident;
    assert_eq!(
        name.to_string(),              When it succeeds, we can retrieve the
        "StructWithNoFieldsBuilder"    properties of the parsed result and
    );                                 see if they match our expectation.
}
```

This is powerful, but once we start outputting more than one item/struct/function, we have to write custom logic for parsing. And when that becomes too complex, we might have to test our tests. That is why the second variation, which uses `quote`, is my favorite of the three, for both clarity and—particularly—ease of use. Besides testing token stream output, white-box testing is very useful for verifying the output of helper functions. Since you are expected to be familiar with the basics of testing in Rust, examples of such tests are not shown here.

Still, despite their usefulness in multiple scenarios, white-box tests are by themselves insufficient for fully testing macros. Yes, they can show us that the output of our code is what we think it should be. But what we really want to know is whether the generated code *will do what we want it to do*. In this case, will it allow us to create our struct? To verify that sort of behavior, we need to adopt an outsider's perspective.

6.4 Black-box unit tests

As we mentioned earlier, black-box tests take an outsider's view. They only want to know whether the code produces the required result, without knowing *how* it achieves this. This is often a good idea since the value of code is in what it can produce rather than how. Do we really care that values are temporarily stored somewhere when we `build` our struct? Is it important to verify that this happens? As a consequence of their approach, black-box tests are less tied to implementation details than white-box tests. This means they change less often when you are only modifying code internals.

6.4.1 A happy path test

We start with some happy path testing, which verifies that the code works *when everything goes according to plan*. We add the test to `builder-usage` since this crate is one of the users of our macro. Alternatively, we could add everything to a new `tests` folder in the root of `builder-usage`. In normal projects, this is a good place for black-box tests because code in `tests` does not have privileged access—it can only use the public API of its project. But in our case, the code we are testing is in an entirely different project. So `main.rs` is fine.

Our first, most basic test verifies compilation of the code and nothing more.

Listing 6.8 A first black-box test (in `builder-usage`, `main.rs`)

```
use builder_macro::Builder;

fn main() {}

#[cfg(test)]
mod tests {
                                              When we create a struct annotated
                                                 with #[derive(Builder)] ...
    #[test]
    fn should_generate_builder_for_struct_with_no_properties() {
        #[derive(Builder)]
        struct ExampleStructNoFields {}                        ◄─
```

```
        let _: ExampleStructNoFields = ExampleStructNoFields::builder()
            .build();      ◁──┐ . . . we expect our macro to
    }                          │  create a builder function.
}
```

Our test defines a struct annotated with our macro, and we are asserting that calling
`::builder().build()` will return an instance of that struct. By doing this, we are
asserting that the code will compile, proving that the functions we are expecting are
generated. Even without assertions, the code already complains: `function or asso-
ciated item builder not found for this struct`. So let's turn our test green by
adding everything we need for this first use case.

Listing 6.9 Adding enough implementation to turn our test green

```
// earlier imports

pub fn create_builder(item: TokenStream) -> TokenStream {
    let ast: DeriveInput = syn::parse2(item).unwrap();
    let name = ast.ident;
    let builder = format_ident!("{}Builder", name);

    quote! {                         │ We already had
        struct #builder {}    ◁──────┘ this builder struct.

        impl #builder {
            pub fn build(&self) -> #name {        But now it has an implementation,
                #name {}                          containing a build method that will return
            }                                     an instance of the annotated struct.
        }

        impl #name {
            pub fn builder() -> #builder {        And the original struct gets a method
                #builder {}                       that returns the builder struct.
            }
        }
    }
}
```

All changes are located in the `quote` macro. Instead of generating an empty struct, we
have added an implementation block for both the builder and the original struct. In
these blocks, we define the two functions that we are calling in our test.

Some errors you may come across writing this piece of code (or similar) are as
follows:

- `expected value, found struct ExampleStructNoFields`—This error is caused
  by forgetting to add `{}` behind `#name` inside `build`. The error message is helpful
  but—as usual—points to the macro instead of a specific line. One way to track
  down the error is to search for places where you are using `#name` since you know
  its value is the `ExampleStructNoFields` that appears in the message. You could
  also use `cargo expand` to visualize what the generated code looks like. The

command is a bit different now because it is *tests* that are being expanded—in this case, `cargo expand --tests --bin builder-usage`, which you can run inside `builder-usage`.

- `expected () because of default return type`—This error is less clear until you realize that you have functions that should return things. So you probably forgot to specify a return type (e.g. `-> #name`).

- `expected identifier, found "ExampleStructNoFieldsBuilder"`—You will get this error if you forget that you need identifiers instead of strings for the names of structs. You may recall that we encountered similar problems in the previous chapter.

- `cannot find value build in this scope`—A typo inside `quote` means that we have a hashtag in combination with an unknown variable. Rust won't like that. So check for hashtags that do not match anything. An IDE will probably give you autocomplete for these hashtags, helping you track down or avoid this problem.

We have turned our first type happy path test—call it a "compile test"—green! This is a good first step. Even if the code does not do what we expect, at the very least it verifies that our generated code does not crash and burn. Note that these implementation changes will cause our second white-box test to fail, as we are now producing more output. You can fix it or disable it for now. I would also advise disabling the third (parsing) test because, as predicted, it now requires too much custom parsing effort vis-à-vis its value. Meanwhile, the first white-box test shows that there is value in simplicity: it just keeps on working.

6.4.2 A happy path test with an actual property

What would be a useful second test? How about a struct with a single property?

Listing 6.10   A test for keeping Fenrir at bay (still in `main.rs, builder-usage`)

```
#[test]
fn should_generate_builder_for_struct_with_one_property() {
    #[derive(Builder)]
    struct Gleipnir {
        roots_of: String,
    }

    let gleipnir = Gleipnir::builder()
        .roots_of("mountains".to_string())
        .build();

    assert_eq!(gleipnir.roots_of, "mountains".to_string());
}
```

This will fail with `no method named roots_of found for struct Gleipnir`. What do we need to do to fix this? Well, our builder has to expose one method for every field in the struct, which will save the value. Our `build` method will use that saved information to create the struct (`Gleipnir`, in our case). The associated `builder` function will create the initial builder as before, but now we have to make sure the builder defines properties for saving all the required values. It seems safe to conclude that we need to retrieve the struct fields to work our magic. More specifically, we need to know their names and types to generate our functions.

NOTE   We are following TDD philosophy, trying to write just enough code to make our tests turn green. So it is okay for now to assume that we only have to deal with a `string`. We will make the code more generic—and performant— in the next section.

The implementation is shown in the following listing.

Listing 6.11 `builder-code` **implementation (without white-box tests and imports)**

```
pub fn create_builder(item: TokenStream) -> TokenStream {
    // AST, retrieving name and creating builder identifier

    let fields = match ast.data {
        Struct(
            DataStruct {
                fields: Named(
                    FieldsNamed {
                        ref named, ..
                    }), ..
            }
        ) => named,
        _ => unimplemented!(
            "only implemented for structs"
        ),
    };

    let builder_fields = fields.iter().map(|f| {
        let field_name = &f.ident;
        let field_type = &f.ty;
        quote! { #field_name: Option<#field_type> }
    });
    let builder_inits = fields.iter().map(|f| {
        let field_name = &f.ident;
        quote! { #field_name: None }
    });
    let builder_methods = fields.iter().map(|f| {
        let field_name = &f.ident;
        let field_type = &f.ty;
        quote! {
            pub fn #field_name(&mut self, input: #field_type) -> &mut Self {
                self.#field_name = Some(input);
                self
            }
        }
    });
```

```
let set_fields = fields.iter().map(|f| {
    let field_name = &f.ident;
    let field_name_as_string = field_name
        .as_ref().unwrap().to_string();
    quote! {
        #field_name: self.#field_name.as_ref()
            .expect(
                &format!("field {} not set", #field_name_as_string))
            .to_string()
    }
});

quote! {
    struct #builder {
        #(#builder_fields,)*
    }
    impl #builder {
        #(#builder_methods)*

        pub fn build(&self) -> #name {
            #name {
                #(#set_fields,)*
            }
        }
    }
    impl #name {
        pub fn builder() -> #builder {
            #builder {
                #(#builder_inits,)*
            }
        }
    }
}
}
```

This is a lot to unwrap. Let's go over it bit by bit. We start with retrieving the fields of the incoming struct, like we did several times before. Once that is done, we use these fields in four different ways.

First, we make sure our helper struct has the same properties as the original struct. That way, we can temporarily store all field information. But when we first create this helper, when `builder()` is called, we do not have any values to store. So we will wrap the types in an `Option`. (And we will ignore complexities such as what to do when a type is already an `Option`.) That is what is happening in the code fragment in the following listing.

Listing 6.12 Adding fields to the builder struct definition

```
let builder_fields = fields.iter().map(|f| {
    let field_name = &f.ident;
    let field_type = &f.ty;
    quote! { #field_name: Option<#field_type> }
});
```

NOTE You may at some point think that creating these temporary variables (`field_name` and `field_type` in this instance) is a waste. Can't we just inline this stuff and use `f` directly inside `quote` (e.g., `#f.ident`)? Unfortunately, no. The `quote` macro is great, but, as stated earlier, it won't retrieve struct fields for you.

Next, when `builder()` is called, we have to *initialize* the fields, setting each one to `None` since we do not have a value yet.

Listing 6.13   Initial values for the builder fields

```
let builder_inits = fields.iter().map(|f| {
    let field_name = &f.ident;
    quote! { #field_name: None }
});
```

Now we want to generate public methods with a name equal to that of a field, for setting that field to something other than `None`. They will take a parameter of the same type as the field and save it in an `Option`. As an example, take the `roots_of` field of type `String`: the method name will be `roots_of`, and the input will be of type `String` and will be saved as an `Option<String>` in a builder struct field called `roots_of`. The method will return the builder (`Self`). That way, we can have a fluent builder that sets value after value: `builder().first_field(…).second_field(…).build()`.

Listing 6.14   Generating methods for setting the value of a property

```
let builder_methods = fields.iter().map(|f| {
    let field_name = &f.ident;
    let field_type = &f.ty;
    quote! {
        pub fn #field_name(&mut self, input: #field_type) -> &mut Self {
            self.#field_name = Some(input);
            self
        }
    }
});
```

Finally, when we call `build`, we want to retrieve all the stored values and create the annotated struct. With the code in listing 6.15, we create this initialization for each field. Since we are dealing with optionals, we use `expect` to get the actual value, and the operation might fail since a user could forget to set a value. So we will return an informative error using `field_name_as_string`. Once that is done, we have the actual field. But as we can't just "move" out of the field, we do a `to_string` to get a copy of the value.

Listing 6.15   Initializing the actual struct

```
let set_fields = fields.iter().map(|f| {
    let field_name = &f.ident;
```

```
    let field_name_as_string = field_name
        .as_ref().unwrap().to_string();
    quote! {
        #field_name: self.#field_name.as_ref()
            .expect(&format!("field {} not set", #field_name_as_string))
            .to_string()
    }
});
```

These are all loose pieces, which we need to bring together in `quote`. If you have trouble visualizing this, run `cargo expand` on the test or consult figure 6.3.

Listing 6.16   Final output

```
quote! {
    struct #builder {
        #(#builder_fields,)*           ◁───   The builder has the same fields
    }                                          as the annotated struct, but the
    impl #builder {                            type is wrapped in an Option.
        #(#builder_methods)*           ◁─────  It has one setter
                                               method for every field.
        pub fn build(&self) -> #name {
            #name {                            And its build function can be
                #(#set_fields,)*               used to create the struct.
            }
        }
    }
    impl #name {
        pub fn builder() -> #builder {
            #builder {                         To create a new builder with all
                #(#builder_inits,)*            fields initialized to None, we add a
            }                                  builder() to the original struct.
        }
    }
}
```

When writing this code, I encountered one annoying error:

```
22 |            #[derive(Builder)]
   |                     ^^^^^^^
   |                     |
   |                     item list starts here
   |                     non-item starts here
   |                     item list ends here
```

Printing information and expanding did not give me any real insights. I suspected that the problems lay in my "builder methods" and confirmed this by temporarily disabling that part of the code. Then it dawned on me that I had written `#(#builder_methods,)*`—and functions are not separated by commas! Removing the comma did the trick.

Figure 6.3 shows an overview of the output generated by the different parts of our code and how everything fits together. From a simple struct with a single field, we generate a builder with a property, its initialization, a method to set its one field, and a `build` method where the original `Gleipnir` struct is created.

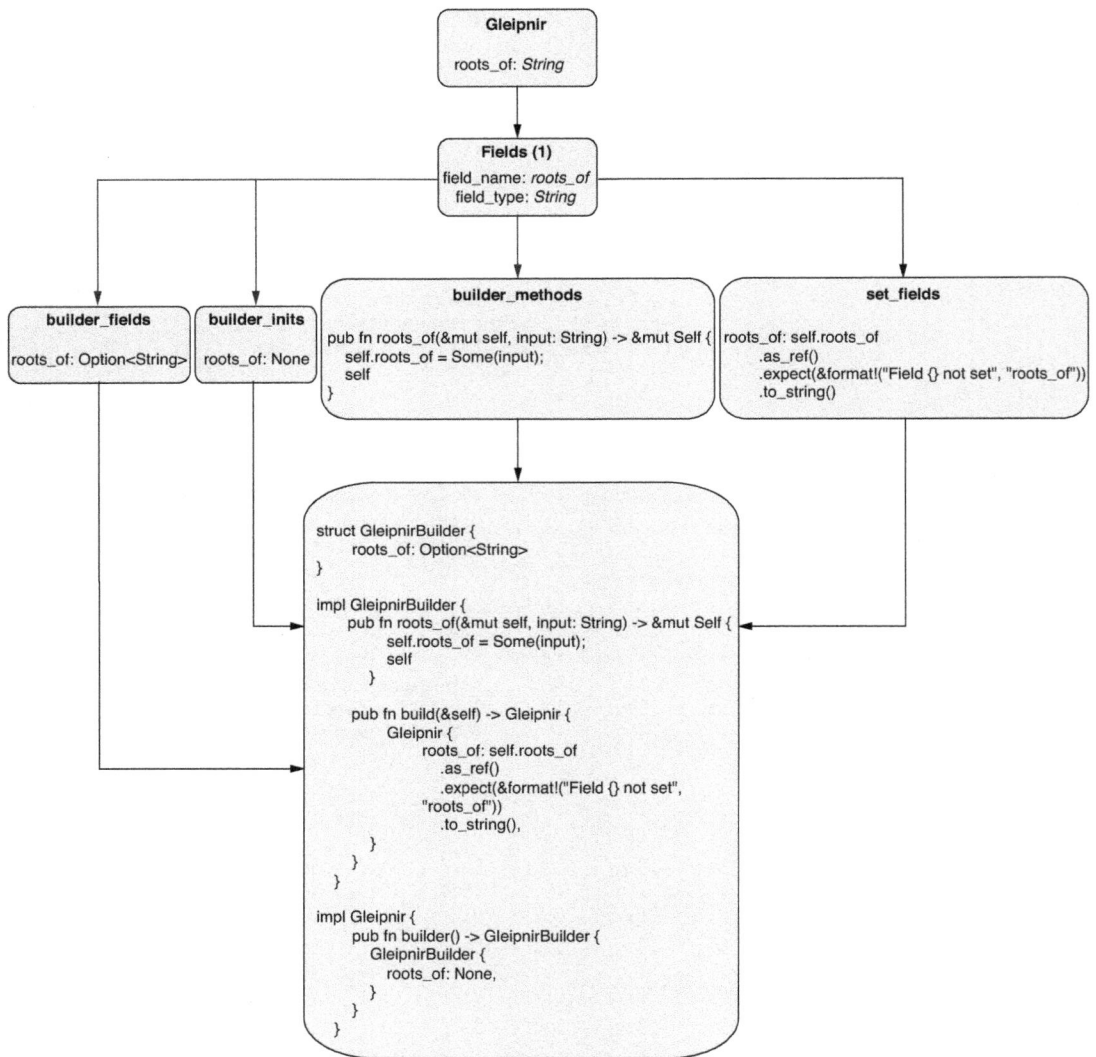

Figure 6.3   An overview of transformations for our example struct

6.4.3   *Testing enables refactoring*

The previous code is far from perfect. But the good news is that tests make it easier and safer to refactor. As long as the black-box tests stay green, we know that our behavior is still the same, albeit only for empty structs and those with one field. Let's make use of that freedom. Until now, we have often placed all our code in one file and one function. While that is good enough for simple examples, this one is now quite big—a single function containing almost 70 lines of code. If we expect the implementation to grow even further, it makes sense to split things up.

Ideally, refactoring happens step by step, and we should verify that our code keeps working after every minor step. We can start by extracting some functions. Each of these does an iteration over the fields to do one thing (field definitions, initializations, etc.). With IDE tooling, this is a piece of cake.

> **Listing 6.17 Code fragment from our refactored `create_builder` function**

```
let builder_fields = builder_field_definitions(fields);
let builder_inits = builder_init_values(fields);
let builder_methods = builder_methods(fields);
let original_struct_set_fields = original_struct_setters(fields);
```

The tests are still green. Retrieving the field name and type is something we do in both `builder_field_definitions` and `builder_methods`, so we can deduplicate. The following listing shows the code for the helper and how it is used in another function.

> **Listing 6.18 Adding a helper function for getting the field name and type**

```
use syn::{Ident, Type}; // plus other imports

fn builder_field_definitions(fields: &Punctuated<Field, Comma>)
                        -> impl Iterator<Item = TokenStream2> + '_ {
    fields.iter().map(|f| {
        let (name, f_type) = get_name_and_type(f);       ⟵ Gets the field name
        quote! { pub #name: Option<#f_type> }               and type from the
    })                                                      helper function
}

fn get_name_and_type<'a>(f: &'a Field) -> (&'a Option<Ident>, &'a Type) {
    let field_name = &f.ident;
    let field_type = &f.ty;
    (field_name, field_type)
}
```

In one of the exercises, we had a very concrete return type for a function like `builder_field_definitions`: `Map<Iter<Field>, fn(&Field) -> TokenStream>`. That works, but this `impl Iterator<Item = TokenStream2> + '_` is more idiomatic when you return iterator types. Instead of specifically telling Rust that the function gives back a `Map`, we say it is something that iterates over token streams: `impl Iterator<Item = TokenStream2>`. The `'_` is obligatory, as Rust will tell you if you forget to add it. The error it throws is quite clear in its explanation: our parameter `fields`, a reference, has an anonymous lifetime. This is captured by us but not mentioned as part of the bounds of the return type `impl Iterator<Item = TokenStream2>`. So we have to make this explicit, which we can do with a *placeholder lifetime*. That's possible because there is only a single lifetime. If we had multiple reference parameters for this function, things would be more complicated.

We also had to add lifetimes to `get_name_and_type`. This is because the *lifetime elision rules*, which allow Rust to infer the proper lifetime, could not be applied to this function with two outputs. In any case, the tests are still running.

Next, there's too much code in a single file, so we should split off some functionality. We could do this in two ways. First, we could create a subdirectory (perhaps called "implementation"?—names are hard), and add a file with the code and a `mod.rs` that determines what is exported (and thus usable in our root library file). This has the advantage of a bit more power and flexibility—which we don't need at the moment—at the cost of a little more effort. Instead, we go with the second option: putting the helpers in a separate file, which is the more "modern" way of doing things in Rust anyway (even though directory + `mod.rs` is still widely used).

That means we have to create a new file, called `fields.rs`, in the `src` directory of our macro code. We can move all the functions except `create_builder` to that file, leaving the tests untouched. When this is done, we need to add `mod fields` to `lib.rs` and import our functions.

Listing 6.19   Part of the new `fields.rs` file

```
// imports

pub fn original_struct_setters(fields: &Punctuated<Field, Comma>)
                        -> impl Iterator<Item = TokenStream2> + '_ {

    fields.iter().map(|f| {
        let field_name = &f.ident;
        let field_name_as_string = field_name.as_ref()
            .unwrap().to_string();

        quote! {
            #field_name: self.#field_name.as_ref()
                .expect(
                    &format!("field {} not set", #field_name_as_string))
                .to_string()
        }
    })
}
```
One of the four functions that are now public (pub) so we can use them elsewhere

```
// three more functions

fn get_name_and_type<'a>(f: &'a Field) -> (&'a Option<Ident>, &'a Type) {
    let field_name = &f.ident;
    let field_type = &f.ty;
    (field_name, field_type)
}
```
This helper can stay private because it is only used by functions in this file.

Listing 6.20 Using the functions in `lib.rs`

```
mod fields;          ←┐  Uses
                      │  our file
use crate::fields::{
    builder_field_definitions,
    builder_init_values,          Imports the
    builder_methods,              functions we need
    original_struct_setters
};

// other imports and code
```

Moving the field-related code has made our library cleaner and has hidden a helper (get_name_and_type) that is only of interest to the field-related functions. This is good: more information hiding and less "surface" area. Having separate functions instead of one big blob also opens the door for additional unit testing. The following listing shows an example of our helper.

Listing 6.21 An example test for `get_name_and_type`

```
#[test]
fn get_name_and_type_give_back_name() {
    let p = PathSegment {
        ident: Ident::new("String", Span::call_site()),
        arguments: Default::default(),
    };
    let mut pun = Punctuated::new();
    pun.push(p);
    let ty = Type::Path(TypePath {
        qself: None,
        path: Path {
            leading_colon: None,
            segments: pun,
        },
    });
    let f = Field {
        attrs: vec![],
        vis: Visibility::Inherited,
        mutability: FieldMutability::None,
        ident: Some(Ident::new("example", Span::call_site())),
        colon_token: None,
        ty,
    };

    let (actual_name, _) = get_name_and_type(&f);

    assert_eq!(
        actual_name.as_ref().unwrap().to_string(),
        "example".to_string()
    )
}
```

As you can see, constructing the parameters for this function requires a lot of boiler-plate. And in this case, our trick with `quote + parse2` can't help us since `Field` does not implement `Parse`. So perhaps you will decide against white-box testing at this level of detail. But if you need it, it's available.

6.4.4 *Further improvements and testing*

With this first bit of refactoring out of the way, we should focus on our implementation, because we are still only able to accept strings. We can verify this behavior with a test, as real, hard-core TDD practitioners should.

Listing 6.22 **A test with two properties, including one that is not a** `String`

```
#[test]
fn should_generate_builder_for_struct_with_two_properties() {
    #[derive(Builder)]
    struct Gleipnir {
        roots_of: String,
        breath_of_a_fish: u8
    }

    let gleipnir = Gleipnir::builder()
        .roots_of("mountains".to_string())
        .breath_of_a_fish(1)
        .build();

    assert_eq!(gleipnir.roots_of, "mountains".to_string());
    assert_eq!(gleipnir.breath_of_a_fish, 1);
}
```

As expected, this fails at compilation time (`expected u8, found struct String`) because we are doing a `to_string` on our values:

```
quote! {
    #field_name: self.#field_name.as_ref()
        .expect(&format!("field {} not set", #field_name_as_string))
        .to_string()
}
```

There are several ways to fix this. One extremely easy solution is to replace `to_string` with `clone`, which will make Strings, primitives, and all structs that implement `Clone` work automagically. And if we get a field that does not implement this trait, we will get an error pointing that out (`YourCustomStruct does not implement Clone`). Neat. But it does require you to implement `Clone` for every struct property, which you may not want.

There are two other solutions. One of them requires additional code and has limited capabilities. The other is shorter and more elegant but requires more thinking in advance about our goal and the rules of Rust. (Obviously, the first solution is the one I thought of first before stumbling on the second one, which works by consuming the builder.) But why on earth would we explore the first alternative when it sounds worse than what we already have? Well, in a book about macros, this solution has the advantage that it requires us to dive into the AST!

So let's begin. One problem with our current solution is that to_string only works for one type. Primitive types like u8 don't require anything like that, since they implement Copy. This means we could check the type we receive and leave out the to_string bit when we have a primitive or when we do not have a String.

To do that, we want a helper that can tell us whether something is a String. But where inside the type can we find that information? Since Type is a large enum, let us print out part of the AST we get in our test:

```
Path(TypePath {
    qself: None,
    path: Path {
        leading_colon: None,
        segments: [
            PathSegment {
                ident: Ident {
                    ident: "String",
                    span: #0 bytes(226..232),
                },
                arguments: PathArguments::None,
            },
        ],
    },
})
```

So our Type contains a Path and TypePath, with an ident inside path.segments (see figure 6.4). And an identifier can be turned into a string.

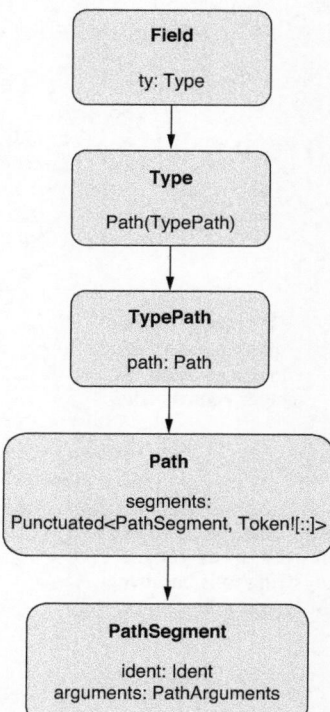

Figure 6.4   A simplified drilling down from Field **to** PathSegment

That means we can write a helper function to retrieve the identifier, turn it into a string, and compare it with a string representation of the type. As you can see, writing this code is a matter of figuring out where to look for useful data.

Listing 6.23 Adding a type helper to `fields.rs`

Only if we have a Type::Path do we dig deeper and compare the identifier as a string with our type_name.

```
fn matches_type(ty: &Type, type_name: &str) -> bool {
    if let Type::Path(ref p) = ty {
        let first_match = p.path.segments[0].ident.to_string();
        return first_match == *type_name;
    }
    false
}
```

Compares the identifier as a string with the type_name parameter, a string representation of the type

We will now use this helper inside `fields.rs`. What we want to do there is to add an `as_ref` and `to_string` call to our `TokenStream` when we have a string, or else we assume we're dealing with a primitive that implements `Copy`, which means we don't have to worry about *moving*.

Listing 6.24 Producing different output depending on our `matches_type` result

```
pub fn original_struct_setters(fields: &Punctuated<Field, Comma>)
                            -> impl Iterator<Item = TokenStream2> + '_ {

    fields.iter().map(|f| {
        let (field_name, field_type) = get_name_and_type(f);
        let field_name_as_string = field_name.as_ref()
                                        .unwrap().to_string();

        if matches_type(field_type, "String") {
            quote! {
                #field_name: self.#field_name.as_ref()
                    .expect(
                        &format!(
                            "field {} not set", #field_name_as_string)
                    ).to_string()
            }
        } else {
            quote! {
                #field_name: self.#field_name
                    .expect(
                        &format!(
                            "field {} not set", #field_name_as_string)
                    )
            }
        }
    })
}
```

Checks whether the type is a string

This is our original quote output, now only used when the helper returns true.

In every other case, we do not need the as_ref and to_string calls because the type can be copied.

If you run our last test again, everything will be green. Huzzah. But the code has a bit of duplication, and if that bothers you, we can get rid of it. The example in listing 6.25 avoids some duplication, though it is also harder to read. It's a tradeoff.

Listing 6.25   Combining `TokenStream` pieces with each other to avoid duplication

```
pub fn original_struct_setters(fields: &Punctuated<Field, Comma>)
                        -> impl Iterator<Item = TokenStream2> + '_ {

    fields.iter().map(|f| {
        let (field_name, field_type) = get_name_and_type(f);
        let field_name_as_string = field_name.as_ref()
            .unwrap().to_string();
        let error = quote!(
            expect(&format!("Field {} not set", #field_name_as_string))
        );

        let handle_type = if matches_type(field_type, "String") {
            quote! {
                    as_ref()
                    .#error
                    .to_string()
            }
        } else {
            quote! {
                #error
            }
        };

        quote! {
            #field_name: self.#field_name.#handle_type
        }
    })
}
```

This is `TokenStream` all the way down, baby! We have said it before: `quote` offers some nice, flexible ways to compose output. So don't think that individual functions need to return a complete, working piece of generated code. It is perfectly possible to build small pieces of a token stream, which will be stitched together in your final output. Or you can ignore things that are not relevant—but more on that later.

6.4.5   *An alternative approach*

Our work is not done yet, as you would find out if you started experimenting with other nonprimitive properties. Remember, right now, we are checking whether a field is a `String` and relying on `Copy` when it's not. But there are a lot of other types out there that are (perhaps) cloneable but not copyable. So let's add another test, for `Vec<String>`.

Listing 6.26 Testing with an additional property that is not `Copy`

```
#[test]
fn should_generate_builder_for_struct_with_multiple_properties() {
    #[derive(Builder)]
    struct Gleipnir {
        roots_of: String,
        breath_of_a_fish: u8,
        other_necessities: Vec<String>,      ◁⎯⎯  We're going to find out
    }                                               whether Vec<String>
                                                    works with our code.
    let gleipnir = Gleipnir::builder()
        .roots_of("mountains".to_string())
        .breath_of_a_fish(1)
        .other_necessities(vec![
            "sound of cat's footsteps".to_string(),
            "beard of a woman".to_string(),
            "spittle of a bird".to_string()
        ])
        .build();

    assert_eq!(gleipnir.roots_of, "mountains".to_string());
    assert_eq!(gleipnir.breath_of_a_fish, 1);
    assert_eq!(gleipnir.other_necessities.len(), 3)
}
```

As expected, compilation fails with `move occurs because self.vec_value has type Option<Vec<String>>` which does not implement the `Copy` trait, because this is a field that is neither `String` nor `Copy`. So maybe we should rewrite our code and clone everything that is not `Copy`? That is certainly one solution to make our current test green. And at the cost of additional code in our macro, it would produce less (and a bit more performant) output code than our original "clone everything" solution, though it would limit our builder macro to types that are `Clone` or `Copy`, and not everything we encounter will be one or the other.

But there is another, less limiting way. Our builder is a *temporary* struct—something to hold onto our data while the struct we want is incomplete. So moving, which we have been trying to avoid, can actually be a good thing. And the most efficient way to deal with the builder is probably to empty it. How do we go about doing this? The answer is by consuming `self` instead of borrowing a (mutable) reference to it. (These changes will once again break our white-box tests. You can get them running again with some minor fixes, but we won't show that here.)

Listing 6.27 Stop borrowing our builder struct (`lib.rs`)

```
pub fn build(self) -> #name {      ◁⎯⎯  &self, a borrow, has been changed
    #name {                              into the consumption of the
        #(#set_fields,)*                 builder by passing on self.
    }
}
```

Listing 6.28 Stop borrowing our builder struct (`fields.rs`)

```
pub fn #field_name(mut self, i: #field_type) -> Self {
    self.#field_name = Some(i);
    self
}
```

> Here the parameter self is no longer a reference, and the return is not a mutable reference anymore

With a couple of minor changes, the code compiles. But we are not done yet: if everything is moved instead of copied, we no longer need to treat strings as something special. And while we are at it, using format for the errors is not ideal, because it does part of its work at run time (expand the code if you do not believe me). In an early chapter, we used the stringify macro to avoid some run-time work. This time, we turn to concat, a macro that concatenates string literals, which should allow us to produce a suitable message.

Listing 6.29 Simplifying `original_struct_setters`

```
pub fn original_struct_setters(fields: &Punctuated<Field, Comma>)
                          -> impl Iterator<Item = TokenStream2> + '_ {

    fields.iter().map(|f| {
        let field_name = &f.ident;
        let field_name_as_string = field_name
            .as_ref().unwrap().to_string();

        quote! {
            #field_name: self.#field_name
                .expect(
                    concat!("field not set: ", #field_name_as_string),
                )
        }
    })
}
```

> matches_type has been removed, the to_string is gone, and we use concat to produce the panic message.

The one downside of this consuming approach is that a builder instance is consumed, meaning you have to clone it if you want to reuse it. Apart from that, our latest solution is shorter and more elegant and should be more performant than what came before. Plus, it doesn't require Clone, since we are moving values instead.

Move performance considerations

With a disclaimer that this is not my area of expertise: like a copy, a move is actually a memcpy in the background—basically a system function that copies byte buffers, generally a cheap operation. Most of these memcpys will probably be optimized away by your compiler, but that is not guaranteed. If they are not optimized away, these copies are not a problem for small types or those that are only pointers plus "bookkeeping," with everything else located on the heap. On the other hand, large types that live entirely on the stack will be costly to copy, and this may cause performance

(continued)

problems. There's a reason it's important to measure performance, because modern computer architecture laughs at our feeble attempts to simplify things ("move is always the best choice").

6.4.6   *Unhappy path*

In unhappy path testing, we want to check failure modes. And for our Rust macros, we are interested in both run-time and compile-time failures. In the first category, our code is expected to panic when a field is missing. We start by verifying that behavior.

Listing 6.30   Testing panic on a missing field

```
#[test]
#[should_panic]                                          We are expecting
fn should_panic_when_field_is_missing() {               a panic.
    #[derive(Builder)]
    struct Gleipnir {
        _roots_of: String,              Our struct has a property,
    }                                   but we are not setting it
                                        before calling build.
    Gleipnir::builder().build();
}
```

`#[should_panic]` tells Rust that we expect this code to panic because we are calling `build` without setting a value for our property. This covers the one place where we panic at run time. But we are also panicking at compile time—for example when we receive something that is not a struct. We should verify this behavior as well. To do that, we will add the crate `trybuild` to our dependencies. Run `cargo add --dev trybuild` or add `trybuild = "1.0.85"` to your `Cargo.toml` dev dependencies (we only need this dependency for testing) in `builder-usage`. Then add a `tests` folder in the root of `builder-usage`, and create a file named `compilation_tests.rs` with the content in the following listing.

Listing 6.31   Our compilation test runner in the `tests` folder

```
#[test]
fn should_not_compile() {                           trybuild will look inside the
    let t = trybuild::TestCases::new();             given directory (tests/fails) for
    t.compile_fail("tests/fails/*.rs");             tests that fail at compile time.
}
```

`trybuild` will verify that everything inside the chosen directory fails to compile. When you run it for the first time for a given test, it will output the error message it received (if any). If the error message matches your expectations, you add the generated output file to the folder your test is in. This approach makes a lot of sense: things can fail to compile for any number of stupid reasons. You want to be sure it fails for the right reason.

Right now, we do not have any failing tests. Add a `fails` directory, and put `build_enum.rs` inside with the content in the following listing.

Listing 6.32 Testing whether running our macro with an enum fails

```
use builder_macro::Builder;

#[derive(Builder)]
pub enum ExampleEnum {}

fn main() {}
```
> Since this is an enum, which we don't handle, we expect compilation to fail.

> A main function is required for trybuild, though it can be empty.

We are annotating an enum with our builder macro, which should fail because we only support named structs. When you run the test, you will get the following error message, as well as a failure file in a `wip` directory inside your project. Either copy the file or take the error message and add it as a file to `fails` under the name `build_enum.stderr`. A newline at the end is important:

```
error: proc-macro derive panicked
 --> tests/fails/build_enum.rs:4:10
  |
4 | #[derive(Builder)]
  |          ^^^^^^^
  |
  = help: message: not implemented: Only implemented for structs
```

This is what we expect to get when applying our macro to an enum: the panic we wrote earlier in this chapter! So that's working—well, failing—as expected. We could add a function example. But derive macros are only allowed on structs, enums, and unions, so Rust is handling that one for us. This means we have now covered the most important unhappy paths for our macro. If you want, you could now move the happy path tests we placed in `main.rs` to the `tests` folder. That way, you have all your tests in one place.

6.5 What kinds of unit tests do I need?

All the unit tests! Ideally. But their importance does vary.

A simple happy path compilation test (a black-box test) seems like the most basic requirement. If your macro won't even compile when you expect it to, what use does it have? Unhappy path compilation failures can be important if you have a lot of failure modes to test. But for a simple macro, there might be few—or you might find ways to work around them.

With regard to white-box unit testing—well, it depends. I really like that Rust allows you to test private functions. That allows you to hide all the information you want while also allowing for easy testing of *pure functions*. This mixes well with my personal preference: keep your impure functions both small in size and number, moving transformations and business logic where possible to pure functions. In the impure parts, where we communicate with outside parties, databases, etc., we can rely on the type system to guide us in the right direction and keep us from doing silly things. (Throw in a few *integration tests* if you have any doubts.) And as pure functions are straightforward to test, I can still get good coverage on a large part of my code base without thinking about things like mocking or how to bring in real dependencies.

> **NOTE** Pure functions are functions that have no side effects and whose returns are determined solely by the input parameters. We'll talk about them again in the next chapter.

That being said, white-box testing for macros is a lot of work. Creating the in- and outputs of helper functions, like the ones in this chapter, is cumbersome. (I am excluding functions that have no macro-specific inputs or outputs from this discussion. For that category, see the brief discussion in the previous paragraph.) In a large project, such tests can help you catch bugs early on. But black-box tests will also detect problems relatively quickly, are easier to set up and reason about, and are less sensitive to minor changes. Even just moving around parts of our output will break white-box tests without changing the workings and meaning of our code. On the other hand, the error you get from a black-box test might be unclear, requiring you to follow a long trail of breadcrumbs (hope you were running your tests after every small addition of code!). So in a larger and more complex application, internal tests *at strategic locations* can be very worthwhile.

6.6 *Beyond unit tests*

We have spent an entire chapter writing unit tests, but this exploration is only scratching the surface of testing. For example, you have tests that take a broader perspective:

- *Integration tests* verify that the integration between parts of your system works as expected. They are generally slower than unit tests because they cover more code and might draw in real dependencies, but they cover more ground and give you more certainty that your code will do what it should do.
- *End-to-end tests* verify the workings of your entire system, meaning most or even all dependencies will be real. A test suite like this offers a lot of value during continuous deployment, making sure that your code probably doesn't break anything—if you can keep it working, because end-to-end tests can be brittle and hard to maintain.
- *Smoke tests* are a sort of variant of end-to-end testing. They focus on a limited number of important paths and make sure that what you deploy is not completely broken. (Is there smoke coming from the servers?) If your app is constantly crashing without doing anything, these tests will tell you.

Other tests feature a different approach or focus:

- *Performance testing* verifies that the system has certain speed and reliability characteristics under various kinds of load. For Rust, you can use Criterion.rs (https://github.com/bheisler/criterion.rs).
- *Load testing* is similar, but its main goal is to verify that your application keeps working without degrading under heavy load.
- *Contract testing* checks that a producer is returning data in the agreed-upon format (i.e., is adhering to its existing public API). This avoids accidentally breaking consumers because something happened to the data they were expecting to receive.
- *Mutation testing*, a fairly new category, makes minor modifications (mutations) to your code and checks that some unit tests failed because of the change. If changing the implementation did not cause any test to turn red, you may be missing coverage.
- *Fuzz testing* tries to make your application crash by injecting all kinds of invalid or unexpected data. Fixing the mistakes found by fuzzing will make your code safer and more stable. For Rust, you can fuzz by combining libFuzzer (https://llvm.org/docs/LibFuzzer.html) with `cargo fuzz` (https://github.com/rust -fuzz/cargo-fuzz).
- *Property-based testing* is popular in the functional programming world and is ideal for testing code that has certain mathematical guarantees in its contract. It generates a whole range (hundreds, thousands) of values, using these to verify that your code always upholds its guarantees. For example, for a function that sums numbers, it would generate two random values (say, `x` and `y`) and check whether the return value equals `x + y`.

There are even some Rust-specific testing variants:

- *Doctests,* short for documentation tests, are Rust unit tests embedded within documentation.
- The *miri interpreter* can be used to check for some types of undefined behavior in your code, making your application even safer.
- *Loom* is a tool for verifying the correct behavior of concurrent programs by exploring "all possible valid behaviors."

Obviously, we cannot explore all these kinds of testing in depth. That would double the size of this book! But what kinds of tests are useful when you're writing macros? In my opinion, integration tests that check your interaction with other systems, like APIs or databases, can be useful depending on the type of macro you are creating. For our current example (builder), unit tests are all we need. But if you are writing a macro for interacting with a database, surely you would want something beyond unit tests—something that actually puts things in a real database that's running locally or—ideally—on a server or in the cloud. So, in another chapter, we will come back to integration testing. At that time, we will also talk about documentation, so doctests will make their appearance as well.

6.7 *From the real world*

Very few macro crates have no testing at all. Most have a couple of unit tests, and `trybuild` is often used for failure scenarios (e.g., by Tokio and `lazy_static`). Here we will discuss just two crates that are worth checking out.

The first, Rocket, is one we have encountered before in the introduction as well as in chapter 3. It is a web framework for Rust that uses macros to generate HTTP endpoints. For example, adding the macro `#[get("/hello/<name>")]` to a function will make it the entry point to a URL with path `/hello` and will pass on a path parameter called "name." Rocket's unit tests are black-box and located in the `tests` folder of the project. A large number of happy path unit tests as well as many failure scenarios use `trybuild`. Apart from that, separate packages even have "benchmark" tests with criterion and a fuzzing setup.

The next crate, `serde` (https://serde.rs/), needs no introduction. It is an extremely popular tool for serializing and deserializing data (e.g., changing raw JSON into a custom struct). One way you can tell `serde` to do this is by using its derive macros, one for serializing and one for deserializing. Once you've added those, things will "just work." `serde` has a wide variety of tests. Some are white-box unit tests for simple, pure functions (the following example has been abbreviated):

```
#[test]
fn rename_fields() {
    for &(original, upper, pascal) in &[
        (
            "outcome", "OUTCOME", "Outcome"
        ),
        (
            "very_tasty",
            "VERY_TASTY",
            "VeryTasty",
        ),
    ] {
        assert_eq!(None.apply_to_field(original), original);
        assert_eq!(UpperCase.apply_to_field(original), upper);
        assert_eq!(PascalCase.apply_to_field(original), pascal);
    }
}
```

But these are the exception. Most are black-box unit tests with the familiar mix of happy path and unhappy path using `trybuild`.

One detail you may be wondering about is what implementation these tests run against. After all, `serde` helps you change Rust code into something concrete like JSON. So you need some kind of implementation of `serde`'s traits to have an output to compare against. But testing against a real implementation is fraught with danger. It is also circular, since that dependency would itself depend on `serde`. Instead, `serde_test` contains a simple implementation that can be used to verify behavior.

Exercises

See the appendix for solutions.

1. We never did write any white-box tests for structs that actually have fields, so add one that runs against the final version of our code.

2. We only wrote code for handling structs with named fields, not the unnamed variety, so we should cover that failure case with another `trybuild` compilation test.

3. In Rocket, you can add headers to functions that make them into endpoints for calls. If you add `#[get("/world")]` and `#[catch(404)]` to a function called `world`, you get an error that looks like this:

```
error[E0428]: the name `world` is defined multiple times
  --> hello/src/main.rs:23:1
   |
22 | #[get("/world")]
   | ---------------- previous definition of the type `world` here
23 | #[catch(404)]
   | ^^^^^^^^^^^^^ `world` redefined here
   |
   = note: `world` must be defined only once in the type
 namespace of this module
```

What could be causing this? Can you think of a way this problem might be avoided?

Summary

- The builder pattern allows you to fluently build structs that require multiple parameters.
- By writing a macro to generate a builder, we can avoid a lot of boilerplate code.
- Unit tests are our most important tool for testing macros, and they can be divided into two categories: white-box and black-box.
- White-box unit tests "know" implementation details about the code. This allows for more in-depth testing but can also lead to brittleness and breaking on minor changes.
- Black-box tests only know what they are testing from an outside perspective. Because they are less brittle and verify the desired behavior of a macro, they are an essential check for your macro code.
- In macro code, white-box tests can be useful for tracking down tricky errors or to verify important behavior.
- If your macro communicates with external systems, some integration-level testing is probably a good idea.
- There is a large variety of other testing options available for use in Rust projects.

7
From panic to result:
Error handling

This chapter covers

- Understanding the difference between pure and impure functions
- Understanding the downsides of breaking control flow
- Using `Result` for better error handling
- Writing macros to manipulate function signatures and return values
- Mutating the received `TokenStream` as an alternative to creating a new one
- Creating better error messages with `syn::Error` or `proc_macro_error`

Until now, most of our code has focused on structs and enums, with very basic error handling. All of that changes right now! In this chapter, we will manipulate functions, changing panics into `Results`, which is a better and more idiomatic way of handling errors in Rust. This is a useful segue into seeing how we can manipulate functions with an attribute macro. We will also use this code to explore better ways of returning errors to the user—because panicking works, but the error just points to the macro invocation, making usage harder than it needs to be. But first, as a general introduction to this chapter's macro, let's talk about the problem with exceptions and possible alternatives.

7.1 Errors and control flow

At the time of writing, all the most widely used programming languages (C#, Java, JavaScript, Python) depend heavily on *throwing* exceptions/errors for failure scenarios. Is something wrong with the data you received from your REST endpoint? Throw an exception, catch it upstream, and change it into a 400 response! A database is giving back an exception when you call it? Wrap it in one of your exceptions and throw it! This is a valid approach to handling things that go wrong or failure paths. You can build great software with error throwing. But it is not without downsides.

One important problem is that it breaks control flow. The easiest code to write, read, and reason about is linear. You read from top to bottom:

```
fn simple(a: i32, b: i32) -> i32 {
    let sum = a + b;
    let product = a * b;
    sum + product
}
```

Once you add conditionals, things become a bit harder because you have to keep track of all the possible paths that your code might take:

```
fn a_bit_harder(a: i32, b: i32) -> i32 {
    let sum = a + b;
    let product = a * b;

    if sum > 7 && product == 0 {
        sum + product
    } else {
        sum - product
    }
}
```

Now add loops, nested conditionals, and even more nested loops, because why not? Things will become so complex that your inner developer will be screaming "Refactor!" because the number of things to keep tabs on for you to understand the function just keeps growing. *Cyclomatic complexity* is a way to measure this code complexity, and it depends on the number of "paths" that you can take in a function. Ideally, you want this to be in the single digits—only a few possible paths. By default, ESLint will start warning you at 20.

Exceptions are a cause of cyclomatic complexity: if something can throw an exception, that is yet another path that your code might take. What makes them worse than conditionals and loops is how totally unexpected their behavior can be. In a large codebase, with a core language that likes throwing exceptions, plus a lot of dependencies, almost anything you call might throw an error in the right (well, wrong) circumstances. For example, in Java, `Optional.of` might throw a `NullPointerException`, which is funny—even if there are reasons for having a method like this—because you are using optionals to *avoid* null pointers. There is also not much you can do about it. Are you going to check every line of code from every dependency to see if there's an exception lurking in there somewhere? If not, you have to accept that your code might take an unexpected path. And when it does, where will it go? If you are currently in function X, it might end up in the `catch` of function Y, or function Z, or maybe no one will catch it. Do you know for sure what will happen?

7.2   *Pure and impure functions*

So exceptions make code harder to reason about. The functional programming paradigm has thought long and hard on control flow and reasoning about code. One of its key tenets is that you should prefer *pure functions* in applications.

You might remember from the previous chapter that pure functions are functions without *side effects*, whose output depends solely on the parameters they receive. The following function, which sums its parameters or returns zero, is pure. Give it the same parameters multiple times, and the answer will always be the same:

```
fn sum_if_big_enough(a: i32, b: i32) -> i32 {
    if a > 100 && b > 1000 {
        a + b
    } else {
        0
    }
}
```

Now look at the next function, which calls a database to determine whether to sum the parameters. Because it relies on something outside the function for its output, it is no longer deterministic. Maybe the function returns 0 for arguments 5 and 3 on our first call. Maybe someone changes the database before our second call, and we now get back 8. Maybe the database has problems on our third call and throws an error:

```
fn sum_if_big_enough(a: i32, b: i32) -> i32 {
    if big_enough_according_to_database(a, b) {
        a + b
    } else {
        0
    }
}
```

Because the input no longer determines the output, this is an *impure function* (i.e., not pure). And it is impure even though it relies on another function (`big_enough_according_to_database`) to actually talk with the database. When you call an impure function, your function also becomes impure. The taint spreads (see figure 7.1).

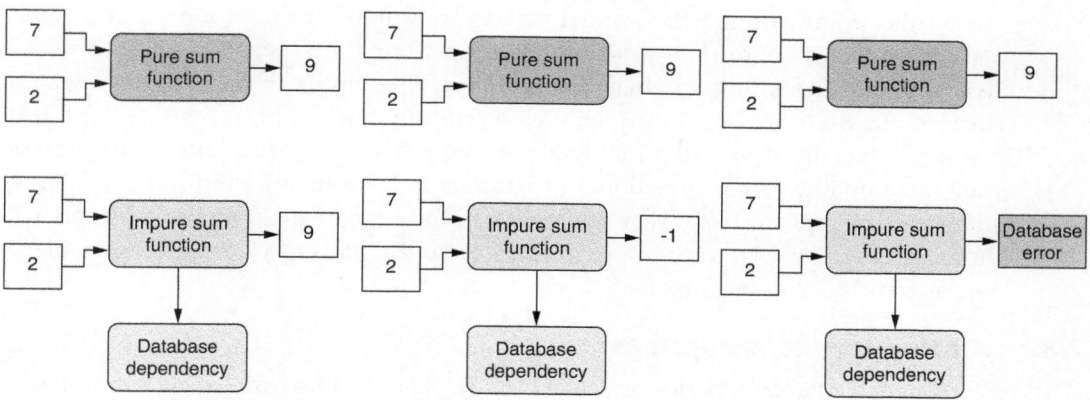

Figure 7.1   Pure functions are consistent and produce the same output for the same parameters. Impure functions are less predictable.

> **NOTE**   Manipulating databases is a side effect: an effect that your function has besides returning a result (which is considered the normal effect of your code). Many other common actions are side effects as well, like calls to other systems. The problem is always the same: what your function does depends on the behavior of an external resource. Even a simple thing like logging is a side effect, as it might fail unexpectedly when the operating system is having problems! That being said, logging is one of the safest (least error-prone) side effects. As far as I'm concerned, you can call your function pure if this is the only sneaky thing it does besides returning things.

Pure functions have nice, mathematical properties like *referential transparency,* which means you can replace a pure function call with its result. This opens the door for optimizations like *memoization,* a caching of function results, which is easy when the answer is always the same as long as the parameters do not change. That means you can return a cached result when you get parameters you've seen before.

There are other qualities that should appeal to programmers. They are easy to reason about because you only need to remember what is happening inside the function. Once we start doing things like calling databases, you need to keep a lot more context in your head. Pure functions are also easy to test, requiring only the most minimal setup, and they are unlikely ever to turn flaky.

Compare this to impure functions like the one from earlier. Reasoning is harder because we need to take into account everything the database might do: return true, return false, throw errors; have connection problems, timeouts, etc. To understand how such a function will behave, we have to dig deep into the underlying functions that it calls, exploring their implementation. Testing also becomes harder because we need mocking or stubbing.

At this point, you may be wondering why we would ever want impure functions. "Want" is the wrong word, however: we *need* these functions, because everything useful is a side effect: sending an email to customers, updating a database with the latest orders, etc. So the goal is not to eliminate impurity but rather to limit its impact. If most of our code consists of pure functions, that will make reading and testing most of our functionality easier. Functional programming, with its focus on pure functions, tries to limit impurity by moving side effects to the edge of an application. Hexagonal architecture, similarly, might move side effects to the ports of your application, keeping a "pure" core of business logic in the center.

7.3   Alternatives to exceptions

We have talked about the downsides of breaking control flow with exceptions. But you do need to handle failure paths. So, if not with exceptions, what alternative is there?

One option, available in every language and sometimes seen in the wild, is to use Booleans to signify success or failure. If you need to return a value and your language does not like tuples, just wrap the Boolean and the actual return value in a custom object. While this works, it has several downsides. It is clunky, requiring a lot of conditional checks instead of try-catch blocks, as well as wrapping and unwrapping. Plus, nothing forces you to handle the Boolean you receive. Just ignore it if you want to! At least exceptions were actively stopping you from doing bad things, albeit at run time. (Or partly at compile time in the case of Java's checked exceptions. These exceptions are hated by developers though, because adding lots of try-catch statements is very clunky, and there is often no good way to handle the checked exception.)

In a variation to the Boolean approach, Go has the convention of returning two values from a call that might fail: a value and an error, with only one of those being present and the other being nil. The convention is good, and it makes Go code easier to understand once you are used to this approach. Seeing errors as ordinary values instead of something exceptional (pun intended) is a good idea as well. But the other problems are still there: boilerplate—all those error nil checks—and no forced handling of the error. Just ignoring the errors is once again a perfectly valid approach but probably not a good idea.

There is another approach, originating largely from the functional programming paradigm. We will focus on a part of that solution, a part that has great support in Rust: *algebraic data types* (ADTs). Whatever language you currently use, you have some experience with these, because one type of ADT is the product type, which you may know under the name "object" or "struct." Basically, a product type has a total number of possible "states" equal to the *product* of its properties. So a struct with two properties, a u8 (which as a number has a total of 256 possible values) and a boolean (two values, either true or false) has $2 \times 256 = 512$ possible states. That makes sense: a struct with 120 and true is different from one with 119 and true. This large range of values can be a downside. You may need to do a lot of work (e.g., a lot of conditionals) to determine whether the state of a product type matches your requirements.

The other major algebraic data type is the *sum type*. As the name suggests, here the number of possible states is the sum of its properties (think of the Union type in C). You could see a Boolean as a sum type. It is *either* true *or* false—not something in between (see figure 7.2). This sounds like a limitation, but as I have said before, it might prove to be a strength because the restricted number of states makes these types ideal targets for pattern matching. Rust offers a very powerful sum type in the shape of enums. They have properties and methods, plus great pattern-matching support.

A product type, the product of all possible values that the properties might take

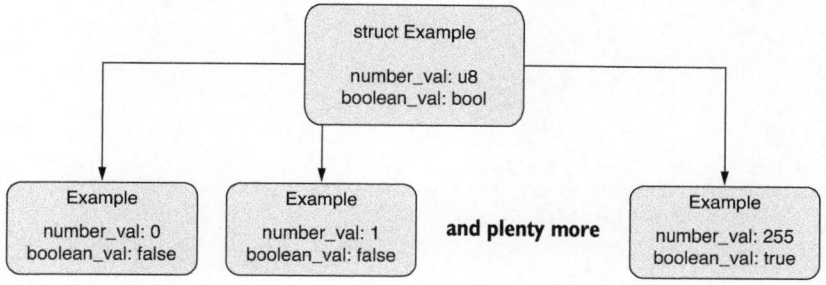

A sum type, the sum of all its values

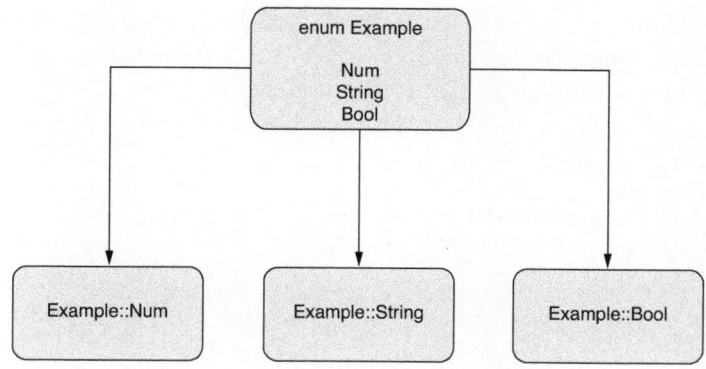

Figure 7.2 **The myriad of options of a product type versus the simplicity of the sum type**

But how does all this help us with our error-handling challenge? Well, reformulate the problem at hand: "We need a way to make clear to the developer and type system that the result of this call is either a success or a failure. If it is a success, it should contain the result; if not, an error (message)." Note we said *either* success or failure—error handling requires a sum type. And enums are ideally suited for that since they can contain properties like a result or error. What we should do is create an enum called

Either, which returns a success or a failure. That, in fact, is the name for this "pattern" in several languages, like Scala and Haskell. For simplicity's sake, the error message is always a string; the result can be anything you want:

```
enum Either<T> {
    Success(T),
    Failure(String),
}
```

If we have a function that returns this Either, we have to take into account failures because the answer we seek is wrapped in a variant. Pattern matching is one convenient way to handle all eventualities:

```
fn calculate_answer_to_life() -> Either<i32> {
    Either::Success(42)
}

fn main() {
    match calculate_answer_to_life() {
        Either::Success(answer) => {
            println!("Got the answer: {answer}");
        }
        Either::Failure(_) => {
            println!("Should handle failure");
        }
    }
}
```

We could add additional convenience methods to make handling the result contained within easier. A map method, for example, manipulates the "success value" if it is present and relies on pattern matching internally (see figure 7.3):

```
impl<T> Either<T> {
    fn map(self, function: fn(T) -> T) -> Either<T> {
        match self {
            Either::Success(answer) => {
                return Either::Success(function(answer))
            }
            // if it's not a success, no need to do anything
            _ => self
        }
    }
}

fn main() {
    let two = Either::Success(1).map(|v| v + 1);
}
```

And that solves all our problems! We have a type that elegantly encapsulates the result of a function that might fail. It is helpful to the type system, and it forces you to deal with failures. Plus, we can add all kinds of methods that help us transform and use the encapsulated result. There is just one problem: we've just reinvented Rust's Result type.

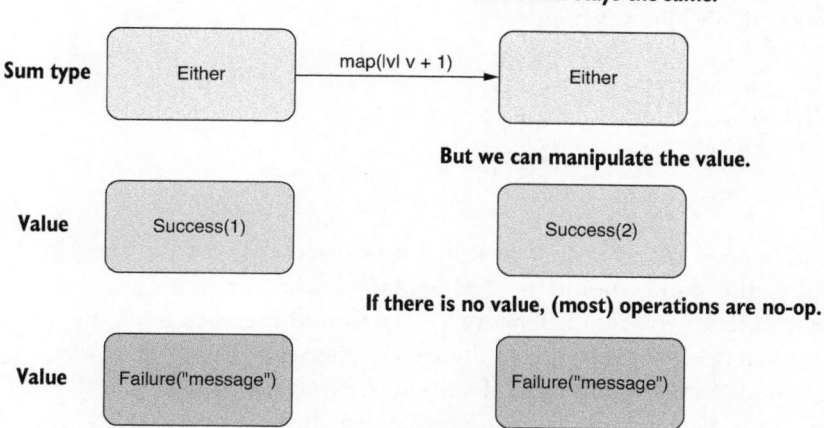

Figure 7.3 "What's in the box?" Manipulating the value

7.4 Rust's Result and panics

So, yes, this was a long-winded path to "This is why I think `Result` is pretty neat." At the center of Rust's standard library, we have two sum types with a million (bazillion?) use cases. As you know, `Result` is an enum with either a value (`Ok`) or an error (`Err`). This means that your error has now become a value that you can handle and manipulate *and* the error is embedded in your type system, which will force you to acknowledge that you might have an error. The signature of your function also becomes living documentation: just from seeing `Result` in the return type, you know that there are failure cases. Suddenly, there's information on almost every possible place where a failure might occur, and the type system forces you to think about them.

The reader also knows that there is an alternative to `Result`: just `panic!` In theory—similar to Go—panic is reserved for situations where you think it is best to stop the program altogether because something that really should not happen happened. A normal failure case is a customer not having enough money in their account or an order being out of stock. Panicking is what you would do if a customer just purchased an order worth infinite dollars. At this point, you may want to stop your application before it starts charging their credit card (or, depending on your moral stance, you could try to charge them as much as possible, I guess). As a more realistic example, consider a server that has just booted and discovers that some of its essential configuration is missing. Since that makes it impossible to do anything useful, panicking becomes a valid course of action.

Panics can also be good for handling situations where you have a *good reason to assume something cannot happen.* `unreachable`, for example, can be used for such situations. Another example: within the following function, we call `unwrap`, which will panic when our character is not a number. But as we just checked that the character is a number, that will never happen:

```
fn get_digit(ch: char) -> u32 {
    if char::is_digit(ch, 10) {
        return char::to_digit(ch, 10).unwrap()
    }
    0
}
```

In "real" code, it would be wise to switch over to `expect` and add a message about why you think the panic should never happen (`expect("value to be digit since we checked with is_digit")`). That way, when something does go wrong, tracking down the problem becomes easier, plus the `expect` message also serves as a bit of documentation. And it allows you to think deeply about your invariants.

unwrap and `expect` are also useful when you are writing a POC or a quick script or doing some exploratory work—any time you are experimenting and do not want proper error handling to get in the way. When and if you have to improve that aspect of your code, do a search for `unwrap` and `expect` and get busy! Besides using these two methods, you can use `panic` and variants like `unimplemented` to handle unforeseen situations in exploratory code. In the code in the following listing, we simply panic when we receive invalid arguments.

Listing 7.1   A function that panics when validation fails

```
fn create_person(name: String, age: i32) -> Person {
    if name.len() < 2 {
        panic!("name should be at least three characters long!")
    } else if age > 30 {
        panic!("I hope I die before I get old");
    }
    Person {
        name,
        age,
    }
}
```

Most of those panics should disappear once you get serious with your code. An `unreachable` still has its place, but the validation of input should be done with `Result`. If you've used a lot of `panic` in your code, that might be a boring refactor, though, which is our motivation to write a macro that can do this for us. Whenever it finds a `panic`, it will replace it with `Result`.

NOTE   This example should not be taken too seriously. It showcases how macros can alter functions and how to give feedback to users. In some rare real use cases, it may even prove useful. But simply rewriting the code to get rid of its panics is obviously preferable.

Because we are changing existing code, we can't go for a derive macro. But an attribute macro can work with functions and change code, so that's ideal.

7.5 Setup of the panic project

This chapter takes a middle ground between the simple setup with one subdirectory from earlier chapters and the more complex builder setup with three subdirectories. Instead, we now have two subdirectories: one with the macro and one with the code for verifying our code (see figure 7.4).

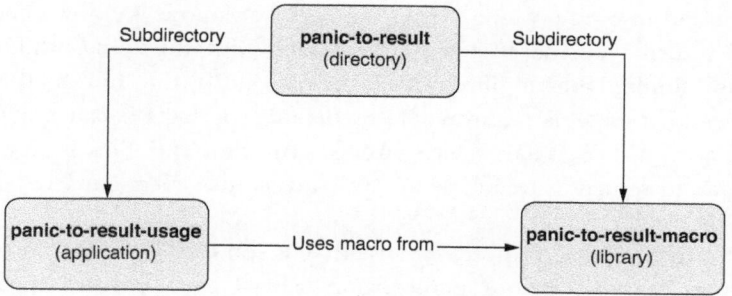

Figure 7.4 Avoiding both extremes, we have realized the middle path.

So, to start, we will create a `panic-to-result-usage` directory and a `panic-to-result-macro` directory. The first is an executable; the second is a library.

Listing 7.2 `toml` file for the macro

```
[package]
name = "panic-to-result-macro"
version = "0.1.0"
edition = "2021"

[dependencies]
quote = "1.0.33"
syn = { version = "2.0.39", features = ["full", "extra-traits"]}

[lib]
proc-macro = true
```

Listing 7.3 Dependencies for the application's `toml`

```
[dependencies]
panic-to-result-macro = { path = "../panic-to-result-macro" }
```

Next we have the first (dummy) version of the macro code, which takes the incoming tokens and returns them.

Listing 7.4   Macro code (first version)

```
use proc_macro::TokenStream;
use quote::{ToTokens};        ◁── This trait gives us the to_token_stream
use syn::ItemFn;                    method, which we use later.

#[proc_macro_attribute]
pub fn panic_to_result(_a: TokenStream, item: TokenStream) -> TokenStream {
    let ast: ItemFn = syn::parse(item).unwrap();          ◁── Uses parse with type
    ast.to_token_stream().into()   ◁── Turns the result into    ItemFn to get the
}                                      a standard TokenStream    function stream
```

Using `parse` instead of `parse_macro_input` is a slight variation. We now need to use
`ItemFn` as the return type, because we are working with functions, which makes
`DeriveInput` and similar types an ill fit. This is the reason why the "full" feature of `syn`
is required, because `ItemFn` is not available by default (perhaps because macros for
structs/enums are more popular macro targets). Another variation is that we use
`to_token_stream` to return a stream, which we convert into a standard `TokenStream`
with `Into`.

Our `main.rs` in the "usage" directory already has some basic code and tests that
verify the current behavior of our panic-prone `create_person` function. To keep
things simple, the function only has validation on the `age` field, panicking if it gets a
value over 30.

Listing 7.5   Application code (usage directory) with tests for `create_person`

```
use panic_to_result_macro::panic_to_result;

#[derive(Debug)]
pub struct Person {
    name: String,
    age: u32,
}

#[panic_to_result]
fn create_person(name: String, age: u32) -> Person {
    if age > 30 {
        panic!("I hope I die before I get old");
    }                                              This is the example
    Person {                                       function we will be
        name,                                      using to test our macro.
        age,
    }
}

fn main() {}

#[cfg(test)]
mod tests {
    use super::*;
```

```
#[test]
fn happy_path() {
    let actual = create_person("Sam".to_string(), 22);

    assert_eq!(actual.name, "Sam".to_string());
    assert_eq!(actual.age, 22);
}

#[test]
#[should_panic]
fn should_panic_on_invalid_age() {
    create_person("S".to_string(), 32);
}
}
```

This test verifies that the function only works for people younger than 30.

7.6 Mutable or immutable returns

We will work on the implementation before investigating macro errors properly. Our current situation is a bit more complicated than those of previous chapters. When we were doing derives, all we needed from the original input was a bit of handpicked information for generating entirely new code. And our attribute macro for the public fields macro was only slightly more complicated. Yes, we had to reconstruct the original struct with every field set to public, but that was relatively simple because struct definitions often don't contain all that much of interest besides fields. After all, a lot of stuff is added via implementation blocks.

But now we will be working with a function, changing the signature, and meddling with part of its content—which means we are back to this conundrum: what is the best way to create our output when it replaces the input? We have already seen that we can take the original object, or a clone, and give that back. But since functions are a bit more complex when it comes to content, the easier solution here is mutating the existing function, changing what we want, and then returning everything as an output. In other languages, mutability has downsides due to being more error prone. But, thanks to the Rust compiler, mutability is quite safe here.

As an example, the following is some code to make a function public. We make our AST mutable, and then we can change the visibility (vis) to public (Visibility::Public):

```
// other imports
use syn::{ItemFn, Visibility};

#[proc_macro_attribute]
pub fn panic_to_result(_a: TokenStream, item: TokenStream) -> TokenStream {
    let mut ast: ItemFn = syn::parse(item).unwrap();
    ast.vis = Visibility::Public(Default::default());
    ast.to_token_stream().into()
}
```

We set the abstract syntax tree to be mutable.

The visibility of ast is changed—in place—to public. Default makes it easy to generate the boring pub_token (which literally contains pub).

At this point, the immutable approach is not that much more complicated. We just create a new ItemFn and add the visibility. Because we would like everything else to remain unchanged, we are *spreading* the existing struct, which will fill in the existing properties while overriding the ones we defined ourselves (i.e., `vis`):

```
// other imports
use syn::{ItemFn, Visibility, VisPublic};


#[proc_macro_attribute]
pub fn panic_to_result(_a: TokenStream, item: TokenStream) -> TokenStream {
    let ast: ItemFn = syn::parse(item).unwrap();
    let new_ast = ItemFn {
        vis: Visibility::Public(Default::default()),
        ..ast
    };
    new_ast.to_token_stream().into()
}
```

> Creates a new ItemFn that has public visibility, taking all other functionality from the existing function, which we are spreading

While this is a viable alternative, it requires a bit more boilerplate. And in this particular example, it might also be confusing to have both an `ast` and `new_ast`. I can easily see myself changing the first and expecting that to effect a change in the generated code. Finally, the immutable approach seems a bit redundant: in both the immutable and mutable approaches, we are replacing the input with the output. The end result is the same, and *internal* mutation is generally safe.

> **DEFINITION**   By internal mutation, I mean any mutation that has no *visible* effect outside its function. An example would be a counter (`let   mut counter...`) that never leaves the function (is not returned, not saved in a database, etc.). This kind of mutation is not very harmful because the limited scope means the code makes it less error prone and easier to understand. And since everything is internal to the function, parallelization will—probably—not cause additional, weird bugs to rear their ugly heads. The inverse of internal mutation is a global mutable variable, like the ones you might encounter in JavaScript or Python. The scope of a global variable is huge (possibly the entire program), and all objects and functions can change its value: a proper nightmare. Read-only global variables avoid these problems by not being mutable. In between these extremes are mutable values that are passed to and from functions. These are not as harmful as global mutable variables but are still dangerous in the wrong circumstances.

7.7   Getting results

Let's get back to the task at hand: a macro that replaces panics with results. Let's do this step by step. First, we will make our function return a `Result`. For the error type, we will go with a simple `String`. The value will have to match the current return type of the function. Once we have changed the signature, the final expression—currently returning a `Person`—will have to be wrapped in an `Ok`. We will ignore more complex situations with multiple possible return expressions. The good thing is that nothing is keeping us from making these changes and still having a panic in our function—meaning we can leave replacing that for later in this chapter.

If we look at `ItemFn`, we can see that the `sig` property is hiding the signature information (see figure 7.5). One level deeper, `output` contains what is returned. And `ReturnType` is not that complex. It is either the default (when the function returns "nothing," though in practice it will still return a unit, `()`) or an arrow followed by the actual type:

```
pub enum ReturnType {
    Default,
    Type(Token![->], Box<Type>),
}
```

Figure 7.6 shows how we go from `ItemFn` to `ReturnType`.

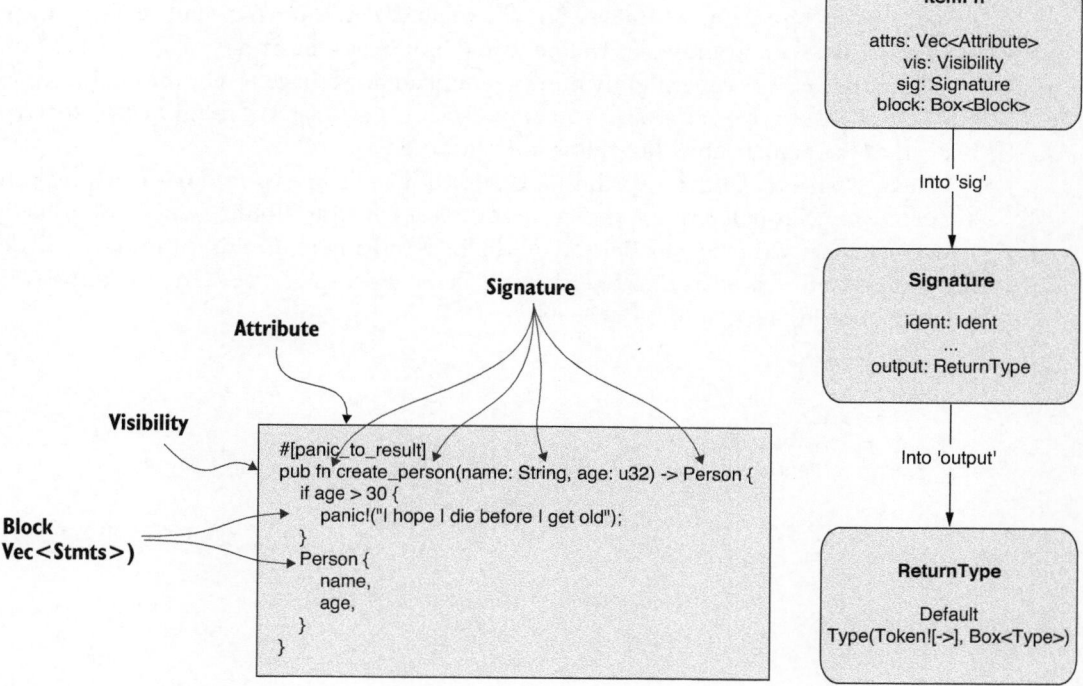

Figure 7.5   Parts of a function with their `ItemFn` names

Figure 7.6   Drilling down into `ItemFn`

What we want to do is to change the output to `Result<(), String>` when there is no return type, or set it to `Result<OriginalReturnType, String>` when we have a type. With `quote` and a bit of thinking, that's not too hard to do.

Listing 7.6   Changing the signature

```
let output = match ast.sig.output {
    ReturnType::Default => {
```

```
        quote! {
                -> Result<(), String>          If we have a default signature,
        }                                      the value is the unit type ().
    }
    ReturnType::Type(_, ty) => {
        quote! {
                -> Result<#ty, String>         Otherwise, we have a type, and
        }                                      we should put that inside Result.
    }
};
ast.sig.output = syn::parse2(output).unwrap();    ◁──┐ We can use parse2 to turn the
                                                       TokenStream into the proper type.
```

We match on `sig.output`, which is either a default (with an explicit `-> ()` signature or an ellipse of the signature) or a type. In the first case, we have an empty return value that needs to be put in a `Result`. So we create a signature for that: `-> Result<(),  String>`. (As we mentioned, we will be using `String` as an error.)

The other case is only slightly more complicated: we have to get the real type, `ty`, and add it to our `TokenStream`. You can also use `ref` to get a reference to the type instead of the actual value, but that's not required.

Next, we use `parse2` to do the hard work for us, converting our tokens into the `ReturnType`. As usual, `parse2` knows what the return type should be because it has to match the type of the `output` field. Would it be annoying to do this without `quote`? See for yourself. Here is what the tokens for `-> Result<Person,  String>` look like (with some properties left out for conciseness):

```
Type(
    RArrow,
    Type::Path {
        path: Path {
            segments: [
                PathSegment {
                    ident: Ident { ident: "Result" },
                    arguments: PathArguments::AngleBracketed {
                        args: [
                            GenericArgument::Type(
                                Type::Path {
                                    path: Path {
                                        segments: [
                                            PathSegment {
                                                ident: Ident {
                                                    ident: "Person"
                                                }
                                            },
                                        ],
                                    },
                                },
                            ),
                            GenericArgument::Type(
                                Type::Path {
                                    path: // path for "String"
                                }
```

```
                                    )]
                        }
                    }
                ]
            }
    })
```

That `"Person"` identifier in there is our `ty`. So we get that one for free. But all the other stuff we would have to write ourselves. It's doable, but it is also a *lot* of boiler-plate code. `quote` makes it easier to both write and read this bit of code.

Now our return value should become a `Result`. This time we have to go looking in `block`, which contains the actual function code, and retrieve the statements inside the function. For this particular function (which has no early returns, etc.), we only need the final statement, so we pop it (removing it from the vector), wrap it in an `Ok`, and put the result back in the vector.

Listing 7.7 Changing the return value

```
use proc_macro::TokenStream;
use quote::{quote, ToTokens};
use syn::{ItemFn, ReturnType, Stmt};

#[proc_macro_attribute]
pub fn panic_to_result(_a: TokenStream, item: TokenStream) -> TokenStream {
    let mut ast: ItemFn = syn::parse2(item).unwrap();

    let output = // code for changing the signature
    ast.sig.output = syn::parse2(output).unwrap();

    let last = ast.block.stmts.pop().unwrap();        // Removes the last statement from the function
    let last_modified = quote! {
        Ok(#last)                                     // Modifies it by wrapping it inside an Ok
    };
    let last_modified_as_expr = Stmt::Expr(           // Parses the token stream we created as
        syn::parse2(last_modified).unwrap(),          // an expression (which is a variant of the
        None                                          // statement enum) with no semicolon
    );
    ast.block.stmts.push(last_modified_as_expr);      // And pushes it to the back of the function statements

    ast.to_token_stream()
}
```

As you can see, putting the result back in the block is slightly more complex than retrieving the statement. The simplest way to do it would be to push the parse result. Sadly, that fails with `unexpected end of input, expected semicolon`. Digging down into the source code, the reason becomes clear: `stmts` is a vector of `Stmt` and the `Parse` implementation of `Stmt` does not allow statements without a semicolon. Instead, we have to give Rust some more context and tell it that this is a specific variant of a statement, an *expression*. And as our (the function's final) expression does not end in a semicolon, we pass in `None` as the second optional, representing that missing semicolon.

If you happen to be using major version 1 of `syn`, this code will not compile, because two variants (`Semi` and `Expr`) were merged in version 2. In this particular case, the change is easy, though: just leave out the `None`.

Listing 7.8 `Stmt` source code in versions 1 and 2

```
// syn version 1
pub enum Stmt {
    Local(Local),
    Item(Item),
    Expr(Expr),
    Semi(Expr, Token![;]),
}

// syn version 2
pub enum Stmt {
    Local(Local),
    Item(Item),
    Expr(Expr, Option<Token![;]>),
    Macro(StmtMacro),
}
```

Now our happy path test is failing because we return a `Result` instead of a `Person`. Perfect! Adding an `unwrap` is a good solution to fix the test because if we don't get the expected `Person`, this will panic and cause the test to fail.

Listing 7.9 `unwrap` the return

```
#[test]
fn happy_path() {
    let actual = create_person("Sam".to_string(), 22).unwrap();

    assert_eq!(actual.name, "Sam".to_string());
    assert_eq!(actual.age, 22);
}
```

Now how about some refactoring? We can move parts of our implementation into separate functions. If you want to clean up even more, you can also move functions to separate files. But this will do for now.

Listing 7.10 Functions for changing the signature and the return value

```
// imports

fn signature_output_as_result(ast: &ItemFn) -> ReturnType {
    let output = match ast.sig.output {
        ReturnType::Default => {
            quote! {
                -> Result<(), String>
            }
```

```
            }
            ReturnType::Type(_, ref ty) => {
                quote! {
                    -> Result<#ty, String>
                }
            }
        };
        syn::parse2(output).unwrap()
}

fn last_statement_as_result(last_statement: Option<Stmt>) -> Stmt {
    let last_unwrapped = last_statement.unwrap();
    let last_modified = quote! {
        Ok(#last_unwrapped)
    };
    Stmt::Expr(syn::parse2(last_modified).unwrap(), None)
}

#[proc_macro_attribute]
pub fn panic_to_result(_a: TokenStream, item: TokenStream) -> TokenStream {
    let mut ast: ItemFn = syn::parse(item).unwrap();

    ast.sig.output = signature_output_as_result(&ast);
    let last_statement = ast.block.stmts.pop();
    ast.block.stmts.push(last_statement_as_result(last_statement));

    ast.to_token_stream().into()
}
```

We now have a bit of nice, readable code that transforms the return type and value of the function. But the panic is still, well, a panic. We still need to replace it with an `Err`.

7.8   Don't panic

Getting rid of the panic is more complex than changing the final statement in our body: this time we can't just `pop` a statement because we don't know where the panic is hiding. So for a general solution, we would have to loop over all statements to see if they contain a panic. In this section, however, we will write code for retrieving `panic` from an if statement, leaving some implementation for the exercises.

7.8.1   Changing the panic into a Result

We will iterate over the statements in our `block` and use `map` with a separate function to transform expressions. Statements that are not expressions will just pass through the mapping. Once the iteration is done, we replace the existing `block` statements with our new ones.

> Listing 7.11   Code fragment from `lib.rs` for mapping statements

```
let new_statements: Vec<Stmt> = ast.block.stmts
    .into_iter()
    .map(|s| match s {
```

```
        Stmt::Expr(e, t) => handle_expression(e, t),    ◁─┐ ┌─ We will map all expressions
        _ => s,              ◁────┐  But any other kind of statement  │  to new statements via a
    })                            │  will just be returned.          │  custom function.
    .collect();
ast.block.stmts = new_statements;    ◁──┐ Finally, we assign the new and the
                                         │ unchanged statements to the block.
```

The reason we focus on expressions is that `if` is an expression, and we know the panic is in there. If we wanted to find every possible panic, we would also have to handle `Semi` (statements that end with a semicolon).

Now let's move on to the transformation of all the other expressions in `handle_expression`, where we look for panics and change them to results.

Listing 7.12 Transforming an expression from panic to error

```
fn handle_expression(expression: Expr, token: Option<Semi>) -> Stmt {
    match expression {
        Expr::If(mut ex_if) => {                    ◁── We are only
            let new_statements: Vec<Stmt> = ex_if.then_branch.stmts    interested in if
                .into_iter()                                           expressions.
                .map(|s| match s {
                    Stmt::Macro(ref expr_macro) =>    ◁──┘ And in if expressions, we
                        extract_panic_content(expr_macro)    only want to check macros.
                            .map(|t| quote! {         ┌── If it is a panic,
                                return Err(#t.to_string());    │  we map it
                            })                        │  to a Result.
                            .map(syn::parse2)
                            .map(Result::unwrap)
                            .unwrap_or(s),
                    _ => s
                })
                .collect();
            ex_if.then_branch.stmts = new_statements;    ┌── We update the statements in
            Stmt::Expr(Expr::If(ex_if), token)    ◁── the if/then branch and rewrap
        },                                            as an expression, passing
        _ => Stmt::Expr(expression, token)    ◁──┐  along the optional semicolon.
    }                                            │  In all other cases, we rewrap
}                                                │  the expression and token.
```

We go through the statements in the then_branch, and, if we find a macro, we check whether it's a panic.

We know the `if` is panicking, so we are only matching on that one variant (see listing 7.14), simply returning all other statements. In a more generic case, we would have to greatly extend the number of match "arms" to handle things like loops, whiles, yields, and the like.

Next, we search for macro statements inside the conditional (`Stmt::Macro`). At that point, the helper, `extract_panic_content`, which we will discuss momentarily, can be used to give back an option with the panic's message—or none if the macro was not a panic. Once we have the message, we use it to replace the panic with an `Err` containing the original message. As before, we use `parse` to get back the right type, a statement, which Rust can infer because we specified the result should be `Vec<Stmt>`.

DEFINITION The shorthands `map(syn::parse2)` and `map(Result::unwrap)` are called *point-free style* in functional lingo. Java calls them method references. This saves us some typing and is quite readable: "Take the (one) parameter you receive and use it to call this function."

If no panic was present, we instead return the statement and add it to our list. Once our iteration is finished, we replace the existing statements with our new ones, which are the ones we already had, except that the panic has been transformed into a `Result`. Finally, we have to wrap everything in our original structure: an `if` expression inside an expression.

This is another piece of code that would behave differently on the first major of `syn` (although you should be using version 2). For one, we would not have to pass around optional tokens in version 1. Bigger changes are required for the match inside `map`, because back then macros were a `Expr::Macro` inside a "semi" (a statement ending with a semicolon) or expression.

Listing 7.13 Code for `syn` version 1

```
Stmt::Semi(Expr::Macro(ref expr_macro), _) =>
    extract_panic_content(expr_macro)
        // ...
```

Listing 7.14 `Stmt`'s variant `Expr`, another enum

```
pub enum Expr {
    Array(ExprArray),
    // ...
    If(ExprIf),
    // ...
    Macro(ExprMacro),
    // ...
}
```

In all other cases, except the one we just discussed, we just return the original statement without any changes.

The `extract_panic_content` function is relatively simple. It looks for an identifier matching the string "panic" inside the macro. If we have a panic, we get the input from `tokens`, clone it, and give it back.

Listing 7.15 Helper for determining if the macro is a panic

```
fn extract_panic_content(expr_macro: &StmtMacro) ->
    Option<proc_macro2::TokenStream> {
    let does_panic = expr_macro.mac.path.segments.iter()
        .any(|v| v.ident.to_string().eq("panic"));

    if does_panic {
        Some(expr_macro.mac.tokens.clone())
    } else {
```

```
        None
    }
}
```

This time around, our failure path test has to change. It now expects an `Err` instead of a `panic`.

```
// happy path unchanged

#[test]
fn should_err_on_invalid_age() {
    let actual = create_person("S".to_string(), 33);

    assert_eq!(
        actual.expect_err("this should be an err"),
        "I hope I die before I get old".to_string()
    );
}
```

We changed the name of the test and removed the should_panic annotation.

We have now successfully enhanced our function with proper error handling!

7.8.2   *Debugging observations*

While writing this code, I bumped into an annoying problem that I spent way too much time staring at. I was refactoring this part of the code:

```
extract_panic_content(expr_macro)
    .map(|t| quote! {
            Err(#t.to_string());
        })
    .map(syn::parse2)
    // ...
}
```

But I kept getting the following error:

```
10 | #[panic_to_result]
| ^^^^^^^^^^^^^^^^^^ cannot infer type of the type parameter `T` declared
  on the enum `Result`
|
= note: this error originates in the attribute macro `panic_to_result`
  (in Nightly builds, run with -Z macro-backtrace for more info)
help: consider specifying the generic arguments
|
10 | #[panic_to_result]::<T, String>
|                      +++++++++++++
```

I figured it had something to do with the `Result` that was returned by `parse2` and Rust somehow not being able to guess the correct types. But a `cargo check` of the macro code worked fine. This was a vital clue that I was looking in the wrong place because

Rust can verify your macro library but not the code you generate. You can put any nonsense in there, and you will only notice when compiling a project that actually uses the macro, not during the compilation of the macro itself.

So, finally, I took a look at `cargo expand` and had Rust / IntelliJ show me the problem: I had written `Err(#t.to_string());` without a `return`. Without that return, `Err(#t.to_string());` was an ordinary statement. But Rust needs to know what type it is, and all it can guess from this piece of code is the value of the error (`E`), a string, but not the return type (`T`). As it has no idea what the value should be, the compiler is asking us what `T` should be. Once you add the return, Rust knows that the `Result` value and error should match those in the signature. Lesson learned: carefully read your error message (which was pointing to the correct `Result`) and think about what `cargo check` and `cargo expand` tell you about the error(s).

7.9 Error-handling flavors

While the aforementioned solution is only a partial one, it is sufficient for now because it's really time we get started with the chapter's main topic: error reporting. On the other hand, right now, our macro has only a few error cases except for the occasional `unwrap` for parsing. To make things interesting, we will add some additional error cases.

For example, it makes sense that our macro should only work for functions that do not yet return `Result`. The most important reason is extra complexity: we want to return a `Result` with a string for the error type. What if the existing `Result` has a different type? Instead of figuring out how to handle that, we will give back a nice error when someone tries to inappropriately use our macro. To verify that the return type is not a `Result` already, we add a simple check to verify that this type is not present in the function's signature.

Listing 7.17 Panicking when the return type is `Result`

```
fn signature_output_as_result(ast: &ItemFn) -> TokenStream {
    match ast.sig.output {
        // default return code...
        ReturnType::Type(_, ref ty) => {
            if ty.to_token_stream().to_string().contains("Result") {
                unimplemented!("cannot use macro on a function with
 Result as return type!");
            }
            Ok(quote! {
                -> Result<#ty, String>
            })
        }
    }
}
```

Right now, this is still poor man's error handling, throwing a panic. We will get to that. But first, we should verify that the function fails.

Listing 7.18   An example function that should fail (add this to `main.rs` for now)

```
#[panic_to_result]
fn create_person_with_result(name: String, age: u32)
    -> Result<Person, String> {              ⟵      Same function as before, with a
    if age > 30 {                                    different return type and name
        panic!("I hope I die before I get old");
    }
    Ok(Person {
        name,
        age,
    })
}
```

If you now run `cargo check` in panic-to-result-usage, you get an error similar to the following:

```
error: custom attribute panicked
  --> src/main.rs:21:1
   |
21 | #[panic_to_result]
   | ^^^^^^^^^^^^^^^^^^
   |
   = help: message: not implemented: Cannot use macro on a function with
 Result as return type!
```

It's an okay message, and the user might understand it. But this is definitely less beautiful and helpful than the built-in messages. And it just points to the macro. Pointing to the signature would make more sense. There are alternatives that give better results.

7.9.1   *Using syn for error handling*

First up is syn error handling, which requires changes to both `signature_output_as_result` and our `panic_to_result` entrypoint.

Listing 7.19   `syn` error handling (partial code from `lib.rs`)

```
// other imports
use syn::spanned::Spanned;                ⟵      We need this trait to be in
                                                  scope if we want to call span().
fn signature_output_as_result(ast: &ItemFn)
    -> Result<ReturnType, syn::Error> {
    let output = match ast.sig.output {
        // default return code...
        ReturnType::Type(_, ref ty) => {
            if ty.to_token_stream().to_string().contains("Result") {
                return Err(
                    syn::Error::new(
syn::Error requires  ⟶      ast.sig.span(),
    a span ...              format!(
                                "this macro can only be applied to a function
                                that does not return a Result. Signature: {}",
```

```
                                quote!(#ty)
                            )
                        )
                    );
                }
                quote! {
                    -> Result<#ty, String>
                }
            }
        };
        Ok(syn::parse2(output).unwrap())
}

#[proc_macro_attribute]
pub fn panic_to_result(_a: TokenStream, item: TokenStream) -> TokenStream {
    // other code
    match signature_output_as_result(&ast) {
        Ok(output) => ast.sig.output = output,
        Err(err) => return err.to_compile_error().into()
    };
    // other code
}
```

... and a message, which we build using format, passing along the faulty signature

When we get back an Ok, everything is the same as before. When we receive an error, we convert it to a stream and return early.

Our `signature_output_as_result` now returns an `Err` if the signature contains a `Result`. Inside that, `Err` is a value of type `syn::Error`. The constructor of that error type requires us to pass back a span and a message (which should implement `Display`). We've encountered span before and noted how it points back to the original code. That might finally be useful! One idea is to pass the span of `sig`, allowing Rust to point to the signature. In the message, we give some information about what we found plus the current signature as a reference. As usual, we use `quote`, which `format!` will automatically add to the string for us.

But we still have to do something with the `Result` that `signature_output_as_result` is returning. And, unlike `main` functions that can return a unit or a `Result`, a proc-macro can only return a `TokenStream`. So we do a match. If everything is okay, we proceed as before by adding the new signature to our AST. If we have an error, we convert it into a compile error (a `proc_macro2::TokenStream`) and `into` a standard stream.

Now we get a better error message in our application:

```
error: this macro can only be applied to a function that does not
return a Result. Signature: Result < Person, String >
  --> src/main.rs:22:1
   |
22 | fn create_person_with_result(name: String, age: u32)
   |     -> Result<Person, String> {
   | ^^
```

This is more informative than the previous message. We're pointing the user to *where* the problem occurs, the signature (which starts with `fn`), and telling them exactly what is wrong.

Let's use our new `syn` error for a second example. We've found it useful to transform existing panics into an `Err` with a message. But what if there is no message to add? Well, our current code will panic if we don't have a message. Great. We can test by adding another function that will fail to compile. You can either disable the other failing example or add `trybuild` and move it into a compilation test.

Listing 7.20 Another failing function

```
#[panic_to_result]
fn create_person_with_empty_panic(name: String, age: u32) -> Person {
    if age > 30 {
        panic!();          ◁──┐  Empty panic, which will
    }                          provoke a compilation failure.
    Person {
        name,
        age,
    }
}
```

We should return a useful error when we encounter that situation instead of a vague custom attribute `panicked`.

Listing 7.21 Handling empty panic content (partial code from `lib.rs`)

```
// imports

fn handle_expression(expression: Expr, token: Option<Semi>)
    -> Result<Stmt, syn::Error> {
    match expression {
        Expr::If(mut ex_if) => {
            let new_statements: Result<Vec<Stmt>, syn::Error> = ex_if
                .then_branch.stmts.into_iter()
                .map(|s| match s {
                    Stmt::Macro(ref expr_macro) => {
                        let output = extract_panic_content(expr_macro);

                        if output.map(|v| v.is_empty()).unwrap_or(false) {
                            Err(syn::Error::new(
                                expr_macro.span(),
                                "please make sure every panic \
                                in your function has a message"
                            ))
                        } else {
                            Ok(extract_panic_content(expr_macro)
                                // code to change panic to result
                            )
                        }
                    }
                    _ => Ok(s)
                })
                .collect();
```

We check whether we have an option with empty content. If so, we return an error.

This code is now wrapped in an Ok but otherwise unchanged.

```
                    ex_if.then_branch.stmts = new_statements?;    ◁——┐ We now have a Result
                    Ok(Stmt::Expr(Expr::If(ex_if), token))             │ instead of a Vec, so we
                }                                                      │ use ? to get to the value
                _ => Ok(Stmt::Expr(expression, token))                 │ (if it's present).
        }
}

#[proc_macro_attribute]
pub fn panic_to_result(_a: TokenStream, item: TokenStream) -> TokenStream {
    // ...
    let new_statements: Result<Vec<Stmt>, syn::Error> = ast.block.stmts
        .into_iter()
        .map(|s| match s {
            Stmt::Expr(e) => handle_expression(e),
            _ => Ok(s),
        })
        .collect();
    match new_statements {                              ┌ Similar to before, we
        Ok(new) => ast.block.stmts = new,               │ match on the Result and
        Err(err) => return err.to_compile_error().into()│ create an error token
    }                                                   └ stream if we have an error.
    // ...
}
```

That is a lot of minor changes. In `handle_expression`, we now return a `Result`, so we've added a lot of `Ok` wrappers. We have also extended the macro check: when we get back the optional value from `is_panic`, we now check whether the content we received is empty. If it is, we return a `syn::Error` with a fitting message, and we use the span of the macro to point the user to the relevant panic. Since our `new_state-ments` are now a `Result`, we return early if there is an error using `?`. Otherwise, we have our statements and can re-add them to the function.

Traverse

Another cool Rust feature makes its appearance in the previous code. As you can see, we map over statements and return a `Result` for each one. That means our output should be `Vec<Result<Stmt, syn::Error>>`. But the output type I defined for `new_statements` in `handle_expression` is `Result<Vec<Stmt>, syn::Error>`! In the functional world, this is called *traverse*, which allows stacking your enums (actually, *monads*, but let's not get into that) in different ways. The reason this works in Rust is that there is a generic `FromIterator` implementation for `Result` for values that turn into something that also implements `FromIterator`, like a vector.

The details are not important, but you should grasp that this is very convenient. I don't have to unwrap all the results myself. Instead, I get either an error or a list of statements. To be fair, the two are not *entirely* equivalent: there is no room for multiple errors in `Result<Vec<Stmt>, syn::Error>`, meaning every error but the first one will be discarded. To gather all the errors, you would need something like a vector. And preferably you would wrap that vector in some custom struct and make that implement `std::error::Error`, as any good error type should (even if it's not strictly required).

In panic_to_result new_statements is now a Result<Vec<Stmt>, syn::Error>. So we transform the error into a token stream and give it back or continue processing if everything is okay. If we now run our faulty function, we get back a new kind of error:

```
error: please make sure every panic in your function has a message
  --> panic-to-result-usage/src/main.rs:13:9
   |
13 |         panic!();
   |         ^^^^^
```

We are pointing to the correct line and the failing statement, with a clear error message. If you want, you can add some extra context:

```
Err(syn::Error::new(
    e.span(),
    format!("please make sure every panic in your function \
            has a message, check: {}",
    quote!(#statement)
)))
```

```
error: please make sure every panic in your function has a message,
check: if age > 30 { panic! () ; }
  --> panic-to-result-usage/src/main.rs:13:9
   |
13 |         panic!();
   |         ^^^^^
```

If our user still can't find the problem, they only have themselves to blame! The only downside with this code is that if the user makes multiple mistakes, there will only be a warning for one of them. Though it requires a bit of extra work, we can use the combine method to fix that.

Listing 7.22 Using `combine` for reporting multiple errors

```
// imports and other functions

#[proc_macro_attribute]
pub fn panic_to_result(_a: TokenStream, item: TokenStream) -> TokenStream {
    // ...
    let signature_output = signature_output_as_result(&ast);
    let statements_output: Result<Vec<Stmt>, syn::Error> = // unchanged

    match (statements_output, signature_output) {            // We match on
        (Ok(new), Ok(output)) => {                           // both of our results.
            ast.block.stmts = new;          If everything is okay,
            ast.sig.output = output;        we can assign to the
        },                                  statements and output.
        (Ok(_), Err(signature_err)) => {
            return signature_err.to_compile_error()
                .into()
        },                                                   If we get one error,
        (Err(statement_err), Ok(_)) => {                     we give it back.
            return statement_err.to_compile_error()
                .into()
```

```
        },
        (Err(mut statement_err), Err(signature_err)) => {
            statement_err.combine(signature_err);
            return statement_err.to_compile_error()
                .into()
        }
    };
    // popping and creating the output
}
```

> And if we have two errors,
> we combine them.

First, a minor change: we have moved the signature output above the statement iteration. This is an easy way to avoid a partial move problem with `ast.block`. (In an earlier version, our work with `block` was done by the time we started handling the
signature, hence why we didn't have problems before.)

Instead of handling the statements and signature separately, we now check their
combined outputs in a match arm, which will allow us to take action when we have
multiple errors. We handle the happy path by mutating the AST. Separate errors are
also handled in the same way as before, by returning the one error. The final match is
for when we have two errors. If that is the case, we `combine` them before returning.
Now when you create a function that returns a `Result` and has an empty panic, you
will get two errors in one go.

7.9.2   Using proc_macro_error for error handling

Our error handling has clearly improved thanks to `syn::Error`. Can we do even better? Maybe! And that's thanks to `proc_macro_error` (http://mng.bz/Adxe). First, add
`proc-macro-error = "1.0.4"` to our `panic-to-result-macro`. Next, we need to add
an attribute to our macro, as in the following listing.

> **Listing 7.23   Adding the extra attribute macro to our public `lib.rs` function**

```
use proc_macro_error::proc_macro_error;

#[proc_macro_error]
#[proc_macro_attribute]
pub fn panic_to_result(_a: TokenStream, item: TokenStream) -> TokenStream {
    // ...
}
```

> Imports the
> error macro

> Annotates our function
> with the error macro

If you don't do this, you will get an error with a helpful message: `proc-macro-error`
`API cannot be used outside of entry_point invocation, perhaps you forgot`
`to annotate your #[proc_macro] function with #[proc_macro_error]`. And now
we are ready to use the macros (yes, it's turtles stacked on turtles) that this crate gives
us. First up is `abort!`. This one allows us to pass in a `syn` struct, from which a `span`
will be taken, as well as several useful messages. We will refactor our `handle_`
`expression` function. Instead of returning a `Result`, it will now abort on a missing
panic message.

> **Listing 7.24 Aborting (some unchanged functions not shown)**

```
// other imports
use proc_macro_error::{abort};

fn handle_expression(expression: Expr, token: Option<Semi>) -> Stmt {
    match expression {
        Expr::If(mut ex_if) => {
            let new_statements: Vec<Stmt> = ex_if.then_branch.stmts
.into_iter()
                .map(|s| match s {
                    Stmt::Macro(ref expr_macro) => {
                        let output = extract_panic_content(expr_macro);

                        if output.map(|v| v.is_empty()).unwrap_or(false) {
                            abort!(
                                expr_macro,
                                "panic needs a message!".to_string();
                                help =
                                "try to add a message: \
                                panic!(\"Example\".to_string())";
                                note =
                                "we will add the message to Result's Err"
                            );
                        } else {
                            // continue
                        }
                    }
                    _ => s
                })
                .collect();
            // return statement
        }
        _ => Stmt::Expr(expression, token)
    }
}

#[proc_macro_error]
#[proc_macro_attribute]
pub fn panic_to_result(_a: TokenStream, item: TokenStream) -> TokenStream {
    // ...
    let new_statements = ast.block.stmts
        .into_iter()
        .map(|s| match s {
            Stmt::Expr(e, t) => handle_expression(e, t),
            _ => s,
        })
        .collect();
    ast.block.stmts = new_statements;
    // ...
}
```

Calls abort, passes in the macro tokens for its span, and adds a message, help, and note

The Result wrappers are gone again.

You can see how `abort` allows us to do all kinds of things, like adding a `help` and `note`, separated by semicolons, in addition to the message. The resulting error applied to our empty panic function looks pretty neat. We are really doing our best to be helpful.

(Aside: As you can see from the location of the fail, I've moved my test function with the empty panic to the `tests` directory):

```
error: panic needs a message!

          = help: try to add a message: panic!("Example".to_string())
          = note: we will add the message to Result's Err

  --> tests/fails/create_person_with_empty_panic.rs:13:9
   |
13 |          panic!();
   |          ^^^^^^^^^
```

But we could go a step further—why not give feedback on all possible problems? For that, we will need `emit_error!`. The difference between these two is that `abort` stops processing, whereas `emit_error` allows you to keep looking for problems, similar to what `combine` allowed us to do for `syn` errors but with less work involved. Let's use this one for both the empty panic and the faulty signature.

Listing 7.25 Using `emit_error` (partial, two unchanged functions not shown)

```
//imports

fn signature_output_as_result(ast: &ItemFn) -> ReturnType {
    let output = match ast.sig.output {
        // default return
        ReturnType::Type(_, ref ty) => {
            if ty.to_token_stream().to_string().contains("Result") {
                emit_error!(ty,
                    format!(
                        "this macro can only be applied to a function \
                        that does not yet return a Result. Signature: {}",
                        quote!(#ty)
                    )
                );
                ast.sig.output.to_token_stream()
            } else {
                quote! {
                    -> Result<#ty, String>
                }
            }
        }
    };
    syn::parse2(output).unwrap()
}

fn handle_expression(expression: Expr, token: Option<Semi>) -> Stmt {
    match expression {
        Expr::If(mut ex_if) => {
            let new_statements: Vec<Stmt> = ex_if.then_branch.stmts
                .into_iter()
                .map(|s| match s {
                    Stmt::Macro(ref expr_macro) => {
                        let output = extract_panic_content(expr_macro);
```

The signature already contains Result, so we emit an error, with ty for the span and a helpful message.

But we want to continue processing, so we return the existing signature (output).

```
                              if output.map(|v| v.is_empty()).unwrap_or(false) {
                                  emit_error!(
                                      expr_macro,
                                      "panic needs a message!".to_string();
                                      help =
                                      "try to add a message: \
                                      panic!(\"Example\".to_string())";
                                      note =
                                      "we will add the message to Result's Err"
                                  );
                                  s                    ──┐  Similarly, we emit the
                              } else {                     │  error and then return
                                  // continue              │  the original statement.
                              }
                          }
                      }
                      _ => s
                  })
                  .collect();
              // return the statement
          }
          // return
      }
}

#[proc_macro_error]
#[proc_macro_attribute]
pub fn panic_to_result(_a: TokenStream, item: TokenStream) -> TokenStream {
    // ...
    ast.sig.output = signature_output_as_result(&ast);  ◀──┐  The Result wrapper is
    // ...                                                   │  gone, so we pass on
}                                                           │  the return directly.
```

The change in `handle_panic_to_result` is not too complex. We now use `emit_error` for both of our error cases, and we have—again—removed every `Result` wrapper. More interesting is that we are still returning something after emitting an error. That is because we want to go on for as long as possible, emitting errors—but continuing with parsing—until we've done everything we could. And because our code will not stop on the first error, we want to give back something sensible. If multiple functions are manipulating the code (say, the signature) and the first one fails and decides to put a garbage stream of tokens in the signature, the next function receives that garbage and fails for a totally unexpected reason. So returning the original value is an easy solution, even if an empty `TokenStream` could also work in simple examples.

We now add an example function that looks like the one in the following listing.

Listing 7.26   Function with faulty `panic` and signature

```
#[panic_to_result]
fn create_person_two_issues(name: String, age: u32)
    -> Result<String, Person> {
    if age > 30 {
        panic!();
    }
```

```
    Ok(Person {
        name,
        age,
    })
}
```

We get back two errors: the one we already had for empty panics as well as the one for faulty signature:

```
error: panic needs a message!
// rest of the error message from before //

error: this macro can only be applied to a function that does not yet
  return a Result. Signature: Result < String, Person >
  --> tests/fails/create_person_two_issues.rs:11:56
   |
11 | fn create_person_two_issues(name: String, age: u32)
-> Result<String, Person> {
   |     ^^^^^^^^^^^^^^^^^^^^^^^^
```

Besides abort! and emit_error!, the crate offers several other macros. abort_call_site! and emit_call_site_error! are similar to the other two except they contain a default span (pointing to the call site). Meanwhile emit_warning! and emit_-call_site_warning! are used for logging warnings that won't stop compilation. But this is all quite similar to what we already discussed, so we won't go into more detail.

7.9.3   *Deciding between syn and proc_macro_error*

Use syn::Error if you dislike adding another dependency to your project since you probably already use syn. Its Result makes the behavior of your functions very clear, signaling that these are functions with failure cases. On the other hand, the proc_macro_error macros have a lot of useful functionality and require less ceremony. In either case, your users will be glad you didn't go for vanilla panicking.

7.10   *From the real world*

Most macro crates handle errors by using one of these two approaches. Tokio, for example, is one of the libraries that uses syn::Error. Say you've added the Tokio macro to a function that is not actually async. The following piece of code will inform you of your mistake:

```
if input.sig.asyncness.is_none() {
    let msg = "the `async` keyword is missing from the function declaration";
    return Err(syn::Error::new_spanned(input.sig.fn_token, msg));
}
```

syn::Error::new_spanned is an alternative to syn::Error::new. The difference is that the latter works with a span and the former allows you to pass in anything that implements ToTokens, which allows for more advanced errors. But, in this case, the output produced will be exactly the same as with syn::Error::new(input.sig .fn_token.span(), msg).

As an example, the following is a somewhat more creative use of `new_spanned`:

```
let msg = "a message";
let token = ast.sig.fn_token;
let name = ast.sig.ident;
let fn_token_plus_function_name = quote!(#token #name);

syn::Error::new_spanned(fn_token_plus_function_name, msg)
    .to_compile_error()
    .to_token_stream()
    .into()
```

If this was used in this chapter's macro, we would get back something like this:

```
error: a message
  --> src/main.rs:11:1
   |
11 | fn create_person(name: String, age: u32) -> Person {
   | ^^^^^^^^^^^^^^^^^^^^
```

Note how the message is pointing to both the function token and function name.

Yew similarly relies on `syn` errors. Interestingly, it does throw an `unimplemented` panic when the input is not a struct:

```
impl Parse for DerivePropsInput {
    fn parse(input: ParseStream) -> Result<Self> {
        let input: DeriveInput = input.parse()?;
        let prop_fields = match input.data {
            syn::Data::Struct(data) => match data.fields {
                syn::Fields::Named(fields) => {
                    // code
                }
                syn::Fields::Unit => Vec::new(),
                _ => unimplemented!("only structs are supported"),
            },
            _ => unimplemented!("only structs are supported"),
        };
        // more code
    }
}
```

Shuttle, an "infrastructure from code" project that we mentioned in chapter 1, relies on `proc_macro_error`. Here they are checking the return type—just like us! Besides a hint, Shuttle also adds a reference to documentation with `doc`:

```
fn check_return_type(signature: &Signature) {
    match &signature.output {
        ReturnType::Default => emit_error!(
            signature,
            "shuttle_service::main functions need to return a service";
            hint = "See the docs for services with first class support";
            doc = "https://docs.rs/shuttle-service/latest/..."
        ),
        // another check and emit error
```

```
        }
    }
```

Leptos uses `proc_macro_errors` as well. In the following code, `abort` is used when there's a useful span to point to, or `abort_call_site` when it is lacking:

```
#[proc_macro_error::proc_macro_error]
#[proc_macro]
pub fn view(tokens: TokenStream) -> TokenStream {
    // getting cx and comma
    match (cx, comma) {
        (Some(TokenTree::Ident(cx)), Some(TokenTree::Punct(punct)))
            if punct.as_char() == ',' =>
        {
            // more code
            let global_class = match (&first, &second) {
                (Some(TokenTree::Ident(first)), Some(TokenTree::Punct(eq)))
                    if *first == "class" && eq.as_char() == '=' =>
                {
                    match &fourth {
                        Some(TokenTree::Punct(comma))
                            if comma.as_char() == ',' =>
                        {
                            third.clone()
                        }
                        _ => {
                            abort!(
                                punct,
                                "To create a scope class with the view! \
                                macro you must put a comma `,`...";
                                help =
                                r#"e.g.,view!{
                                cx,class="my-class", <div>...</div>
                                }"#
                            )
                        }
                    }
                }
                _ => None,
            };
            // more code
        }
        _ => {
            abort_call_site!(
                "view! macro needs a context and RSX: e.g., view! {{ cx, \
                <div>...</div> }}"
            )
        }
    }
}
```

Rocket, meanwhile, uses Diagnostics from `proc_macro2_diagnostics`, which has some neat extension traits for `proc_macro2`. They add an `error` and `help` to a `span` when checking a signature:

```
if catch.function.sig.inputs.len() > 2 {
    return Err(catch.function.sig.paren_token.span
        .error("invalid number of arguments: must be zero, one, or two")
        .help("catchers optionally take `&Request` or `Status, &Request`"));
}
```

Those two return a `Diagnostic` that you can add more information to. You turn it into an output using `emit_as_item_tokens()`:

```
let uri_display = match uri_display {
    Ok(tokens) => tokens,
    Err(diag) => return diag.emit_as_item_tokens()
};
```

Tokio, Leptos, Shuttle, Rocket—all of them report errors in a way that should be at least superficially familiar to you after reading this chapter. So, congratulations: you now have the tools to give awesome feedback to the users of your macros.

7.11   Exercises

See the appendix for solutions.

1 Rewrite the public fields macro to mutate the incoming `TokenStream` instead of creating a brand-new one.
2 Our function-like macro for generating methods throws `unimplemented` for non-struct inputs. Use `syn::Error` instead. You can point to the span of the name.
3 Now avoid the `unimplemented` with `proc_macro_error`.
4 Expand our "panic checks" to also transform panics in `while` expressions.

Summary

- Pure functions, whose return only depends on the parameters they receive, are easier to understand, test, and use than impure, side effect–producing functions.
- Exceptions make code harder to understand because they break control flow, making Rust's `Result` enum an excellent alternative for error handling.
- Panics should only be used for situations that cannot happen or should never happen or when you are exploring ideas.
- Besides creating entirely new token streams, you can manipulate the ones you receive, changing only what is necessary while leaving the rest of the code untouched.
- With `ItemFn`, we can view the signature and body (statements) of a function.
- Using panics for error handling in a macro works, but the resulting compilation error is not very useful to your users.
- `syn::Error` gives you an error type for use in `Result` that can be transformed into a much more informative output.
- `proc_macro_error` offers additional power in reporting helpful errors.
- With `emit_error`, you can easily report multiple errors in one go.

Builder with attributes 8

This chapter covers

- Working with field-level custom attributes to rename methods
- Using root-level custom attributes to decide on error handling
- Making a builder easier to use with type state
- Exploring how derive and attribute macros differ
- Parsing (document) attributes inside function-like macros

Every macro we created thus far had its behavior set in stone. Nothing was customizable. But sometimes you want overridable behavior, because that greatly increases flexibility, or you may need it to meet some requirements. In this chapter, we focus on customization via attributes, which are available for both derive and attribute macros. We will see how we can add information to a macro attribute and other parts of your code, like the individual properties of a struct.

As always, we need a project to illustrate these possibilities. Instead of introducing something new, let's save some time by expanding on the builder example we created previously. How can we make it more versatile? Perhaps we can start by allowing users to rename the setter methods that will appear on our builder. This is quite typical functionality (Serde, for example, allows renames), because sometimes there is a mismatch between what your data looks like and what you need it to be to conform to standards or requirements. Even if the default works for most cases, it's something you may want to make possible.

8.1   A rename attribute

The setup for this chapter is easy since we already have a macro ready to go. If you're following along, disabling the existing tests might be a good idea, as we won't make an effort to keep those running. We will, however, still write test scenarios for our new code, which we will add to `main.rs` in the usage folder.

8.1.1   Testing the new attribute

What we need is a test that shows we can rename a property. This should also change the relevant setter method name. These two assertions come together in the test in the following listing.

Listing 8.1   Verifying the desired behavior with a test

```
#[test]
fn should_generate_builder_for_struct_with_one_renamed_property() {
    #[derive(Builder)]
    struct Gleipnir {
        #[rename("tops_of")]        ←┐ This attribute is new and
        roots_of: String,            │ specifies a custom name.
    }

    let gleipnir = Gleipnir::builder()
        .tops_of("mountains".to_string())   ←┐ Because of this, the builder method is
        .build();                            │ now called tops_of instead of roots_of.

    assert_eq!(
        gleipnir.roots_of,        ←┐ The actual property
        "mountains".to_string()    │ remains as is.
    );
}
```

The one new thing in this test is the `#[rename("tops_of")]` attribute, which we are using inside a struct annotated with `#[derive(Builder)]`. Try to run this test. You will get back an error: `cannot find attribute rename in this scope`. This is because we haven't told Rust that our macro has attributes. Modify the `lib.rs` file in `builder-macro`.

Listing 8.2   Adding the `rename` attribute

```
#[proc_macro_derive(Builder, attributes(rename))]    ←┐ attributes(rename) tells the
pub fn builder(item: TokenStream) -> TokenStream {    │ derive macro that it has an
    create_builder(item.into()).into()                │ attribute called "rename."
}
```

A derive macro's attributes are called "derive macro helper attributes." They are *inert*, meaning they will not remove themselves during attribute processing. You can see this for yourself by running `cargo expand` on a derive macro with attributes—the output still contains the attributes. This makes sense, as derive macros cannot change their input. The only purpose of these attributes is to be fed into a derive macro that can use them to change behavior and output.

All attributes, including our `rename`, should be specified in the macro declaration under `attributes` (as seen earlier). `rename` is now a known attribute. But it is still without implementation, causing the test to fail with `no method named tops_of found...`. We are ready to start fixing that.

8.1.2   Implementing the attribute's behavior

Our game plan is as follows:

1 Loop over our fields as before.
2 Check whether we have a `rename` attribute.
3 Change the method name if we do.
4 Fallback to our default if we don't.

Before we continue, a quick refresher: the following are all the properties of `syn::Field`. You have already learned to work with `vis`, `ident`, and `ty`. `colon_token` simply indicates whether there is a : in the field definition (in `example: String`, that `Option` will be `Some`). `mutability` is a new field in `syn` version 2 and is—at the time of writing—always `None`. That means `attrs`, the attributes placed above the field, is the only relevant property we haven't used yet. And now we will:

```
pub struct Field {
    pub vis: Visibility,
    pub ident: Option<Ident>,
    pub ty: Type,
    pub colon_token: Option<Token![:]>,
    pub mutability: FieldMutability,
    pub attrs: Vec<Attribute>,
}
```

Since we want to modify the generation of methods, expanding `builder_methods` makes sense. The relevant code is in the following listing.

Listing 8.3   Original `builder_methods` code

```
pub fn builder_methods(fields: &Punctuated<Field, Comma>)
    -> impl Iterator<Item = TokenStream2> + '_ {
    fields.iter().map(|f| {
        let (field_name, field_type) = get_name_and_type(f);
        quote! {
            pub fn #field_name(&mut self, input: #field_type) -> &mut Self {
                self.#field_name = Some(input);
```

```
                self
            }
        }
    })
}
```

We need to make quite a few changes to use attributes, but the good news is that all the changes are scoped to the `fields.rs` file. `lib.rs` will remain untouched. We will start simple and write a helper that uses `find` to look within the field's attributes for a name that matches our string.

Listing 8.4 Helper method in `fields.rs` to find a field attribute with a given name

```
fn extract_attribute_from_field<'a>(f: &'a Field, name: &'a str)
    -> Option<&'a syn::Attribute> {
        f.attrs.iter().find(|&attr| attr.path().is_ident(name))
}
```

The `path` method gives back the attribute's path, which is the part right after the `#[` bit (i.e., "rename"). Because this is an identifier, we should use its `is_ident` to compare with our string. Alternatively, we could have done a bit more work and compared path segments: `attr.path().segments.len() == 1 && attr.path().segments[0].ident == *name`. This works because there is a generic implementation of equality for `Ident`, `PartialEq<T>`, for anything `where T: AsRef<str>`. `find` will return the attribute wrapped in `Some`, defaulting to `None` if nothing was found.

Now on to the meat of our code in `builder_methods`. We are still iterating over the fields and retrieving name and type, except we now have additional logic for retrieving the attribute, analyzing it, and deciding on output depending on the result of that analysis.

Listing 8.5 New `builder_methods` code in `fields.rs`

```
// earlier imports
use syn::{Meta, LitStr};

pub fn builder_methods(fields: &Punctuated<Field, Comma>)
    -> Vec<TokenStream> {
    fields.iter()
        .map(|f| {
            let (field_name, field_type) = get_name_and_type(f);
            let attr = extract_attribute_from_field(f, "rename")    ←┐ Calls the
                .map(|a| &a.meta)                                      │ helper
                .map(|m| {
                    match m {
                        Meta::List(nested) => {
                            let a: LitStr = nested
                                .parse_args()
                                .unwrap();
```

```
                              Ident::new(&a.value(), a.span())
                          }
                          Meta::Path(_) => {
                              panic!(
                                  "expected brackets with name of prop"
                              )
                          },
                          Meta::NameValue(_) => {
                              panic!(
                                  "did not expect name + value"
                              )
                          }
                      }
                  }                   Tries to retrieve the override
              });              ◁─┘    from the rename attribute

          if let Some(attr) = attr {
              quote! {
                  pub fn #attr(mut self, input: #field_type) -> Self {
                      self.#field_name = Some(input);
                      self
                  }
              }
          } else {
              quote! {
                  pub fn #field_name(mut self, input: #field_type) -> Self {
                      self.#field_name = Some(input);
                      self
                  }
              }
          }
      }).collect()
  }
```

If we have an override, produces a method name with that value

If not, falls back to the default output

We use our helper to retrieve the attribute if it exists. But that is not enough. We also need to do some additional mapping to retrieve what we are really interested in: the desired method name (see figure 8.1). Most of an attribute's interesting information is located inside meta, an enum with three variants: List, Path, and NamedValue:

- NamedValue is when you put keys with values in the brackets behind your attribute (e.g., #[rename(name=tops_of)]).
- Path is when you have (a path of) attribute information *without brackets*.
- List is for a list of values between brackets: #[rename("first","second")].

In our case, the last one, a list of exactly one element, is correct. We will keep things simple by panicking when we receive the wrong attribute format. But I would be amiss if I didn't point out that meta has a couple of useful methods for this very situation. require_list will return the nested MetaList if it is present or an Err if we received a different enum variant. And there are similar methods for the other two: require_path_only and require_name_value. So require_list is a great alternative for a simple panic.

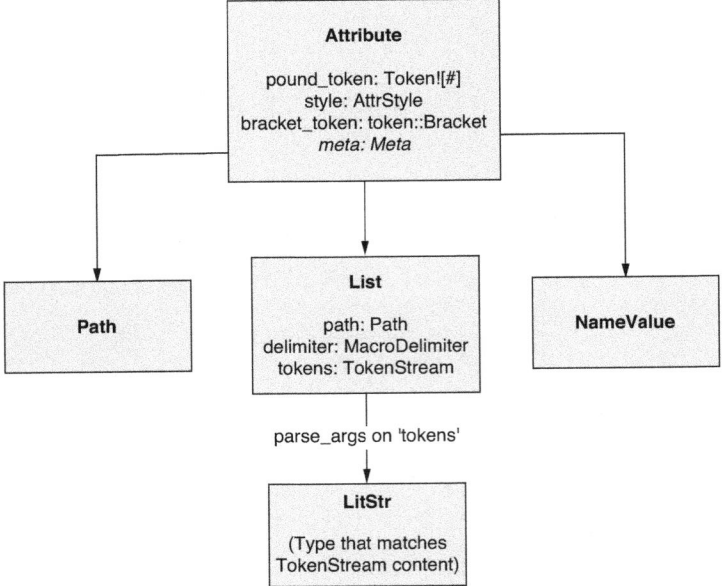

Figure 8.1   Diving into the `Attribute` type

`List` contains `tokens`, which is a `TokenStream` with the information we want. The easiest way to get a useful type out of that stream is to use the `parse_args` method, specifying the expected return type. For us, `LitStr` is a convenient return as we literally—feeble pun intended—expect a string!

Now all that is left is to transform this literal into an identifier we can use to construct the method name. For that we use the `value` helper method and the `span` of the existing literal, passing them to the `new` method. It may seem like retrieving the token, changing it into a string, and taking a reference (i.e., `&nested_lit.token().to_string()`) would also work. Unfortunately, that code will error: `"\"tops_of\""` is not a valid `identifier`. Those escapes around your literal are not what you want for your identifier, and `value` gets rid of them for you.

Once we are done changing the attribute into a custom method name, we use `if let` to get the value from the `Option` if it is present. In every other case, we default to our previous implementation, where the field and method names are the same.

8.1.3   *Parsing variations*

As always, there are many possible variations for this macro and its implementation. For example, maybe you think the quotation marks around `"tops_of"` are a needless distraction when invoking the macro. Maybe you prefer it without quotes, like

#[rename(tops_of)]. In that case, we don't have a `LitStr` wrapping and the tokens inside our brackets are exactly what we need. So the alternative code within `match` looks like the following.

Listing 8.6   Alternative code within our `match`

```
Meta::List(nested) => {
    &nested.tokens
}
```

With an ident instead of a string, we could also have turned to `parse_nested_meta`, a method on `Attribute`. In that case, instead of two nested maps (`map(|a| &a.meta)` plus the map that does a `match`), we would have what appears in the following listing.

Listing 8.7   Alternative with `parse_nested_meta`

```
let mut content = None;

a.parse_nested_meta(|m| {          Calls parse_nested_meta to get
    let i = &m.path.segments.first().unwrap().ident;   the content of the attribute
    content = Some(Ident::new(&i.to_string(), i.span()));   We know that a
    Ok(())                                                  rename should contain
}).unwrap();                                                a single identifier, so
                      This returns a unit result, which we should   we retrieve it.
                      handle (in this case by unwrapping).

content.unwrap()          content should now be an Option<Ident>,
                          so we unwrap it and return the identifier.
```

In major version 1 of `syn`, there was another useful `parse_meta` method under the parsing feature, but that seems to have been removed.

To make sure that everything works, you can add additional tests to `main.rs.`, such as one with multiple properties but only one of them with a custom name or a test where multiple properties have custom names.

Listing 8.8   Additional test (example)

```
#[test]
fn should_generate_builder_for_struct_with_two_props_one_custom_name() {
    #[derive(Builder)]
    struct Gleipnir {
        #[rename("tops_of")]
        roots_of: String,
        breath_of_a_fish: u8,
    }

    let gleipnir = Gleipnir::builder()
        .tops_of("mountains".to_string())
        .breath_of_a_fish(1)
        .build();
```

```
    assert_eq!(gleipnir.roots_of, "mountains".to_string());
    assert_eq!(gleipnir.breath_of_a_fish, 1);
}
```

These tests, and the existing ones, should compile and succeed.

8.2   *Alternative naming for attributes*

Before moving on, we will explore the alternative of using a key plus value for our
`rename` attribute. Several libraries use yet another approach, creating a single library
attribute with the specific command added between parentheses—for example,
`#[serde(rename = "name")]`. But we'll leave that for the exercises.

Start with a unit test to verify the required behavior. (You should disable the other
tests. We are going to replace the existing attribute behavior.)

Listing 8.9   Testing for an alternative attribute-naming strategy

```
#[cfg(test)]
mod tests {
    #[test]
    fn should_generate_builder_for_struct_with_one_renamed_prop() {
        #[derive(Builder)]
        struct Gleipnir {
            #[rename = "tops_of"]        Instead of parentheses, we use
            roots_of: String,           an equals sign to separate the
        }                               "command" from its value.

        let gleipnir = Gleipnir::builder()
            .tops_of("mountains".to_string())
            .build();

        assert_eq!(gleipnir.roots_of, "mountains".to_string());
    }
}
```

Now for the implementation. Again, we only have to focus on `fields.rs` and `builder_
methods`. While there are only a few essential changes, the solution does take a more
"streaming" approach to mapping. Instead of using `if let`, we map until we have our
output, using `unwrap_or_else` to get the default. `unwrap_or` is an alternative, but
`unwrap_or_else` accepts a closure and is *lazily evaluated*, which could give a minor performance boost, especially if there are a lot of renames.

Listing 8.10   Implementation for the alternative approach

```
// other code, imports

pub fn builder_methods(fields: &Punctuated<Field, Comma>) ->
  Vec<TokenStream> {
    fields.iter()
```

```
.map(|f| {
    let (field_name, field_type) = get_name_and_type(f);

    extract_attribute_from_field(f, "rename")
        .map(|a| &a.meta)
        .map(|m| {
            match m {
                Meta::NameValue(
                    MetaNameValue { value: Expr::Lit(ExprLit {
                        lit: Lit::Str(literal_string), .. }), ..
                }) => {
                    Ident::new(
                        &literal_string.value(),
                        literal_string.span()
                    )
                }
                _ => panic!(
                    "expected key and value for rename attribute"
                ),
            }
        })
        .map(|attr| {
            quote! {
                pub fn #attr(mut self, input: #field_type) -> Self
                {
                    self.#field_name = Some(input);
                    self
                }
            }
        })
        .unwrap_or_else(|| {
            quote! {
                pub fn #field_name(mut self, input: #field_type)
-> Self {
                    self.#field_name = Some(input);
                    self
                }
            }
        })
}).collect()
}
```

We look for the string value inside Meta::NameValue.

Continues mapping and creates the TokenStream

Defaults to the normal output with unwrap_or_else

Besides the additional mappings, the only real difference with the previous code is that we now have to look for NameValue in the metadata (see figure 8.2). As mentioned, that is the variant we get for key-value attributes. The match is quite long (Meta::NameValue(MetaNameValue { value: Expr::Lit(ExprLit { lit: Lit::Str (literal_string), .. }), .. })), and if you find it to be too complicated, you can split it up into multiple, nested matches. Personally, I like how I can get to the desired value with a single, readable pattern match.

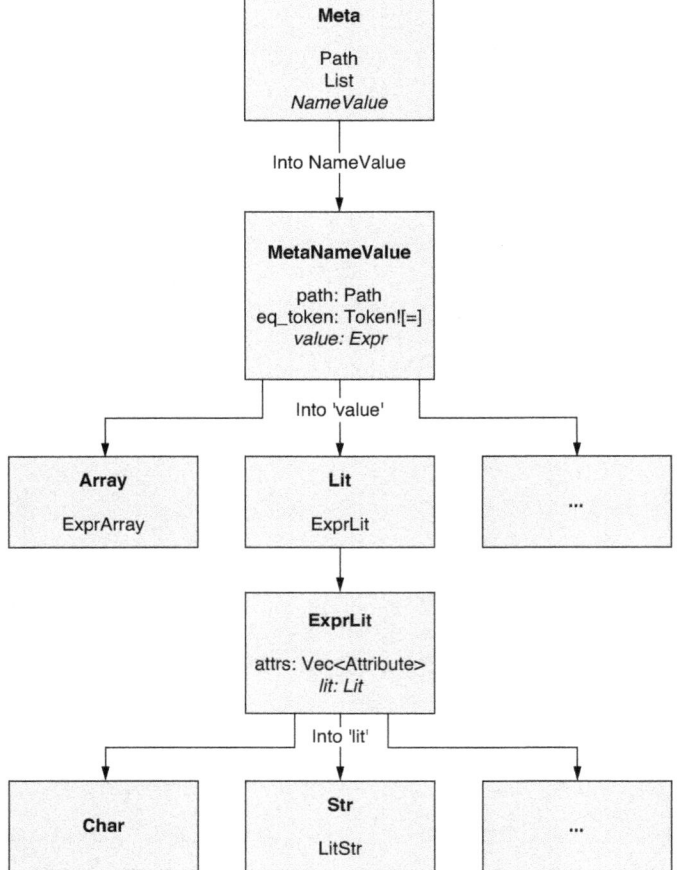

Figure 8.2   Simplified view of the `meta` property for our use case

Lazy and eager evaluations

Eager and lazy evaluations are two approaches to writing code. *Eager evaluation* means the code you write will be invoked when it is encountered. *Lazy evaluation* means that evaluation is postponed until it proves necessary. In listing 8.10, `unwrap_or_else` is lazy because the closure that creates the default `TokenStream` *will only be called if we end up in the* `unwrap_or_else` *call*. If every field has a `rename` attribute, and we never end up in `unwrap_or_else`, we never pay the cost that comes with creating the default stream. `unwrap_or`, on the other hand, is eager, meaning that if we used that method, the default `TokenStream` would be constructed every time, even when that is unnecessary.

Eager evaluation can have the advantage of being simpler to reason about. There is simplicity in the knowledge that everything is always ready for use. Besides offering possible performance advantages, lazy evaluation is the only approach suitable to some programming constructs, like infinite data structures. If you have a stream that will produce data without ever stopping, eager evaluation would call it forever, whereas with a lazy approach, you would only invoke that stream when you really need data. Languages often have a built-in preference for one kind of evaluation, even if this is seldom exclusive. JavaScript is generally eager, whereas Haskell is lazy. We have actually already encountered lazy evaluation in this book. The `lazy_static` crate has a macro for "declaring lazily evaluated statics."

8.3   Sensible defaults

Remember how we talked about proper error handling, in a previous chapter? How you should not panic or throw exceptions at every turn? Then why on earth do we panic whenever a user forgets to fill in a field?

There are alternatives. Instead of panicking, we could output a `Result` when calling `build`, giving back an `Err` if a field is missing. This is standard Rust practice for method calls that might fail. Or we could try to make panics impossible—a radical idea that we will save for later. Another idea, which we will explore now, is to use defaults as a fallback. We will use the nifty `Default` trait to do that. In the unlikely event that you have never heard of this trait before: by implementing `Default`, you specify a default value for a given type. Most built-in types already have sensible defaults out of the box, like numbers `(0)`, strings `(empty)`, Booleans `(false)`, and `Option (None)`. Defaults are also easily implemented with a derive macro.

In this section, we add an attribute to our macro, which will determine whether to use defaults. The following listing shows a test.

Listing 8.11   A test for defaults

```
#[test]
fn should_use_defaults_when_attribute_is_present() {
    #[derive(Builder)]
    #[builder_defaults]
    struct ExampleStructTwoFields {
        string_value: String,
        int_value: i32,
    }

    let example: ExampleStructTwoFields =
 ExampleStructTwoFields::builder()
            .build();

    assert_eq!(example.string_value, String::default());
    assert_eq!(example.int_value, Default::default());
}
```

When you try to run this test, it fails because Rust does not know about an attribute called `builder_defaults`. This is easy to fix.

Listing 8.12   Adding the missing attribute

```
#[proc_macro_derive(Builder, attributes(rename,builder_defaults))]
pub fn builder(item: TokenStream) -> TokenStream {
    create_builder(item.into()).into()
}
```

Now our test panics because we haven't written our implementation yet. So we should retrieve the attribute. If it is present, we fall back to defaults. The code change in our `lib.rs` file is simple: it checks whether we have to use defaults and passes the Boolean on to the method that needs it.

Listing 8.13   `lib.rs` code changes: checking the attributes for `builder_defaults`

```
// mode, imports
use syn::Attribute;

const DEFAULTS_ATTRIBUTE_NAME: &str = "builder_defaults";

pub fn create_builder(item: TokenStream) -> TokenStream {
    let ast: DeriveInput = parse2(item).unwrap();
    let name = ast.ident;
    let builder = format_ident!("{}Builder", name);
    let use_defaults = use_defaults(&ast.attrs);        ◁──┐ Sends the root
    // ...                                                  │ attributes to a helper
    let set_fields = original_struct_setters(
        fields,
        use_defaults        ◁──┐ And passes its Boolean result
    );                         │ to the function that needs it
    // ...
}

fn use_defaults(attrs: &[Attribute]) -> bool {
    attrs
        .iter()
        .any(|attribute|
            attribute.path().is_ident(DEFAULTS_ATTRIBUTE_NAME))
}
```

As you can see, attributes are present both at the root level of `DeriveInput` and at the field level. Previously, we were adding attributes to individual fields. This time we placed one on top of our struct. So we should look in the root. Our `use_defaults` helper is simple. It checks whether any attribute identifier matches the name `builder_defaults`. The result is given to `original_struct_setters`, the only method that needs to know about it. Meanwhile, in `fields.rs`, we have more work to do, because we want to behave differently depending on this Boolean value.

Listing 8.14   `fields.rs` code changes

```
// imports and other code
```

```
pub fn original_struct_setters(fields: &Punctuated<Field, Comma>,
  use_defaults: bool)
    -> Vec<TokenStream> {
    fields.iter().map(|f| {
        let field_name = &f.ident;
        let field_name_as_string = field_name
            .as_ref().unwrap().to_string();

        let handle_type = if use_defaults {          If use_defaults is true,
            default_fallback()                       generates a default fallback
        } else {
            panic_fallback(field_name_as_string)  ◄─┐ Otherwise, we fall
        };                                           │ back to panics.

        quote! {
            #field_name: self.#field_name.#handle_type
        }
    })
        .collect()
}


fn panic_fallback(field_name_as_string: String) -> TokenStream {
    quote! {
        .expect(concat!("field not set: ", #field_name_as_string))
    }
}


fn default_fallback() -> TokenStream {
    quote! {
        unwrap_or_default()
    }
}
```

We have added some code and refactored a bit. We moved the "panic" generation, the fallback, to a separate method:

```
fn panic_fallback(field_name_as_string: String) -> TokenStream {
    quote! {
        expect(concat!("Field not set: ", #field_name_as_string))
    }
}
```

As we mentioned before, it is perfectly fine for streams to be bits of code that cannot function on their own. That is the case here. This expect is not valid, standalone Rust code, but we will combine it with other bits of code until it can be parsed as valid. We also need to generate code for the default fallback. What is nice is that Option has an unwrap_or_default() method created just for this use case:

```
fn default_fallback() -> TokenStream {
    quote! {
        unwrap_or_default()
    }
}
```

Now we need to use the "defaults" Boolean to determine the behavior, which we do with a simple `if-else`, combining the result with code for filling in the field. By combining all these fragments, we are one step closer to valid Rust, though we still need to do some transformations in `lib.rs` before everything is in place:

```
pub fn original_struct_setters(fields: &Punctuated<Field, Comma>,
 use_defaults: bool) -> Vec<TokenStream> {
    fields.iter().map(|f| {
        let field_name = &f.ident;
        let field_name_as_string = field_name
            .as_ref().unwrap().to_string();

        let handle_type = if use_defaults {
            default_fallback()
        } else {
            panic_fallback(field_name_as_string)
        };

        quote! {
            #field_name: self.#field_name.#handle_type
        }
    })
        .collect()
}
```

For our convenience, we are returning a `Vec` instead of a `Map` or `impl`. All three are valid inputs for `quote`, but `Map` now becomes a lot more annoying to use. As we are passing the `use_defaults` Boolean to map, this means that the function inside that map is now *capturing a variable from its environment*. That makes it a *closure*, which means our previous signature (`Map<Iter<Field>`, `fn(&Field) TokenStream>`) is invalid, as fn is a function pointer, not a closure. Change it to `Fn`, and you will get a complaint about sizes not being known at compile time. In brief, the following listing shows everything we have to do to keep our `Map`.

Listing 8.15   Do not pass go, do not collect: alternative to returning a `Vec`

```
pub fn original_struct_setters<'a>(fields: &'a Punctuated<Field, Comma>,
 use_defaults: bool)
        -> Map<Iter<'a, Field>, Box<dyn Fn(&Field) -> TokenStream>> {   ←┐
    fields.iter().map(Box::new(move |f| {   ←┐ Box our              Lifetimes,
        // same as before                    │ closure           boxing, and dyn
    }))                      ←┤ No more collect
}
```

The signature requires an `Fn` because of the closure and a `Box` to let Rust know the compile-time size. That means we actually have to box our closure: `Box::new(move |f| …)`. The `move` is needed because of our original problem; that is, we need to take ownership of `use_defaults`. So it's a lot of busy work, a complex signature, and possibly worse performance because of the boxing.

On the other hand, `impl Iterator<Item = TokenStream> + '_` is still an acceptable alternative solution. Its signature stays the same, and we only have to add a `move` to our mapping for the same reason as stated previously.

With one of these solutions in action, the test that we wrote should compile and pass. If you want to make sure no previous code was broken, add a test that still panics for missing properties.

8.4 A better error message for defaults

What happens when we have properties that do not implement `Default`? Add `trybuild` to the project, copy the `compilation_tests.rs` we used before, and put this under `tests/fails`.

> **Listing 8.16** Testing what happens when a property does not implement `Default`

```
use builder_macro::Builder;

struct DoesNotImplementDefault;        ←──┐ This struct does not
                                           │ implement Default.
#[derive(Builder)]
#[builder_defaults]
struct ExampleStruct {
    not: DoesNotImplementDefault       ←──┐ But we use it in a struct that
}                                          │ uses the default fallback.

fn main() {}
```

Rust throws an error:

```
??????????????????????????????????????????
6 | #[derive(Builder)]
  |          ^^^^^^^ the trait `Default` is not implemented for
 `DoesNotImplementDefault`
  |
note: required by a bound in `Option::<T>::unwrap_or_default`
 --> $RUST/core/src/option.rs
  |
  |         T: ~const Default,
  |            ^^^^^^^^^^^^^^ required by this bound in
 `Option::<T>::unwrap_or_default`
...
```

The error is clear enough for a user to figure out what the problem is. But the lack of precision in the message, pointing to the macro instead of the faulty property, is annoying.

In a chapter 7, we learned how we could use custom errors to give back a clearer error message, with `span` allowing us to point to a specific location in our source code. We can try to use that to our advantage here. One approach, inspired by examples from the `syn` library, is to generate an empty struct, giving it a `where` clause that requires a field's type to implement `Default`. To generate that code, we use `quote_spanned` because it allows us to pass in a `span` that will be applied to the generated code.

Listing 8.17   Example usage of `quote_spanned` with a `where` clause

```
quote_spanned! {ty.span()=>
    struct ExampleStruct where SomeType: core::default::Default;
}
```

We are also passing in the full path for `Default`, `core::default::Default`, which avoids confusion with other traits with the same name that live in other crates (or in the user's codebase). This is a best practice that we have been avoiding until now for simplicity's sake and that will feature in more detail in a later chapter.

What we want to do now is loop through our fields with `iter` and `map`, adding structs with `where` clauses that claim a field's type implements `Default`. If this is not the case, well—feel the wrath of the compiler, which will use the span we passed in (the one from the offending type) to point the user to their mistake. The struct's name starts with two underscores, another best practice for avoiding collisions with user code.

Listing 8.18   Additional code in `fields.rs`

```
// other imports
use quote::{format_ident, quote, quote_spanned};   │ We need this trait to be
use syn::spanned::Spanned;                          │ present when calling span().

pub fn optional_default_asserts(fields: &Punctuated<Field, Comma>)
    -> Vec<TokenStream> {
        fields.iter()
            .map(|f| {
                let name = &f.ident.as_ref().unwrap();
                let ty = &f.ty;
                let assertion_ident = format_ident!(
                    "__{}DefaultAssertion",              │ Creates an identifier
                    name                                 │ for our empty struct
                );

                quote_spanned! {ty.span()=>
                    struct #assertion_ident where #ty: core::default::Default;
                }
            })
            .collect()
    }
```

Tells Rust that it implements Default, passing along the span of the field's type (annotation pointing to the `quote_spanned!` block)

Now all we need to do is to add this `Vec` to our final output, using the hashtag style for multiple items, when the "default" annotation is present. Otherwise, we add an empty vector of tokens, which generates nothing at all.

Listing 8.19   Code in `lib.rs` (builder-code)

```
pub fn create_builder(item: TokenStream) -> TokenStream {
    // ...
    let default_assertions = if use_defaults {
```

```
          optional_default_asserts(fields)    ←
   } else {
      vec![]                                    ←
   };
```

If defaults are in use, we want to add the assertions. If not, an empty vector is all we need.

```
   quote! {
      // generate the struct, builder, etc.
      #(#optional_default_assertions)*          ←
   }
}
```

Adds the default assertion structs

Now if you try to pass in a nested struct that does not implement `Default`, you get a more informative error pointing to the exact location of the offender:

```
error[E0277]: the trait bound `DoesNotImplementDefault: Default`
 is not satisfied
 --> tests/fails/no_default.rs:9:10
  |
9 |     not: DoesNotImplementDefault
  |          ^^^^^^^^^^^^^^^^^^^^^^^^ the trait `Default` is not implemented
  for `DoesNotImplementDefault`
  |
  = help: see issue #48214
help: ...
```

As a footnote to this section: I stumbled upon a variation to this approach while answering a Stack Overflow question. A user was using a macro to generate a function that required a trait implementation for its argument. One problem they were having was that the error message for when the type did not implement the trait was unhelpful. It pointed to the macro invocation. Sound familiar? The solution was a nice variation on using spans for error messages. Instead of hardcoding the trait, generate an identifier with the span of the type that does not implement the trait:

```
let trait_ident = Ident::new("MyTrait", problematic_type.span());
```

Now if you use `trait_ident` in a `where` clause and something goes wrong, Rust will point to the span and the faulty type.

8.5   *Build back better*

How about a slight detour before soldiering on with attributes? I promise it is somewhat relevant—and, even if it's not, the technique is interesting.

8.5.1   *Avoiding illegal states and the type state pattern*

What may be bothering you is how we seem to have only three choices to deal with missing properties: defaults, panics, and a `Result` return type. We have implemented the first two, and the latter option sounds nice and idiomatic. But it is not a perfect fit because there is no reason to allow mistakes in building our example structs. You either have all their required properties or you don't. In the former case, the operation is always a success. In the latter case, it never is. That means there is no reason to allow anyone to skip properties when our fallback is panicking. And the "default varia-tion" forces developers to implement a trait, as well as carries a risk: did the user really want a default, or did they forget to set the property? (See figure 8.3.)

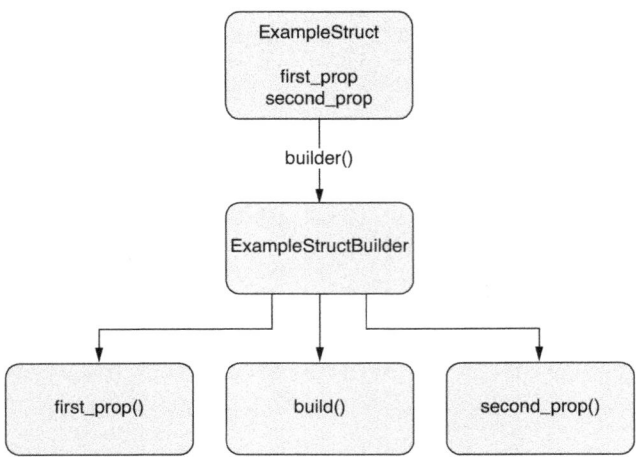

Figure 8.3   **Current situation: too much room for errors. We generate a builder that can immediately call** `build`, **even without setting the fields.**

The best solution would be to move our check to the type system, to *make illegal states unrepresentable*. What I mean by that is that the best kind of application does not allow programmers to create run-time problems. Instead, we can try to mold the type sys-tem, to make the compiler stop users when they make mistakes. Any type system offers this functionality to users in a basic form. It can, for example, make sure that numeric things like age cannot be strings, negative numbers, or very large.

This may sound familiar, because we talked about this idea when we were discuss-ing newtypes, which are one way to extend the power of your type system, making it more specific to your domain. Specifically, in the case of our builder, we want to force users to fill in every required property, only allowing them to call `build` when this has been done.

We can use the *type state pat-tern* to do that, encoding the state of our system in a type parameter. A simple example might help illustrate the idea. We have a traf-fic light that is either green or red. When it is red, turning red a second time does not make sense (see figure 8.4).

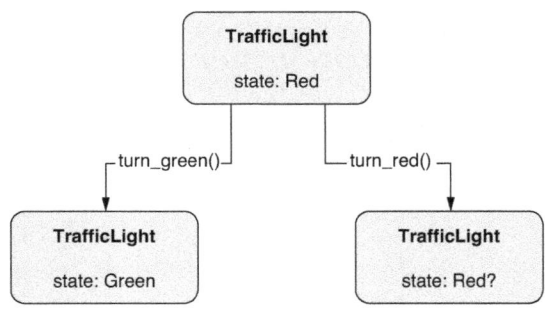

Figure 8.4   **It makes no sense for a traffic light to turn red when it already is that color. We are allowing illegal states.**

No, a red light should only change to green—green only to red (green → red → green → ; it's a *state machine*) (see figure 8.5).

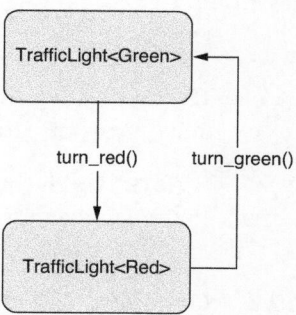

Listing 8.20 shows some code for enforcing this behavior at compile time, using a *marker trait,* a trait that has no methods or properties but serves to "mark" types as being something and some structs that implement that marker. Because Rust does not allow unused generic properties, we have to add `PhantomData<T>` (from the standard library) to `TrafficLight` as a signal: "I have compile-time plans for this generic." Next, we write implementation blocks that differ *depending on the type of our generic.* Only when the generic parameter is `Green` do we have the `turn_red` method, which

Figure 8.5   The situation presented here is preferable: only valid states are allowed.

returns a traffic light with the `Red` struct as a parameter. And the implementation block for `TrafficLight<Red>` only has `turn_green`, which returns `TrafficLight<Green>`.

Listing 8.20   Traffic light

```
trait Light {}

struct Green {}                    We will use the Light marker
struct Red {}                      trait, plus the Green and Red
                                   structs, to encode state.
impl Light for Green {}
impl Light for Red {}

struct TrafficLight<T: Light> {    Our traffic light has a generic
    marker: PhantomData<T>         parameter that implements
}                                  Light (i.e., the previous structs).

impl TrafficLight<Green> {
    fn turn_red(&self) -> TrafficLight<Red> {
        TrafficLight {
            marker: Default::default(),
        }
    }
}
                                              Here we put our structs to
impl TrafficLight<Red> {                      good use (e.g., only
    fn turn_green(&self) -> TrafficLight<Green> {   TrafficLight<Green>
        TrafficLight {                         implements turn_red).
            marker: Default::default(),
        }
    }
}

fn main() {
    let light = TrafficLight { marker: Default::default() };
```

```
light.turn_red().turn_green();
}
```
⟵ **Rust infers that we started green and only allows this sequence of calls.**

The result? A traffic light guaranteed by the compiler to only have valid state transitions! Graydon Hoare would be proud.

> **NOTE** As the story goes, Hoare—the creator of Rust—was inspired to create the language when an elevator in his apartment failed to work because of a software glitch.

8.5.2 *Combining the builder pattern with type state*

We can do the same for our builder (see figure 8.6). We should

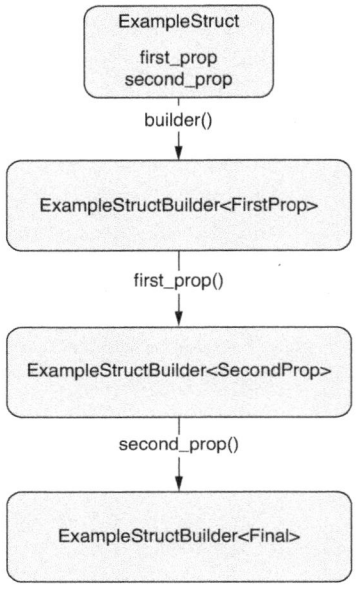

- Create a marker trait.
- Create a struct without properties for every field we receive (we can call them "field structs") and make it implement the marker trait.
- Make our builder accept a generic type that implements the marker trait.
- Make the `builder` method of our struct return a builder *with the generic type set to the first "field struct"* (in the case of Gleipnir, this is `roots_of`).
- Create an implementation block for the builder with that specific generic parameter with a method that accepts a field (`roots_of`) and returns a builder with the next generic parameter (`breath_of_a_fish`).
- Rinse and repeat for all fields.
- The final field does not return the "next" generic parameter since there is none. Instead, it returns a builder with a `build` method.

Figure 8.6   Desired situation: illegal states are unrepresentable. We generate a struct with a different generic type parameter for every method, only allowing the last one to call `build`.

Our setup is that of the previous sections, with the attribute-related things (rename and defaults) stripped out so they don't distract us. The following listing shows a test that should compile because the fields are all called in the correct order.

Listing 8.21 `builder-usage` test with correct order of attributes

```
// macro import

fn main() {}

#[cfg(test)]
mod tests {
```

```
    #[test]
    fn should_work_with_correct_order() {
        #[derive(Builder)]
        struct Gleipnir {
            roots_of: String,
            breath_of_a_fish: u8,
            anything_else: bool,
        }

        let gleipnir = Gleipnir::builder()
            .roots_of("mountains".to_string())
            .breath_of_a_fish(1)
            .anything_else(true)
            .build();

        assert_eq!(gleipnir.roots_of, "mountains".to_string());
    }
}
```

That tests the compilation and saving of at least one field value. For the error scenario, we add a test in the `tests` folder, with this code under `fails/missing_prop.rs`.

Listing 8.22 `builder-usage` **compile test, under** `tests`

```
use builder_macro::Builder;

#[derive(Builder)]
struct Gleipnir {
    roots_of: String,
    breath_of_a_fish: u8,
    anything_else: bool,
}

fn main() {
    Gleipnir::builder()
        .roots_of("mountains".to_string())
        .breath_of_a_fish(1)
        // missing final property
        .build();
}
```

This should fail with a compile-time error because we forgot to add one of the attributes (namely, `anything_else`). Meanwhile, our `builder-macro` remains the same. The builder code has a lot of changes, though. `lib.rs` becomes simpler because more responsibility has been delegated to separate functions. All of those functions now need a reference to the name of a struct. We will see why in a moment.

Listing 8.23 `lib.rs` **in** `builder-code`

```
pub fn create_builder(item: TokenStream) -> TokenStream {
    // ... get the struct name and its fields
    let builder = builder_definition(&name, fields);
```

```
    let builder_method_for_struct = builder_impl_for_struct(&name, fields);
    let marker_and_structs = marker_trait_and_structs(&name, fields);
    let builder_methods = builder_methods(&name, fields);

    quote! {
        #builder
        #builder_method_for_struct
        #marker_and_structs
        #builder_methods
    }
}
```

Before moving on to the meat of the implementation, listing 8.24 shows `util.rs`, which provides a way to create the identifier for the builder struct and field struct. By using these functions, we can avoid some duplication, and we make changing the names of our builders and additional structs, if we think of better names, much simpler.

Listing 8.24   `util.rs` in `builder-code`

```
use proc_macro2::Ident;
use quote::format_ident;

pub fn create_builder_ident(name: &Ident) -> Ident {
    format_ident!("{}Builder", name)
}

pub fn create_field_struct_name(builder: &Ident, field: &Ident) -> Ident {
    format_ident!("{}Of{}", field_name, builder_name)
}
```

We are going to have to split up the code in `fields` in separate fragments because it contains about 170 lines of code. We will be ignoring `get_name_and_type`, `panic_fallback` and `original_struct_setters`, which are basically unchanged.

First, we create the marker trait and structs. We add a marker trait and generate a struct plus implementation of the trait for every field. We need one additional struct for calling `build`. The trait (`MarkerTraitForBuilder`) and final struct (`Final-Builder`) are hardcoded for brevity's sake. In a production-grade macro, it would probably be best to add the name of the struct and `__` as a prefix to make it more unique. Also, the structs start with a lowercase letter and have underscores, due to the field names, which is something Rust will complain about with a compiler warning.

Listing 8.25   `marker_trait_and_structs` in `fields.rs`

```
pub fn marker_trait_and_structs(name: &Ident, fields: &Punctuated<Field,
  Comma>)
    -> TokenStream {
    let builder_name = create_builder_ident(name);
```

```
let structs_and_impls = fields.iter().map(|f| {
    let field_name = &f.ident.clone().unwrap();
    let struct_name = create_field_struct_name(
        &builder_name,                              Creates the
        field_name                                  right identifier
    );
    quote! {
        pub struct #struct_name {}                  Creates the struct and
        impl MarkerTraitForBuilder for #struct_name {}   implements the
    }                                               hardcoded marker
});

quote! {
    pub trait MarkerTraitForBuilder {}      Adds the trait, structs,
                                            and implementations
    #(#structs_and_impls)*

    pub struct FinalBuilder {}
    impl MarkerTraitForBuilder for FinalBuilder {}    Adds a struct that
}                                                     implements the marker
}                                                     for calling build
```

The builder definition is also fairly easy. We have moved more responsibility into the method and added the generic parameter and `PhantomData` marker. But that's about it.

Listing 8.26   `builder_definition` in `fields.rs`

```
pub fn builder_definition(name: &Ident, fields: &Punctuated<Field, Comma>)
    -> TokenStream {
    let builder_fields = fields.iter().map(|f| {
        let (field_name, field_type) = get_name_and_type(f);
        quote! { #field_name: Option<#field_type> }
    });                                              This is our
    let builder_name = create_builder_ident(name);  previous code.

    quote! {
        pub struct #builder_name<T: MarkerTraitForBuilder> {
            marker: std::marker::PhantomData<T>,     The builder now has a generic
            #(#builder_fields,)*                     parameter that implements
        }                                            the trait we just defined, plus
    }                                                a marker property.
}
```

Now for something more complex. In listing 8.27, we generate the `builder` method, which creates the empty builder struct. The "inits" are the same as before, and we need both the `struct_name` and `builder_name` for our output. But we also need a generic for the builder struct. As we said that this should refer to the first field of our struct, we retrieve the `first` field (and hope there is at least one; in a real use case, we would have to check whether it's empty and act accordingly) and use a utility to get the right struct name.

Listing 8.27   `builder_impl_for_struct` in `fields.rs`

```rust
pub fn builder_impl_for_struct(name: &Ident, fields: &Punctuated<Field,
Comma>)TokenStream {
    let builder_inits = fields.iter().map(|f| {
        let field_name = &f.ident;
        quote! { #field_name: None }
    });
    let first_field_name = fields.first().map(|f| {
        f.ident.clone().unwrap()
    }).unwrap();
    let builder_name = create_builder_ident(name);
    let generic = create_field_struct_name(
        &builder_name,
        &first_field_name
    );

    quote! {
        impl #struct_name {
            pub fn builder() -> #builder_name<#generic> {
                #builder_name {
                    marker: Default::default(),
                    #(#builder_inits,)*
                }
            }
        }
    }
}
```

> This assumes we have at least one field.

> Uses the field identifier we found to build the right "field struct" identifier

> The builder now has a generic type parameter and marker.

Finally, we should generate methods for setting fields. This method is huge, so we will split it up into three parts. In the first, we gather some information. `original_struct_setters` gives us field setters for when we will eventually call `build`, while `get_assignments_for_fields` sets all field properties for the builder struct. And for reasons that may become clear in the next code fragment, I prefer to start with the final field, so we reverse the field vector.

Listing 8.28   `builder_methods` in `fields.rs`: setup

```rust
pub fn builder_methods(name: &Ident, fields: &Punctuated<Field, Comma>)
    -> TokenStream {
    let builder_name = create_builder_ident(name);
    let set_fields = original_struct_setters(fields);
    let assignments_for_all_fields = get_assignments_for_fields(fields);
    let mut previous_field = None;
    let reversed_names_and_types: Vec<&Field> = fields
        .iter()
        .rev()
        .collect();
    // ...
}
```

In the next fragment, we have a map, with conditional branching. When we start iterating, `previous_field` will be empty, so we will end up in the `else` (and while this was not really on purpose, this is the more optimal choice of branching for performance, putting the least likely option last). Since the first field in our *reversed* list is actually the last field of our struct, we should create an implementation block with a setter for the final "field struct."

Because we set the `previous_field` in both branches of the condition, every subsequent call will end up in the `if` branch. Here, like before, we want to generate a setter for the current generic. But this time, the return type should point to the generic parameter of the *next field*. And since we reversed the vector, we have that one available, stored away in `previous_field`.

Listing 8.29 `builder_methods` in `fields.rs`: generating the methods

```
pub fn builder_methods(struct_name: &Ident, fields: &Punctuated<Field,
  Comma>)
    -> TokenStream {
    // ...
    let methods: Vec<TokenStream> = reversed_names_and_types
        .iter()
        .map(|f| {
            if let Some(next_in_list) = previous_field {
                previous_field = Some(f);
                builder_for_field(
                    &builder_name,
                    &assignments_for_all_fields,
                    f,
                    next_in_list
                )
            } else {
                previous_field = Some(f);
                builder_for_final_field(
                    &builder_name,
                    &assignments_for_all_fields,
                    f
                )
            }
        }).collect();

    quote! {
        #(#methods)*

        impl #builder_name<FinalBuilder> {
            pub fn build(self) -> #struct_name {
                #struct_name {
                    #(#set_fields,)*
                }
            }
        }
    }
}
```

We already have a field? That means there is another field after this one, so we return a builder whose generic parameter points to the next "field struct" in our list.

There is no "previous"? That means we have the last field—that is, the first element of our vector. We should point to the final "field struct."

What follows is the implementation of the two functions that were called in the map. The difference between them is subtle. Both generate a method that is added to the builder, which sets a specific field and returns the builder, using the "assignments" to fill in all its properties. This is necessary because we cannot simply return self thanks to the generic type parameter.

The main difference is that the first method (builder_for_field) points to the builder with a type referring to the next field (next_field_struct_name), while the second method (builder_for_final_field) produces one with generic type Final-Builder.

Listing 8.30   The two functions used in builder_methods

```
fn builder_for_field(
        builder_name: &Ident, field_assignments:&Vec<TokenStream>,
        current_field: &Field,
        next_field_in_list: &Field
) -> TokenStream {
    let (field_name, field_type) = get_name_and_type(current_field);
    let (next_field_name, _) = get_name_and_type(next_field_in_list);
    let current_field_struct_name = create_field_struct_name(
        &builder_name,
        field_name.as_ref().unwrap()
    );
    let next_field_struct_name = create_field_struct_name(
        &builder_name,
        next_field_name.as_ref().unwrap()
    );

    quote! {
        impl #builder_name<#current_field_struct_name> {
            pub fn #field_name(mut self, input: #field_type) ->
 #builder_name<#next_field_struct_name> {
                self.#field_name = Some(input);
                #builder_name {
                    marker: Default::default(),
                    #(#field_assignments,)*
                }
            }
        }
    }
}

fn builder_for_final_field(
        builder_name: &Ident,
        field_assignments: &Vec<TokenStream>,
        field: &Field
) -> TokenStream {
    let (field_name, field_type) = get_name_and_type(field);
    let field_struct_name = create_field_struct_name(
        &builder_name,
        field_name.as_ref().unwrap()
    );
```

```
    quote! {
        impl #builder_name<#field_struct_name> {
            pub fn #field_name(mut self, input: #field_type) ->
#builder_name<FinalBuilder> {
                self.#field_name = Some(input);
                #builder_name {
                    marker: Default::default(),
                    #(#field_assignments,)*
                }
            }
        }
    }
}
```

Finally, the function brings everything together, adding the individual implementation blocks as well as the build method.

```
quote! {
    #(#methods)*

    impl #builder_name<FinalBuilder> {
        pub fn build(self) -> #struct_name {
            #struct_name {
                #(#set_fields,)*
            }
        }
    }
}
```

The test in builder-usage should now succeed. And, depending on how well your IDE handles macros, you should only get suggestions for the right methods when using the builder: roots_of, breath_of_a_fish, anything_else, and finally build. As our compile test shows, you won't get the builder to compile if you skip a property. Rust even gives you a clue as to what is wrong, thanks to the generic parameters:

```
error[E0599]: no method named `build` found for struct
 `GleipnirBuilder<anything_elseOfGleipnirBuilder>` in the current scope
  --> tests/fails/missing_prop.rs:16:10
   |
4  | #[derive(Builder)]
   |          ------- method `build` not found for this struct
...
16 |         .build();
   |          ^^^^^ method not found in
 `GleipnirBuilder<anything_elseOfGleipnirBuilder>`
   |
   = note: the method was found for
           - `GleipnirBuilder<FinalBuilder>`
```

This is really cool. You are forcing users of the macro to do the right thing, keeping them from shooting themselves in the foot. And everything is done automatically by a macro, with all the complexity hidden away. Furthermore, the run-time impact should be minimal. The marker trait, empty structs, phantom markers, and generic type parameters only play a role at compile time and can be optimized away. And most of the other code was already present in our previous, more naive builder.

A possible extension to this example: what if you had optional values in your struct (i.e., values wrapped in an option or values where the `Default` implementation is good enough if the user does not pass anything along)? In that case, you could force the user to fill in all required values, but once the final *required* value is filled in, they should be able to call any of the optional setters as well as `build`.

> **How did I write this?**
>
> This is a macro with a lot of moving parts, so you may be wondering how to approach such a complex task. In this particular case, I first sketched out my solution with normal Rust code, identifying all the different parts and how they fit together. Then I wrote code for things that were prerequisites, as well as being relatively simple to generate (the marker trait and structs, for example), looking at the output to check my work. That done, I wrote the rest of the code and made the macro compile. Finally, I ran `cargo expand` on an example struct to identify any remaining problems. For example, I forgot to save the "previous field" value in the `else` branch, so all the setters were pointing to `build` instead of the next setter!

8.6 *Avoiding scattered conditionals*

Gently tying this back to the original builder code, we can see that patterns like this could be used in complex macros. For example, the `if-else` approach to our error handling (panic or default) is fine right now because it is limited to one location. But what if it appeared in a lot of methods? We would have a lot of ugly conditionals in our code, scattering one piece of logic (our fallback behavior) across the application. That makes mistakes easier and refactoring harder. Instead, you could centralize this behavior while making it easier to use.

One idea would be to have a `Strategy` trait with methods for everything that requires a conditional, like generating the proper fallback. Then you could have an enum representing the different approaches that implement the trait.

NOTE The *strategy pattern* is a design pattern from the Gang of Four. It creates separate objects for algorithms and hides the concrete choice behind an interface. This makes it easier to switch out algorithms without changing any other part of your codebase. Here we use a trait instead of an interface and a single enum with two variants instead of multiple objects.

> **Listing 8.32 The `Strategy` trait and an enum that implements its method**

```
trait Strategy {
    fn fallback(&self, field_type: &Type, field_name_as_string: String)
```

```
                    -> TokenStream;
    }

    enum ConcreteStrategy {
        Default,
        Panic,
    }

    impl Strategy for ConcreteStrategy {
        fn fallback(&self, field_type: &Type, field_name_as_string: String)
            -> TokenStream {
            match self {
                ConcreteApproach::Default => {
                    quote! {
                        unwrap_or_default()
                    }
                }
                ConcreteApproach::Panic => {
                    // similar
                }
            }
        }
    }
}
```

Within the macro, you decide on a strategy based on the presence of our defaults attribute, get back the right enum variant, and pass it to the right methods.

Listing 8.33   Example of passing on and using the strategy

```
fn original_struct_setters<T>(strategy: &T, fields: &Punctuated<Field, Comma>)
    -> Vec<TokenStream> where T: Strategy {
    fields.iter()
        .map(|f| {
            let (field_name, field_type) = get_name_and_type(f);
            let field_name_as_string = field_name
                .as_ref()
                .unwrap()
                .to_string();
            let handle_type = strategy.fallback(
                field_type,
                field_name_as_string
            );

            quote! {
                #field_name: self.#field_name.#handle_type
            }
        })
        .collect()
}
```

This is more than enough abstraction for our current macro. But in a more complex setup, where there is more need to steer developers, we could add type state, returning intermediate states from our methods, with only the final state returning the output `TokenStream`. That way, everything that is needed for the macro to work *has* to be present. A useful attribute that helps steer the user is `#[must_use]`, which throws a warning when a required return value goes unused.

8.7   *Attribute tokens and attributes*

We already mentioned that only derive and attribute macros support attributes. (Function-like macros are powerful enough that you could mimic them, as we shall soon see.) But we only discussed derive macros. Are there any differences between the two?

The answer is yes. While derive macro attributes are inert, attribute macros (including any additional attributes) are active, meaning they remove themselves during attribute processing. That is probably the most sensible action, because, for example, an attribute macro might not produce any output (see chapter 9's core example). Does it make sense to keep an attribute in your source code when the item it was attached to has disappeared? Another difference is that you have some additional freedom in the exact format of your attribute macro attributes, whereas for a derive macro, you need to specify attributes in a specific property (`attributes`).

For a simple attribute macro example, we can go back to our "public fields" macro, where we add an "exclude" property that allows you to add properties that should not be made public. We won't go over the entire (unchanged) setup, but listings 8.34 and 8.35 are the two files under `src`. As you can see, we modified our macro invocation. Instead of a simple `#[public]`, we now have additional information within parentheses, `#[public(exclude(fourth, third))]`. We also added a public "constructor" so we can create the struct in other modules. In the following listing, we expect `first` to become public and the visibility of the other properties to stay unchanged.

Listing 8.34   `example.rs`, with a struct

```
use make_public_macro::public;

#[public(exclude(fourth, third))]        ⟵┐  We exclude properties
struct Example {                              third and fourth so they
    first: String,                            will not be made public.
    pub second: u32,
    third: bool,
    fourth: String,
}

impl Example {                    ┌  We need a public method for creating the
    pub fn new() -> Self {   ⟵──┘  struct since some properties are private.
        Example {
            first: "first".to_string(),
            // etc.
        }
    }
}
```

In our main file, we will have a simple test to check compilation.

Listing 8.35 `main.rs`, with some usage of our example struct

```
use crate::example::Example;

mod example;

fn main() {
    let e = Example::new();
    println!("{}", e.first);
    println!("{}", e.second);
    // println!("{}", e.third);
}
```

These will work, because we will make them public.

Here we expect an error: field third of struct Example is private.

Now let's move on to the library code and some notable differences. With a derive macro, we had attributes in the root of the token stream or on individual fields. With an attribute macro, you can still find attributes on the individual fields, and other attributes can still be found in the root of the AST. But one thing is very much unlike a derive macro: our annotation is extremely flexible. A derive macro is always `#[derive(...)]`; an attribute macro's invocation can be molded. But where does all the information about that attribute end up if it is not in the root of the AST? Well, it's finally time to look inside the first `TokenStream` parameter of this macro. And if you were to print it for our current example, you would get back something like this:

```
[Ident { ident: "exclude" }, Group { delimiter: Parenthesis,
 stream: TokenStream [Literal { kind: Str, symbol: "fourth, third",
 suffix: None }]
```

Look at that! It's the property we added to our macro.

Now that we know where to look, we can move on to the macro entry point. Notice how we are now passing the `attr` parameter to a second `parse_macro_input` invocation, putting the result in a custom struct called `ExcludedFields`. Then we use a custom method that we added to that struct to detect whether the field was excluded. If it was, we give back the existing visibility. Otherwise, we make the field public.

Listing 8.36 Our `public` function with a custom struct for parsing the first parameter

```
// imports

#[proc_macro_attribute]
pub fn public(attr: TokenStream, item: TokenStream) -> TokenStream {
    let ast = parse_macro_input!(item as DeriveInput);
    let excluded_fields = parse_macro_input!(
        attr as ExcludedFields
    );
    let name = ast.ident;

    let fields = // still retrieving the fields
```

We parse the attributes TokenStream into a custom struct.

```
let builder_fields = fields.iter().map(|f| {
    let name = &f.ident;
    let ty = &f.ty;
    let vis = &f.vis;

    if excluded_fields.matches_ident(name) {
        quote! { #vis #name: #ty }
    } else {
        quote! { pub #name: #ty }
    }
});

// return output
}
```

We use a custom method to determine whether the field was excluded.

Okay, so it is already clear that, this time around, we have taken a struct approach to parsing our input, with ExcludedFields as a wrapper for a vector of strings. The struct implements Parse because, otherwise, we could not pass it to parse_macro_input. As we know, there is currently only one attribute, and it looks like this: exclude(...). So we know we are dealing with a MetaList and parse it as such. Meta, being one level higher up, would have worked equally well, but that would be pointless, since we are only interested in getting a list, not a path or name value. That means we can skip one layer of abstraction by going directly for MetaList (see figure 8.7).

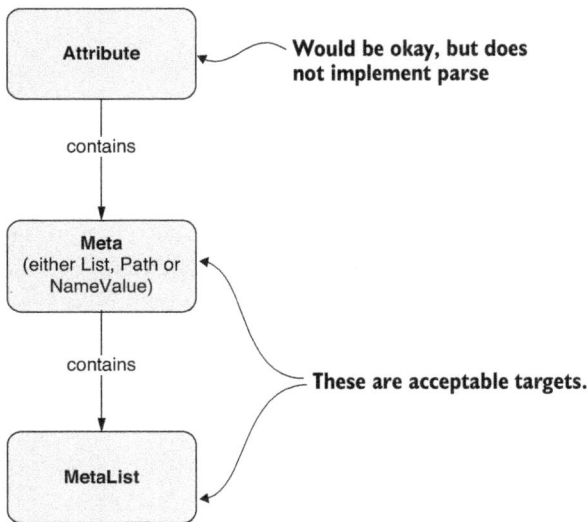

Figure 8.7 Attribute, Meta, or MetaList

Once we have the meta list, we check the path property to see if our exclude annotation is present. If it is, we parse as a Punctuated of identifiers using parse_terminated and change those into strings.

Listing 8.37 `ExcludedFields` **implementation for** `syn` **major version 2**

```
const EXCLUDE_ATTRIBUTE_NAME: &str = "exclude";

struct ExcludedFields {
    fields: Vec<String>
}

impl ExcludedFields {
    fn matches_ident(&self, name: &Option<Ident>) -> bool {
        name.as_ref().map(|n| n.to_string())
            .map(|n| self.fields.iter().any(|f| *f == n))
            .unwrap_or_else(|| false)
    }
}

impl Parse for ExcludedFields {
    fn parse(input: ParseStream) -> Result<Self, syn::Error> {
        match input.parse::<MetaList>() {          Parses our tokens
            Ok(meta_list) => {                      as a MetaList
                if meta_list.path
                    .segments
                    .iter()
                    .find(|s| s.ident == EXCLUDE_ATTRIBUTE_NAME)
                    .is_some()
                {
                    let parser = Punctuated::<Ident, Token![,]>
::parse_terminated;
                    let identifiers = parser.parse(
                        meta_list.clone().tokens.into()
                    ).unwrap();
                    let fields = identifiers.iter()
                        .map(|v| v.to_string())        Retrieves the values from the
                        .collect();                   tokens property and stores them
                    Ok(ExcludedFields { fields })
                } else {
                    Ok(ExcludedFields { fields: vec![] })
                }
            }
            Err(_) => Ok(
                ExcludedFields { fields: vec![] }     If parsing fails, we assume
            )                                         there are no items to exclude.
        }
    }
}
```

Checks that the property is in the path → `.is_some()`

Had we gone for `exclude("fourth", "third")`, it would have been a `Punctuated` of `LitStr` and the map would call the `value` method. The other code would stay unchanged.

Note that this is code written for `syn` major version 2. In version 1, you had a useful—but limiting—struct called `AttributeArgs`, which was an alias for `Vec<NestedMeta>`. To get the excluded items, you could do something like in the following listing (note the "match guard" in the first `match`).

Listing 8.38   Parsing `AttributeArgs` and `MetaList` in syn 1

```
fn properties_to_exclude(args: AttributeArgs) -> Vec<String> {
    args.iter()
        .flat_map(|a| {
            match a {
                Meta(List(MetaList {
                    path: Path { segments, .. },
                    nested,
                    ..
                })) if segments.iter()
                    .find(|s| s.ident == EXCLUDE_ATTRIBUTE_NAME)
                    .is_some() => {
                        nested
                        .iter()
                        .map(|v| match v {
                            Lit(Str(l)) => l.value(),
                            _ => unimplemented!(
                              "expected at least one args between
    brackets"
                            ),
                        })
                        .collect()
                },
                _ => vec![],
            }
        })
        .collect()
}
```

This is quite similar, but not the same, as our current implementation. The big difference is that, inside the `if` branch, we use the `nested` property of `MetaList` (which, in
this code example, contains a list of `LitStr`).

A more up-to-date alternative to our current approach is to use `syn::meta
::parser`. The implementation in listing 8.39 is quite similar to a documentation
example. We `parse_macro_input!(attr with attr_parser)` to pass in a custom
parser for the attributes, which we defined one line above using `syn::meta::parser`.
Actual parsing is a task for our custom struct, which checks whether we have an
exclude attribute in the `path` property, throwing an error if we receive something else.
Within the attribute, we dive one level deeper with `parse_nested_meta` and retrieve
the identifiers, adding them to our `Vector` of fields.

Listing 8.39   Meta parser

```
#[derive(Default)]
struct AlternativeExcludedFields {
    fields: Vec<String>,
}

impl AlternativeExcludedFields {
    fn matches_ident(&self, name: &Option<Ident>) -> bool {
```

```
            // same as ExcludedFields
        }
    }


    impl AlternativeExcludedFields {
        fn parse(&mut self, meta: ParseNestedMeta) -> Result<(), syn::Error> {
            if meta.path.is_ident(EXCLUDE_ATTRIBUTE_NAME) {
                meta.parse_nested_meta(|meta| {
                    let ident = &meta.path.segments.first().unwrap().ident;
                    self.fields.push(ident.to_string());
                    Ok(())
                })
            } else {
                Err(meta.error("unsupported property"))
            }
        }
    }


    #[proc_macro_attribute]
    pub fn public(attr: TokenStream, item: TokenStream) -> TokenStream {
        let ast = parse_macro_input!(item as DeriveInput);
        let mut excluded_fields = AlternativeExcludedFields::default();
        let attr_parser = syn::meta::parser(|meta| excluded_fields.parse(meta));
        parse_macro_input!(attr with attr_parser);
        // everything else is the same
    }
```

One nice thing is that the library takes care of empty attribute streams for us, whereas earlier we had to catch an `Err` and return an empty `Vec`. It should also produce "sensible error messages on unexpected input" (https://docs.rs/syn/latest/syn/meta/fn .parser.html).

8.8 Other attributes

There are other kinds of attributes that we have not looked at in this chapter. The `syn` documentation lists six types of attributes in total:

- Outer attributes like `#[repr(transparent)]`, positioned outside or in front of an item
- Inner attributes—for example, `[#![feature(proc_macro)]`—placed inside the item
- Outer and inner one-line doc comments (`///` and `//!`)
- Outer and inner documentation blocks (`/* */` and `/! */`)

There's nothing special when it comes to the four kinds of documentation attributes. In fact, as the documentation notes, comments are transformed into normal-looking attributes (`#[doc = r"your comment text here"]`) before macros enter the equation. We will use a tiny example to show additional ways of parsing documentation and, by extension, attributes. Since we said function-like macros can mimic attributes if they want to, we will write one of those.

The following listing shows our "usage code," a simple macro invocation on a struct with all four kinds of comments.

```
use other_attributes_macro::analyze;

analyze!(
    /// outer comment
    /** comment block */
    struct Example {
        //! inner comment
        /*! inner comment block */
        val: String
    }
);

fn main() {}
```

Next we parse this input into a struct. The outer comments are the first ones we encounter, and to parse them we can combine `Attribute::parse_outer` with `call` to automatically turn the comments into a vector of (two) attributes. The most interesting field in `Attribute` is `meta`, which contains the comment content—so, in this case, `outer comment` and `comment block`. You can also see traces of the transformation into `#[doc = r"..."]` that happened before we entered the scene:

```
Meta::NameValue { path: Path { ..., segments: [PathSegment { ident: Ident
{ ident: "doc" } }] }, eq_token: Eq, value: Expr::Lit {
attrs: [], lit: Lit::Str { token: " outer comment" } } }
```

To get to the inner comments, we have to get rid of some things, like the `struct` keyword and identifier (`Example`), which is what we do with the first two `parse` calls. Next, we use a macro from `syn` that is specifically designed to handle curly braces: `braced`, which is only available when the parsing feature of `syn` is enabled. `braced` will put the entire content of the curly braces from `input` in the variable we passed along, `content`. Next, we use `Attribute::parse_inner` to retrieve the inner comments. This, again, returns a `Vec<Attribute>`.

```
#[derive(Debug)]
struct StructWithComments {
    ident: Ident,
    field_name: Ident,
    field_type: Type,
    outer_attributes: Vec<Attribute>,
    inner_attributes: Vec<Attribute>,
}

impl Parse for StructWithComments {
    fn parse(input: ParseStream) -> Result<Self, syn::Error> {
```

**Uses Attribute::
parse_outer,
together with
call, to parse
the outer
attributes**

```
let outer_attributes = input.call(Attribute::parse_outer)
    .unwrap();
let _: Token![struct] = input.parse().unwrap();
let ident: Ident = input.parse().unwrap();

let content;
let _ = braced!(content in input);
let inner_attributes = content.call(Attribute::parse_inner)
    .unwrap();
let field_name: Ident = content.parse().unwrap();
let _: Colon = content.parse().unwrap();
let field_type: Type = content.parse().unwrap();

Ok(StructWithComments {
    ident,
    field_name,
    field_type,
    outer_attributes,
    inner_attributes,
})
    }
}


#[proc_macro]
pub fn analyze(item: TokenStream) -> TokenStream {
    let _: StructWithComments = parse_macro_input!(item);
    quote!().into()
}
```

**Calls the braced macro to
get the content within
the curly braces ({ })**

**And Attribute::parse_inner
will help us get the inner
attributes.**

We finish our `Parse` implementation by retrieving the field name and type. As we wanted to give a brief introduction to parsing comments, as well as show some additional utilities for that kind of parsing, we did not take into account complexities like multiple fields, nor do we bother returning any output from the macro.

> **NOTE** As a reminder, when you parse a `TokenStream` into a struct, `syn` expects you to parse everything it finds. If you only retrieve the inner attributes from the braced content and do nothing with the rest, you would receive an `unexpected token` error pointing to the first thing you're not parsing. In our example, we parse everything to avoid this. But when you are not interested in the remainder of the content, you can put everything that remains into an ignored token stream: `let _: TokenStream2 = content.parse().unwrap();`. You can even leave the stream in its `Result`.

8.9   *From the real world*

Let's look at some real-world examples, starting with a simple one from Tokio. When you are inside the test macro (`#[test]`), a check is done to verify that you are not adding the test annotation multiple times:

```
if let Some(attr) = input.attrs.iter().find(|a| a.path.is_ident("test")) {
    let msg = "second test attribute is supplied";
    Err(syn::Error::new_spanned(attr, msg))
```

```
    } else {
        // ...
    }
```

Meanwhile, Yew has logic that decides whether the attributes of the original struct should be used in its builder struct. Like Tokio, it uses the is_ident method to compare with strings:

```
impl Parse for DerivePropsInput {
    fn parse(input: ParseStream) -> Result<Self> {
        let input: DeriveInput = input.parse()?;
        // ...
        let preserved_attrs = input
            .attrs
            .iter()
            .filter(|a| should_preserve_attr(a))
            .cloned()
            .collect();
        Ok(Self {
            // ...
            preserved_attrs,
        })
    }
}

fn should_preserve_attr(attr: &Attribute) -> bool {
    let path = &attr.path;
    path.is_ident("allow") || path.is_ident("deny") || path.is_ident("cfg")
}
```

Serde, as noted, starts every additional attribute with serde, as seen in its derive entry point:

```
#[proc_macro_derive(Deserialize, attributes(serde))]
pub fn derive_deserialize(input: TokenStream) -> TokenStream {
    let mut input = parse_macro_input!(input as DeriveInput);
    // …
}
```

And it has *a lot* of code to handle the different kinds of metadata. The following is a very partial fragment. It starts by checking whether the attribute is that of serde. When that's done, the macro needs to know what is inside the parentheses, so it uses parse_nested_meta (from syn version 1; several libraries, at the time of writing, still use version 1) and reacts to things like RENAME:

```
pub fn from_ast(cx: &Ctxt, item: &syn::DeriveInput) -> Self {
    // ...
    for attr in &item.attrs {
        if attr.path() != SERDE {
            continue;
        }

        if let Err(err) = attr.parse_nested_meta(|meta| {
            if meta.path == RENAME {
```

```
                    let (ser, de) = get_renames(cx, RENAME, &meta)?;
                    // ...
                } else if meta.path == RENAME_ALL {
                    let one_name = meta.input.peek(Token![=]);
                    let (ser, de) = get_renames(cx, RENAME_ALL, &meta)?;
                    // ...
                } else if meta.path == DEFAULT {
                    if meta.input.peek(Token![=]) {
                        // ...
                    } else {
                        // ...
                    }
                } else {
                    let path = meta.path.to_token_stream()
                        .to_string()
                        .replace(' ', "");
                    return Err(
                        meta.error(
                            format_args!(
                                "unknown serde container attribute `{}`", path
                            )
                        )
                    );
                }
                Ok(())
            }) {
                cx.syn_error(err);
            }
        }
        // ...
    }
```

You will find lots more attribute-handling code in popular crates, even if few are as extensively customizable as Serde. Its code will even feature briefly in the solution to the first exercise.

Exercises

See the appendix for solutions.

1 In our rename discussion, we used a simple name for our attribute. However, some libraries specify the crate name within the attribute and have the specific command wrapped inside parentheses—for example, `#[serde(rename = "name")]`. Rewrite our `#[rename("...")]` to instead use `#[builder(rename = "...")]`.

2 Our default assertions generated a warning about naming conventions, `type __notDefaultAssertion should have an upper camel case name`. Fix that warning.

3 Add an uppercase field-level attribute to our builder project, which will uppercase `String` types. As an extension, you could return an informative (syn?) error when the attribute is used on a field that is not a `String`.

Summary

- Macros can have attributes that allow you to further customize their behavior.
- Attributes can be placed on top of a struct or enum or inside (above a field). Depending on this positioning, they will be found in the root of the AST or under the `fields` property.
- Attribute macros, have a custom attribute that might contain additional instructions, unlike derive macros, whose attribute is set in stone.
- Function-like macros can mimic attributes and parse them.
- With the type state pattern, we can eliminate illegal states, making our code easier and safer to use.
- The strategy pattern gives us a way to centralize a piece of logic, making it possible to change or swap out algorithms.

Writing an infrastructure DSL

Most of the macros we have created thus far work within Rust, generating new functions, adding methods to enums, etc. But we also know macros can do more than that. For example, they allow you to generate compile-time checked HTML (Yew), or they create infrastructure for your code based on annotations (Shuttle).

This chapter features a macro that boldly goes beyond the confines of Rust and creates infrastructure in Amazon Web Services (AWS). This is interesting because it allows us to manage both application and infrastructure logic in the same repository and the same language, which might make expanding and maintaining the code easier. And, hopefully, the example also offers inspiration to readers as to what else they might do with procedural macros. But first let's take a step back to make sure we are all on the same page.

9.1   *What is IaC? What is AWS?*

With the rise of cloud providers that allow you to provision or destroy hundreds of servers at the click of a button, a new way of organizing IT infrastructure was needed. In the olden days, sysadmins could administer servers manually or with some light scripting. But that kind of approach is not scalable and works rather poorly in the cloud. It is hard enough to administer hundreds of servers manually, configuring them by logging into each one and entering the right sequence of Bash commands. But now imagine the added ephemeral nature of many cloud resources. The server you get from your cloud provider might be restarted/updated/changed several times a day. What do you do? Manually check your servers every few minutes, reentering your commands when they are replaced?

Never waste a good crisis, engineers thought, and a new philosophy was born—one where servers were no longer treated as pets (i.e., each one special and unique) but rather like cattle (i.e., interchangeable components, easily described based on a few characteristics). The treatment of cattle is also a lot more automated. And so, to enable automation, the configuration of servers and services should be *declared* in a readable format like JSON or some kind of Domain-Specific Language. That way, we have a written specification of what we need (this OS, this much RAM, CPU, storage) for our application. This specification not only enables us to easily destroy and create resources and environments, but it also serves as living, version-controlled documentation of infrastructure. That makes things easier to reason about, since everything is/ should be exactly as described. You don't need to figure out the specs, OS, languages, dependencies, etc. to reproduce a bug on your server if all that information is available in a text file. When everything we need to run an application is in a readable format that can somehow be executed to create said application, we call that *Infrastructure as Code* (IaC).

> **NOTE**   The aforementioned story is a simplification. Automation and version-controlling infrastructure are ideas with a long history. Nevertheless, these ideas have seen a huge uptick in popularity thanks to the cloud.

AWS is the cloud division of Amazon, currently the biggest player in the cloud business and a mile ahead of other big players like Azure and Google Cloud. A large part of the internet (including Netflix) runs on its infrastructure, which becomes painfully obvious when AWS has problems and countless websites go down.

AWS started simple some two decades ago with compute (Elastic Compute Cloud [EC2]), storage (Simple Storage Service [S3]), and queueing (Simple Queue Service

[SQS]—yes, AWS really likes "simple" things). Nowadays, few people can enumerate all the services that it offers.

It has also been one of the cloud providers that has driven IaC, launching its tool for IaC, AWS CloudFormation, more than 12 years ago. CloudFormation lets you describe your infrastructure in JSON or YAML *templates,* which are used to create *stacks* that contain all the actual application infrastructure. Other AWS tools build on the capabilities of CloudFormation. AWS SAM offers a version of CloudFormation that is easier to work with when you create serverless applications. AWS CDK lets you write your infrastructure in a language like Typescript or Python, which will be translated into CloudFormation templates.

There are also many independent tools, like Terraform, Pulumi, or the Serverless Framework, that allow you to create services for multiple cloud providers. The underlying idea stays the same, though: describe what you want in text or code and let the framework make your infrastructure dreams come true! But how do these tools communicate your desires to the cloud providers? Generally, they turn to either REST endpoints that the cloud provides for creating, destroying, and using services or *software development kits* (SDKs) that abstract away irrelevant details and allow you to work with these services directly from your favorite programming language.

> **NOTE** Behind the scenes, CloudFormation also makes service calls to AWS to create and update services. But it is not 100% clear what calls these are: the REST endpoints? Custom endpoints?

In this chapter, we will work on a DSL that uses the AWS SDK for Rust to create resources, focusing on Amazon S3 and AWS Lambda. S3 provides object-based storage via buckets that theoretically have unlimited storage. Lambda functions allow you to run compute without worrying about infrastructure. You provide code and some configuration, like the amount of memory you require and the maximum amount of time the code is allowed to run (timeout), and AWS makes sure that your code is executed and you only pay for the time that your code requires. Neat.

9.2 *How our DSL works*

Besides giving you a beautiful new way to create two AWS services from code, we also want to give users fast feedback. One of the downsides of text-based tools like CloudFormation is that there is no built-in mechanism for feedback when you make mistakes. This almost necessitates using IDE plugins and command-line interface tools as a substitute, because you do not want to start deploying an application just to find out minutes later that your template had a typo.

Rust is different: it likes to give you *a lot* of feedback before stuff starts running, and so do we. Summarized, what we want to offer is a simple language for describing infrastructure that automatically creates the specified resources and warns you when and where things go wrong, preferably as early as possible.

For example, creating a bucket named `unique` might look like this:

```
iac! {
    bucket unique
}
```

That seems simple and easy. As an example of a warning when things go wrong, we will return this error when we type `bucke` instead of `bucket`:

```
error: only 'bucket' and 'lambda' resources are supported
 --> src/main.rs:7:9
  |
7 |         bucke unique
  |         ^^^^^
```

We point to the typo and give additional information. This seems actionable enough (one of the exercises tries to make the message even better).

Besides limiting the number of services, we also limit the number of properties you can pass in, because not only do both buckets and lambdas have a huge number of properties, but the added value of having them in this chapter drops rapidly, since the required code is very similar. What we allow is creating buckets (required property: name), creating lambda functions (required: name; optional: memory and timeout), and sending events from buckets to functions. The latter provides very useful functionality, allowing you to react to the creation or changing of objects, which allows for a wide variety of use cases, like updating databases or triggering business workflows. As such, these bucket events are widely used, even now that Amazon EventBridge has become more of a central intermediary for eventing within AWS.

To summarize, this chapter's macro will parse a DSL that contains instructions for creating a lambda and/or bucket (see figure 9.1). This information will be passed on to clients who will use the AWS SDK to create the specified resources in the cloud.

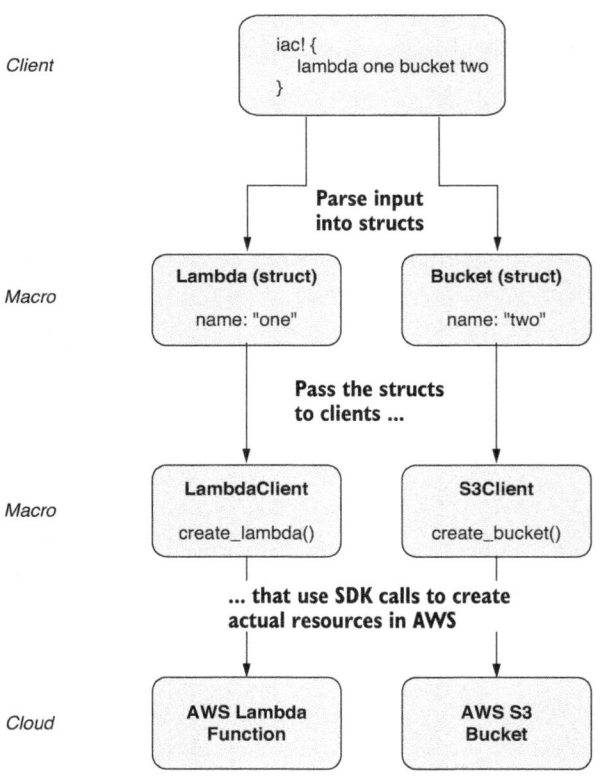

Figure 9.1   Overview of what our macro will eventually do

9.3 Parsing our input

We will write this macro in two phases. In this first phase, we concentrate on parsing the input into custom structs. Only in the second phase will we start doing something with the parsed information.

One reason for working in two phases is that parsing is very different from creating cloud resources, so treating these two separately makes sense. And if we keep the parsing separate, it could—in theory—be made independent of the concrete cloud that is used behind the scenes. If our example had been something like `iac! { object-storage unique }` instead, the naming would have focused on high-level desires that could be resolved in different ways. With an AWS backend, that `object-storage` would create a bucket; with an Azure Cloud backend, it would go for Azure Blob Storage. We would have to write one backend for every cloud *but only one parser.* That being said, in practice there are often subtle differences between cloud providers that make it hard not to leak implementation details in your IaC.

Another reason is of a practical nature: creating real cloud infrastructure adds much complexity, while also requiring an AWS account. By banning the cloud to the second part of this chapter, we minimize the number of code examples where you have to interact with AWS when coding along.

9.3.1 Project setup and usage examples

We can use the two-directory setup from earlier projects, with our macro in a subdirectory called `iac-macro`, and our usage examples in an `iac-macro-usage` directory. The following listing shows the familiar `Cargo.toml` file for the macro itself.

Listing 9.1 The `iac-macro Cargo.toml`

```
[package]
name = "iac-macro"
version = "0.1.0"
edition = "2021"

[dependencies]
quote = "1.0.33"
syn = { version = "2.0.39", features = ["extra-traits"]}

[lib]
proc-macro = true
```

The following listing shows one for the usage project.

Listing 9.2 The `iac-macro-usage Cargo.toml`

```
[package]
name = "iac"
version = "0.1.0"
edition = "2021"
```

```
[dependencies]
iac-macro = { path = "../iac-macro" }

[dev-dependencies]
trybuild = "1.0.85"
```

Our `main.rs` consists of a lot of usage examples: you can create a bucket, a lambda, a bucket with a lambda, or a bucket linked to a lambda via an event. For the last two, we use an arrow (=>) to indicate an event coming from the bucket and going to the lambda.

Listing 9.3   Usage examples

```
use iac_macro::iac;

fn main() {
    iac! {                              Creates
        bucket uniquename  <──┐ a bucket
    }
    iac! {
        lambda a_name                          <───┐
    }                                               Creates a lambda, which takes
    iac! {                                          memory (mem) and a timeout
        lambda my_name mem 1024 time 15  <───       (time) as optional parameters
    }
    iac! {
        lambda name bucket uniquename  <───┐ You can also create both a bucket and a lambda.
    }                                        In this case, the order does not matter.
    iac! {
        bucket uniquename => lambda anothername  <───┐ If you create both, you can have
    }                                                  the lambda listen to (object-
    iac! {                                             created) events from the bucket
        bucket b => lambda l mem 1024 time 15  <───┘   by adding an arrow =>.
    }
}
```

The usage directory also contains compilation tests (in `tests`) for failure cases, which are not shown here.

Our parsing implementation is about 140 lines of code. The entry point delegates the work to a custom struct. When parsing is done, it prints the result and gives back an empty `TokenStream` because we don't have anything sensible to return.

Listing 9.4   Macro entry point in `lib.rs`

```
#[proc_macro]
pub fn iac(item: TokenStream) -> TokenStream {
    let ii: IacInput = parse_macro_input!(item);
    eprintln!("{:?}", ii);
    quote!().into()
}
```

Since we are using a custom struct to do the parsing, we should implement the `Parse` trait for `IacInput`.

9.3.2 Implementing the Parse trait for our structs

In the following code, you can see that `IacInput` is responsible for high-level parsing, leaving the bucket and lambda specifics to other structs. As long as there is input, we keep looking for a bucket and lambda, trying to parse those inputs. (We could easily extend this part of our code to allow for multiple buckets and lambdas if we wanted to.) To do that, we use `peek`, which takes a look at the next token in the stream.

If we receive anything else, we throw an error because we either encountered an unknown resource or there is an unparsable leftover. Here, we turn to `lookahead1`, which allows us not only to see the next token but also to return an error for that particular piece of code. In our case, we take the `span` and return our own, custom error.

Once the input has been fully parsed, we check whether our bucket has the `has_event` property set to `true`. If that is the case, we expect a lambda to also be present, since it is required for receiving those events. Finally, when we retrieve the event from the bucket, the type of the `bucket` variable is not yet clear to Rust, so it can't be inferred, and we have to make it explicit: `let mut bucket: Option<Bucket>`.

NOTE In this chapter, I have done my best to follow the Rust standard of having errors start with a lowercase letter and without trailing punctuation. Capitalization comes more naturally to me, and not every project seems to follow the standard. Even so, it is probably best to follow existing conventions.

Listing 9.5 `IacInput` definition and `Parse` implementation

```
#[derive(Debug)]
struct IacInput {
    bucket: Option<Bucket>,
    lambda: Option<Lambda>,
}

impl Parse for IacInput {
    fn parse(input: ParseStream) -> Result<Self, syn::Error> {
        let mut bucket: Option<Bucket> = None;
        let mut lambda = None;

        loop {
            if input.peek(kw::bucket) {
                bucket = Some(input.parse()?);
            } else if input.peek(kw::lambda) {
                lambda = Some(input.parse()?);
            } else if !input.is_empty() {
                return Err(syn::Error::new(
                    input.lookahead1().error().span(),
                    "only 'bucket' and 'lambda' resources are supported")
                );
            } else {
```

These are custom keywords (discussed later).

If we have a bucket or lambda, delegates parsing to the Bucket or Lambda struct

If we have any other input, returns an error with a helpful span and message

```
                   break;            ◄─┐  No input left;
               }                       │  stops looping
           }

           if bucket.as_ref().map(|v| v.has_event).unwrap_or(false)
           && lambda.is_none() {
               return Err(syn::Error::new(
                   input.span(),
                   "a lambda is required for an event ('=>')"
               ))
           }

           Ok(
               IacInput {
                   bucket,
                   lambda,
               }
           )
       }
   }
```

One thing that is probably still unclear: what are `kw::bucket` and `kw::lambda`? Yes, those two do require a bit of explaining. Within our macro, `lambda` and `bucket` have a special meaning. Both act like a sort of keyword for a "resource declaration," which is followed by—required and optional—resource details. But for Rust/`syn`, there is no reason to treat either of these words as something special. So we can use the `custom_keyword` macro to tell `syn` that these two are keywords within our macro. By convention, such custom keywords are placed in a separate module called `kw` (short for "keywords"), as shown in the following listing.

Listing 9.6   Our four keywords: bucket, lambda, memory, and timeout

```
pub(crate) mod kw {
    syn::custom_keyword!(bucket);
    syn::custom_keyword!(lambda);
    syn::custom_keyword!(mem);
    syn::custom_keyword!(time);
}
```

Behind the scenes, the macro turns the given keywords into structs that implement `Parse`, as well as a method for allowing `peek`. This is useful, since we are using both `parse` and `peek` in the code.

Now we can soldier on to take a look at `Bucket`, the struct that parses the S3 bucket information. The parsing code gets rid of the bucket token, retrieves the name, and sees if an event token (=>) is present.

Listing 9.7 `Bucket` and its `Parse` implementation

```
#[derive(Debug)]
struct Bucket {
    name: String,
    has_event: bool,
}

impl Parse for Bucket {
    fn parse(input: ParseStream) -> Result<Self, syn::Error> {
        let bucket_token = input.parse::<kw::bucket>()
            .expect("we just checked for this token");
        let bucket_name = input.parse()
            .map(|v: Ident| v.to_string())
            .map_err(|_| syn::Error::new(
                bucket_token.span(),
                "bucket needs a name"
            ))?;

        let event_needed = if !input.peek(kw::lambda)
        && input.peek(Token!(=>)) {
            let _ = input.parse::<Token!(=>)>().unwrap();
            true
        } else {
            false
        };

        Ok(Bucket {
            name: bucket_name,
            has_event: event_needed,
        })
    }
}
```

The next identifier should be the bucket name.

We parse the bucket token, which should be present if we end up in this method.

If we have = >, an event is required, so sets has_event to true and gets rid of the arrow

Most of this is familiar: we are parsing the inputs, including those we won't use (the bucket token and arrow) but have to get rid of. Similar to `IacInput`, we have made some effort to provide good error handling. But when we expect things to always work, we use `expect` with a message explaining our thinking.

The code for parsing the lambda is similar but a bit longer due to the additional properties. We parse the token and name. If there is still input *and* the next token is not the start of a bucket declaration, there are optional properties. We loop and check for the `mem` and `time` custom keywords. If we get anything else, we error. As our optional properties can only be numbers, we parse them as `LitInt` (which is very similar to the `LitStr` from earlier chapters). That means the library will return sensible errors when the value is not a number. Finally, we parse the values we received into `u16` (see figure 9.2).

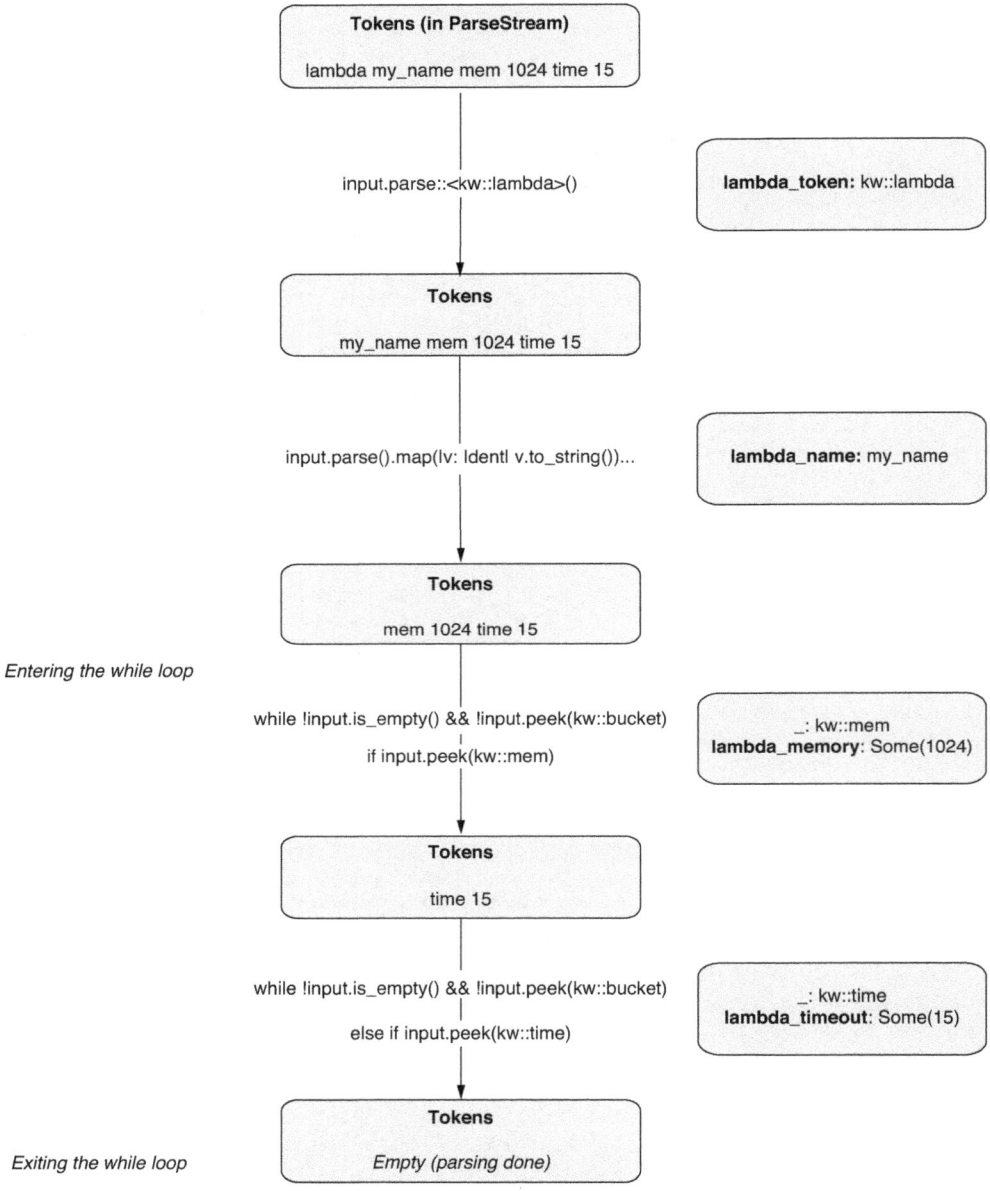

Figure 9.2 Parsing in our `Lambda` struct

Why `u16`? Simple: That way, we can get the compiler to do even more work for us! Both memory and timeout can only be positive numbers, so `i` is not required. And because memory and time can be larger than 255 (the maximum value of `u8`), `u16` is next in line, which will stop illegal values above 65,535. A further improvement to error handling would be to add additional checks on top of what syn and the compiler are doing for us. For example, in the time branch, we would check that the value is <= 900.

Listing 9.8   `Lambda` and its `Parse` implementation

```
#[derive(Debug)]
struct Lambda {
    name: String,
    memory: Option<u16>,
    time: Option<u16>,
}

impl Parse for Lambda {
    fn parse(input: ParseStream) -> Result<Self, syn::Error> {
        let lambda_token = input.parse::<kw::lambda>()
            .expect("we just checked for this token");
        let lambda_name = input.parse()
            .map(|v: Ident| v.to_string())
            .map_err(|_| {
                syn::Error::new(lambda_token.span, "lambda needs a name")
            })?;
        let mut lambda_memory = None;
        let mut lambda_timeout = None;

        while !input.is_empty() && !input.peek(kw::bucket) {
            if input.peek(kw::mem) {
                let _ = input.parse::<kw::mem>()
                    .expect("we just checked for this token");
                lambda_memory = Some(
                    input.parse()
                        .map(|v: LitInt| v.to_string()
                        .parse()
                        .map_err(|_| {
                            syn::Error::new(
                                v.span(),
                                "memory needs positive value <= 10240"
                            )
                        })
                    )??
                );
            } else if input.peek(kw::time) {
                let _ = input.parse::<kw::time>()
                    .expect("we just checked for this token");
                lambda_timeout = Some(
                    input.parse()
                        .map(|v: LitInt| v.to_string()
                        .parse()
                        .map_err(|_| {
                            syn::Error::new(
                                v.span(),
                                "timeout needs positive value <= 900"
                            )
                        })
                    )??
                );
```

Keeps looping while we have input for our lambda

The optional properties should be LitInt values that can be parsed into u16. If that is not the case, we return an error.

```
        } else {
            Err(syn::Error::new(         ◄──────────
                input.span(),
                "unknown property passed to lambda"
            ))?
        }
    }

    Ok(Lambda {
        name: lambda_name,
        memory: lambda_memory,
        time: lambda_timeout,
    })
    }
}
```

> **We don't have any other optional properties besides time and mem, so if we end up here, we should return an error.**

`main` now runs, and its logging shows that everything is parsed:

```
IacInput { bucket: Some(Bucket { name: "uniquename", event: true }),
 lambda: Some(Lambda { name: "my_name", memory: Some(1024),
 time: Some(15) }) }
```

Plus, we warn users of quite a few errors at compile time (bet you are tired of hearing me say that), like when we forget to give a lambda a name,

```
error: lambda needs a name
 --> tests/fails/bucket_and_no_lambda_name.rs:5:23
  |
5 |          bucket unique lambda
  |                        ^^^^^^
```

when we pass a string as a memory property,

```
error: expected integer literal
 --> tests/fails/lambda_time_not_a_number.rs:5:25
  |
5 |          lambda name mem "yes"
  |                          ^^^^^
```

or when the number we pass is invalid:

```
error: memory needs positive value <= 10240
 --> tests/fails/lambda_negative_time.rs:5:25
  |
5 |          lambda name mem -10
  |                          ^
```

So now we have a nice, little, helpful parser, which we will soon put to work.

> **NOTE** This is a helpful parser but not a perfect one, as it allows for some odd behavior. For example, we can pass in multiple buckets, but we will save only one. We won't fix all those oddities here, though the exercises do ask you to make one minor improvement.

9.4 Two alternative parsing approaches

First let me show you a few alternatives. And to make things a little more interesting, we are going to use a slight variation in our DSL syntax. Maybe the current style is a bit too loose, and we could make it clearer where a resource starts and ends. So for the lambda and its multiple properties, we can put everything between parentheses and separate property name and value by an equals sign.

Listing 9.9 Alternative example invocation

```
fn main() {
    iac! {
        bucket uniquename => lambda (
            name = my_name,mem = 1024, time = 15
        )
    }
}
```

Thus, in our alternatives, we focus on the `Lambda` struct, which must change because of the updated syntax.

9.4.1 Using Punctuated with a custom struct

In the first alternative `Parse` implementation, we now have to retrieve the content within the parentheses. And instead of manually parsing these parentheses (which is an option), we introduce the `parenthesized` macro, which will do this work for us. Its usage is very similar to `braced`, which we encountered earlier: give the macro your braced/parenthesized input and a variable to put the content in.

When we have the `content`, we know the properties are separated by commas, with every property consisting of a key separated by a value. That kind of repetition calls for `Punctuated`. So we use it to parse the properties. For the `name = value` part, we create a struct called `KeyValue` (as in key-value pairs), which we will discuss in a moment. When we have all the key-value pairs, we go through the results and compare them with the string value of our keys to find the right properties, throwing an error when we encounter an unrecognized property. An error is also thrown when we do not find the required name property.

Listing 9.10 `Lambda` and its new `Parse`

```
// other imports
use syn::parenthesized;
use syn::punctuated::Punctuated;

impl Parse for Lambda {
    fn parse(input: ParseStream) -> Result<Self, syn::Error> {
        let _ = input.parse::<kw::lambda>()
            .expect("we just checked for this token");
        let mut lambda_name = None;
```

```
let mut lambda_memory = None;
let mut lambda_timeout = None;

let content;
parenthesized!(content in input);

let kvs = Punctuated::<KeyValue, Token!(,)>::parse_terminated(
    &content
)?;
kvs.into_iter().for_each(|kv| {
    if kv.key == "name" {
        lambda_name = Some(kv.value);
    } else if kv.key == "mem" {
        lambda_memory = Some(
            kv.value.parse().unwrap()
        );
    } else if kv.key == "time" {
        lambda_timeout = Some(
            kv.value.parse().unwrap()
        );
    }
});

Ok(Lambda {
    name: lambda_name.ok_or(syn::Error::new(
        input.span(),
        "lambda needs a name"
    ))?,
    memory: lambda_memory,
    time: lambda_timeout,
})
    }
}
```

parenthesized is similar to braced.: it will put whatever is inside the parentheses in content.

Using Punctuated and a custom struct, we parse the content, returning early with ? if there is a problem.

The keys are compared with the string values of our properties.

We should actually return errors, but we are skipping that for brevity's sake.

A name is required, so a missing lambda_name is an error.

Because we do string comparisons this time, we do not need the keywords for mem and time, so those can be removed.

The definition of KeyValue holds few surprises. We save the key and value as strings because that will work for all properties. And, in Parse, we retrieve the key, which should be the first part of our input. Next, we get rid of the = token, which we don't need. But since it is part of our syntax, we do throw an error if it is not present. Note that this is the one place where we check for the equals sign, so if we wanted to use another separator, like a colon, that would be a one-line change.

For the values of the properties, we expect an Ident for the name. If we had used name = "some_name", it would have been a LitStr. LitInt is used for the other two, which should stop several faulty inputs. In all other cases, the property is unrecognized, which means it's error time.

Listing 9.11   lib.rs and the new KeyValue struct

```
#[derive(Debug)]
struct KeyValue {
    key: String,
```

```
        value: String,
    }

    impl Parse for KeyValue {
        fn parse(input: ParseStream) -> Result<Self, syn::Error> {
            let key = input.parse()
                .map(|v: Ident| v.to_string())        ◄──┐ Gets
                .map_err(|_| syn::Error::new(             │ the key
                    input.span(),
                    "should have property keys within parentheses"
                ))?;
            let _: Token![=] = input.parse()
                .map_err(|_| syn::Error::new(
                    input.span(),
                    "prop name and value should be separated by ="
                ))?;

            let value = if key == "name" {
                input.parse()
                    .map(|v: Ident| v.to_string())
                    .map_err(|_| syn::Error::new(
                        input.span(),
                        "Name property needs a value"
                    ))
            } else if key == "mem" || key == "time" {
                input.parse()
                    .map(|v: LitInt| v.to_string())
                    .map_err(|_| {
                        syn::Error::new(
                            input.span(),
                            "memory and time needs a positive value")
                    })
            } else {
                Err(syn::Error::new(
                    input.span(),
                    format!("unknown property for lambda: {}", key
                    )))
            }?;

            Ok(KeyValue {
                key,
                value,
            })
        }
    }
}
```

Annotation left of the `let _: Token![=]` line: **Parses the equals sign just to get rid of it**

Annotation right of the `let value = if key == "name"` block: **Now parses based on the property, returning an error (note the final ?) when the property is unknown**

The happy path for this alternative approach is identical to that of the previous setup, producing the same output. Error handling is basically the same, even if it is slightly abbreviated. The use of parentheses and the equals signs does mean we have some additional messages, like

```
error: prop name and value should be separated by =
 --> tests/fails/lambda_colon_instead_of_equals.rs:5:22
  |
5 |         lambda (name :)
  |                      ^
```

That concludes the first movement (variation). One nice thing is how it avoids the use of a (while) loop for retrieving the properties by making Punctuated do part of the work. And having the content within parentheses does not hurt either. It also shows that keywords are a nice convenience but not obligatory.

9.4.2 *Using Punctuated with a custom enum and builder*

Now, take a look at the next approach. On the surface, it's similar to the previous one: get rid of the token and retrieve the content. Except, this time, we have Lambda-Property in our Punctuated, and we are folding/reducing the results into our output using a builder.

> **Listing 9.12   lib.rs Lambda struct**

```
impl Parse for Lambda {
    fn parse(input: ParseStream) -> Result<Self, syn::Error> {
        let _ = input.parse::<kw::lambda>()
            .expect("we just checked for this token");

        let content;
        parenthesized!(content in input);

        let kvs = Punctuated::<LambdaProperty, Token!(,)>::parse_terminated(
            &content
        )?;
        let builder = kvs
            .into_iter()
            .fold(Lambda::builder(content.span()), |acc, curr| {
                match curr {
                    LambdaProperty::Name(val) => acc.name(val),
                    LambdaProperty::Memory(val) => acc.memory(val),
                    LambdaProperty::Time(val) => acc.time(val),
                }
            });

        Ok(builder.build()?)
    }
}
```

Annotations:
- **Parses into a Punctuated of LambdaProperty, a new struct** → `let kvs = Punctuated::<LambdaProperty, Token!(,)>::parse_terminated(`
- **Folds into LambdaBuilder, another new struct** → `.fold(Lambda::builder(content.span()), |acc, curr| {`
- **Builds, returning early if there are errors** ← `Ok(builder.build()?)`

Listing 9.13 shows part of the builder definition. Thanks to earlier chapters, you should be intimately familiar with both concept and implementation. We save a span in the struct to allow creating an error when the required name parameter is missing. And build returns a Result because, as we just made clear, the operation might fail when the name is not present.

> **Listing 9.13   LambdaBuilder struct, and the Lambda method that instantiates it**

```
struct LambdaBuilder {
    input_span: Span,
    name: Option<String>,
```

```
        memory: Option<u16>,
        time: Option<u16>,
}

impl LambdaBuilder {
    fn name(mut self, name: String) -> Self {
        self.name = Some(name);
        self
    }

    // similar setters for memory and time

    fn build(self) -> Result<Lambda, syn::Error> {
        let name = self.name.ok_or(
            syn::Error::new(
                    self.input_span,
                    "name is required for lambda"
            )
        )?;
        Ok(Lambda {
            name,
            memory: self.memory,
            time: self.time,
        })
    }
}

impl Lambda {
    fn builder(input_span: Span) -> LambdaBuilder {
        LambdaBuilder {
            input_span,
            name: None,
            memory: None,
            time: None,
        }
    }
}
```

⟵ **A name is required, so if it is missing we should return an error with a span pointing to the original code.**

The span that we are storing inside the `LambdaBuilder` comes from `proc_macro2`, since that is the type of span that `syn::Error` requires. That means we need to add `proc-macro2 = "1.0.69"` to our dependencies.

`LambdaProperty` is an enum with the three kinds of known lambda properties, which allows us to immediately pass in the right type of value (a string or a number). Meanwhile, within `parse`, our code is similar to what we had in our first approach. We check whether the property matches any of our keywords. If it does, we get rid of what we do not need and return the proper variant.

Listing 9.14   The `LambdaProperty` enum

```
pub(crate) mod kw {
    // earlier keywords
    syn::custom_keyword!(name);
}
```

```
#[derive(Debug)]
enum LambdaProperty {
    Name(String),
    Memory(u16),
    Time(u16),
}

impl Parse for LambdaProperty {
    fn parse(input: ParseStream) -> Result<Self, syn::Error> {
        let lookahead = input.lookahead1();

        if lookahead.peek(kw::name) {
            let _ = input.parse::<kw::name>()
                .expect("we just checked for this token");
            let _: Token![=] = input.parse()
                .map_err(|_| syn::Error::new(
                    input.span(),
                    "prop name and value should be separated by =")
                )?;
            let value = input.parse()                    ◁━━┓ After getting rid of the keyword
                .map(|v: Ident| v.to_string())                │ and equals sign, parses the name
                .map_err(|_| syn::Error::new(                 │ value to create the right variant
                    input.span(),
                    "name property needs a value")
                )?;
            Ok(LambdaProperty::Name(value))
        } else if lookahead.peek(kw::mem) {
            let value = parse_number::<kw::mem>(        ◁━━┓
                input,                                        │
                "memory needs a positive value <= 10240"      │ Uses a helper to do
            )?;                                               │ the same for the
            Ok(LambdaProperty::Memory(value))                 │ numeric properties
        } else if lookahead.peek(kw::time) {                  │
            let value = parse_number::<kw::time>(      ◁━━┛
                input,
                "time needs a positive value <= 900"
            )?;
            Ok(LambdaProperty::Time(value))
        } else {                                  ┃ Returns an error if the
            Err(syn::Error::new(            ◁━━━━━┛ property is unknown
                input.span(),
                format!("unknown property for lambda")
            ))
        }
    }
}
```

For once, we have a helper for the practically identical parsing required for memory and time, because in both cases, we like to have LitInt as the parsing type to stop errors, necessitating an additional step to turn the result into a u16. That means we cannot just use the function for parsing the name.

The most interesting thing about parse_number is that we made it generic over Parse. That's necessary because we want to parse the memory and time keywords. And

`Parse` is a *trait implemented by custom keywords*. So, as seen earlier, when we want to parse the timeout, we simply call `parse_number::<kw::time>`.

Listing 9.15 The generic `parse_number` helper

```
fn parse_number<T>(input: ParseStream, error_message: &str)
                -> Result<u16, syn::Error>
                   where T: Parse {                  <-- We have a generic T that implements
    let _ = input.parse::<T>()                            Parse, a good fit for our keywords.
        .expect("we just checked for this token");
    let _: Token![=] = input.parse()                  That generic is used to parse
        .map_err(|_| syn::Error::new(                  the mem and time keywords.
            input.span(),
            "prop name and value should be separated by =")
    )?;
    let value = input.parse()
        .map(|v: LitInt| v.to_string()
            .parse()
            .map_err(|_| {
                syn::Error::new(
                    v.span(),
                    error_message,
                )
            })
        )??;
    Ok(value)
}
```

Those are the three implementation options we have on offer today, though you could think of countless more. As usual, the best choice depends on preferences and project specifics. Our first approach was the shortest, mainly because it was leaving a lot of the hard work to a single struct (`Lambda`). And in the case of a macro of this length, it's a perfectly fine solution. The second solution is longer, but the abstraction of adding another struct for parsing might pay off in the long run. The third approach is even longer—definitely overkill for a macro like this. However, having a flexible and use-case-specific enum can become worthwhile if the application keeps growing.

9.5 Actually creating the services

Next up is asking AWS to create the requested services. We can do this with the AWS SDK for Rust.

Caveats

There are several things to be aware of for this part of the project.

Linking the bucket and lambda may occasionally fail because AWS might mistakenly think that the bucket or lambda you created less than a second ago does not exist. A production-grade version of this project would detect such failures and do a retry.

(continued)

This code only *creates* resources. If you run it a second time, you will get an error saying that the resources already exist. Production-grade code would check the existence of these resources by names or by keeping a state—like Terraform. See the exercises for a simple example.

Also, be careful when running this code in certain IDEs. IntelliJ, for example, might expand macros to give you better feedback, except that, in our case, expanding has the side effect of creating resources—which won't cost you anything, because buckets and lambdas are free. But it might cause your code to fail because the name you picked was already claimed by the IDE.

When it comes to IntelliJ, you can try to avoid this by skipping resource creation when you know the IDE is expanding your macros:

```
impl IacInput {
    pub fn has_resources(&self) -> bool {
        !is_ide_completion()
        && (self.bucket.is_some() || self.lambda.is_some())
    }
}

fn is_ide_completion() -> bool {
    match std::env::var_os(
        "RUST_IDE_PROC_MACRO_COMPLETION_DUMMY_IDENTIFIER"
    ) {
        None => false,
        Some(dummy_identifier) => !dummy_identifier.is_empty(),
    }
}
```

Alternatively, you can use the `RUST_IDE_PROC_MACRO_COMPLETION` environment variable, which will be set to `1`. Of course, there are no guarantees that this will work for your IntelliJ setup or future versions of the IDE.

And, a final caveat, we will be using the first approach (of those presented previously) for parsing our input.

Our project now has two very different tasks to perform. It still needs to parse the input, as we have done in previous sections. But it also needs to communicate with AWS. It might be best to split our project into multiple modules/files, with more specialized tasks:

- `lib.rs` still exists as the entry point and coordinator.
- `input.rs` contains everything related to parsing.
- `lambda.rs` has code to handle creating lambdas.
- `s3.rs` similarly contains code for creating a bucket.
- `errors.rs` contains a custom error, translating AWS SDK errors into useful `syn` errors. Errors handled by `input.rs` are already of type `syn`, so we leave those untouched.

- The `example` directory contains a basic JavaScript function `handler.js`, which we will execute in our AWS Lambda.

A minor change, not shown here, is that many of the fields of our parsing structs have become public to allow `lambda.rs` and `s3.rs` to access them when creating resources.

Creating a separate file for errors is not always a good idea. Locality, or having everything related to a piece of functionality—including error handling—in one place can be a big plus. And in a large project, having separate files for errors can become unwieldy. In this specific case, it offers us a nice way to unify the errors from `lambda` and `s3` while also allowing us to discuss all our error handling in one go.

We start by looking at `lib.rs`. Our first step is still to parse that input. When that is done, we use a helper to determine whether we have any resources that need to be created. This is an optimization that helps us avoid some work when it is not necessary.

What kind of work? Well, AWS SDK client initialization (via the `new` method) is asynchronous. Plus, most of the methods exposed by these clients are also `async`. And, for this behavior, the SDK relies on Tokio as an asynchronous runtime (i.e., for executing the asynchronous Rust code).

NOTE We have encountered Tokio before when we talked about the `tokio::main` macro.

So the asynchronous behavior and Tokio runtime from the AWS SDK infect our macro, meaning that when we have resources and need to use the SDK, we have to start a runtime and call `block_on` to wait until the infrastructure has been created.

Listing 9.16 The `lib.rs` entrypoint

```
// mods and imports

#[proc_macro]
pub fn iac(item: TokenStream) -> TokenStream {
    let ii: IacInput = parse_macro_input!(item);

    if ii.has_resources() {
        let rt = tokio::runtime::Runtime::new()
            .unwrap();

        match rt.block_on(create_infra(ii)) {
            Ok(_) => quote!().into(),
            Err(e) => e.into_compile_error()
        }
    } else {
        quote!().into()
    }
}
```

Creates a Tokio runtime and blocks on the create_infra function

If our macro ends without errors, we return an empty TokenStream.

Here we got an error while creating the infrastructure, so we change it into proper tokens.

As we are now using `tokio`, you will need to add it as a dependency to the project. Somewhat surprisingly, the runtime (`rt`) feature is not enough to get this code working: the `new` method is sneakily hiding behind the `rt-multi-thread` flag. We also add the AWS SDK dependencies we need—s3 and lambda, plus one for creating configuration for the clients of these crates:

```
aws-config = "1.1.1"
aws-sdk-s3 = "1.11.0"
aws-sdk-lambda = "1.9.0"
tokio = { version = "1.26.0", features = ["rt", "rt-multi-thread"] }
```

And if you think tokio is too big a dependency for such a simple use case, you may be able to use something more lightweight, like the pollster crate, which has no dependencies and is a fraction of the size of Tokio. Their usage is pretty similar:

```
use pollster::FutureExt as _;

pub fn iac(item: TokenStream) -> TokenStream {
    // ...
    match create_infra(ii).block_on() {
            Ok(_) => quote!().into(),
            Err(e) => e.into_compile_error()
    }
}
```

However, this is not an option for this particular use case because—as we mentioned—the AWS SDK relies on the Tokio runtime. This means you get an error (there is no reactor running, must be called from the context of a Tokio 1.x runtime) when using any alternative runtime.

The async function create_infra is shown in listing 9.17. It creates clients for the SDK calls to Amazon S3 and AWS Lambda. And, as you can see, those are async, since we need to await them—hence the need for an asynchronous function. When the clients are ready, we create the lambda, saving the result in output. Why? Because we will be creating a bucket next, and if it has an event, we need to know the Amazon Resource Name (ARN; a unique identifier) of the lambda so we know where to send the event. We also need to add so-called AWS Identity Access Management (IAM) permissions to tell the lambda that our bucket is allowed to send events. Errors inside the function are changed into IacError, the custom error type that is turned into_compile_error by our entry point.

NOTE You could imagine somehow encoding "we have a linked bucket and lambda" in the parsing phase, maybe with an enum variant called Bucket-LinkedToLambda(Bucket, Lambda). That would make this phase of creating the infrastructure easier and safer. See the exercises.

Listing 9.17 async create_infra function coordinating the infrastructure setup

```
async fn create_infra(iac_input: IacInput) -> Result<(), IacError> {
    let s3_client = S3Client::new()
        .await;                                       ⎫  Creates the AWS
    let lambda_client = LambdaClient::new()           ⎬  SDK clients
        .await;                                       ⎭
    let mut output = None;
```

```
        if let Some(lambda) = &iac_input.lambda {
            eprintln!("creating lambda...");
            output = Some(lambda_client.create_lambda(lambda).await?);
        }
```
If we have a lambda, creates it

```
        if let Some(bucket) = &iac_input.bucket {
            eprintln!("creating bucket...");
            s3_client.create_bucket(bucket).await?;
```
Creates the bucket

```
            if bucket.has_event {
                eprintln!("linking bucket and lambda by an event...");
                let lambda_arn_output = output
                    .expect("when we have an event, we should have a lambda");
                let lambda = iac_input.lambda
                    .expect("when we have an event, we should have a lambda");

                let lambda_arn = lambda_arn_output.function_arn()
                    .expect("creating a lambda should return its ARN");
                lambda_client.add_bucket_permission(
                    &lambda, &bucket.name
                ).await?;
                s3_client.link_bucket_with_lambda(
                    bucket, lambda_arn
                ).await?;
            }
        }
        Ok(())
}
```
If has_event is true, we should have a lambda, and we can set its permissions and configure the bucket to send an event.

To summarize: Once our input has been parsed, we check whether we have any resources that need creating. When we have a bucket and/or lambda, we start a runtime, block on an asynchronous function, and wait for it to build our resources using the two SDK clients.

9.6   The two AWS clients

All that is left to do is to dive into the code for the two clients. We use `aws_config` (that additional crate) to create the right configuration, relying on locally available credentials and an AWS region that we pass in (eu-west-1; i.e., in Ireland—you may want to pick another region if you are not in Europe). That is, to run this code locally, make sure you have active AWS admin creds.

Listing 9.18   The `LambdaClient` new method

```
// imports

pub struct LambdaClient {
    client: Client,
}
```
aws_config uses local credentials to load configuration. We set the region to Ireland.

```
impl LambdaClient {
    pub async fn new() -> Self {
        let config = aws_config::defaults(BehaviorVersion::latest())
```

```
                    .region(Region::new("eu-west-1"))
                    .load()
                    .await;
            LambdaClient {                        ◄─────
                client: Client::new(&config),
            }
        }
    }
```

With that config ready, we create the AWS client and our LambdaClient.

In a real project, we could turn to `Default` for a default setup, allowing users to pick a region when calling `new`.

Next are the functions we already saw in action. `create_lambda` uses a builder to send lambda configuration information to AWS. We set the name and optionally add a time and memory size. We also have to fill in several other properties, including a role (which already exists in my account) and a zip with the code, which was already uploaded to a bucket (`"my-lambda-bucket"`) in my account.

Listing 9.19   `create_lambda`

```
pub async fn create_lambda(&self, lambda: &Lambda)
        -> Result<CreateFunctionOutput, SdkError<CreateFunctionError>> {
    let mut builder = self.client
        .create_function()
        .function_name(&lambda.name)
        .role("arn:aws:iam::11111111111:role/change")    ◄───
        .code(FunctionCode::builder()
            .s3_bucket("my-lambda-bucket")
            .s3_key("example.zip")                  ◄────┘
            .build()
        )
        .runtime(Runtime::Nodejs18x)
        .handler("handler.handler");                  ◄──────

    if let Some(time) = lambda.time {
        builder = builder.timeout(time.into());
    };
    if let Some(mem) = lambda.memory {
        builder = builder.memory_size(mem.into())
    };

    builder
        .send()
        .await                      ◄──┐
}
```

Sets the name ├───▷

Sets the role (and the Lambda should be able to "assume" it).

Since the code in the zip is JavaScript, the runtime should be Nodejs. └──▷

Tells AWS that the code for this function is in a bucket object called "example.zip"

The zip contains a file called "handler," which has a function that is also called "handler." So we point AWS to handler.handler.

Sets the memory and timeout if they are present

Waits for AWS to create your resource

The following code is the `handler.js` file within `example.zip`. If you only want the macro to work (and not the Lambda that we are creating), you can even upload an empty file:

```
exports.handler = async () => {
    return {
        hello: 'world'
```

```
    };
};
```

To make the method more unit testable, you could extract the builder, which is pure, into a separate function that contains most of the code and has no need for mocking. The `send`, which is impure, would be in a different function:

```
pub async fn create_lambda(&self, lambda: &Lambda)
        -> Result<CreateFunctionOutput, SdkError<CreateFunctionError>> {
    self.create_lambda_builder(&lambda)        <──┐ The helper function contains
        .send()                                    │ most of the code and is pure.
        .await
}
```

The second function, `add_bucket_permission`, allows the bucket to invoke the lambda. It, too, uses a builder and `send` to talk to AWS. Inside we do some basic AWS IAM things, like allowing anyone (`"*"`) to invoke the lambda *as long as the source of that invocation is our bucket.* That way, the bucket can invoke the function when it has an event ready to go.

Listing 9.20   `add_bucket_permission`

```
pub async fn add_bucket_permission(&self, lambda: &Lambda, bucket: &str)
        -> Result<AddPermissionOutput, SdkError<AddPermissionError>> {
    self.client.add_permission()
        .function_name(&lambda.name)
        .principal("*")                          <──┤ Allows anyone . . .
        .statement_id("StatementId")
        .action("lambda:InvokeFunction")         <──┤ . . . to invoke this lambda . . .
        .source_arn(
            format!("arn:aws:s3:::{}", bucket)   <──┐ . . . as long as the source of
        )                                           │ the invocation is our bucket
        .send()
        .await
}
```

Now let's look at the `S3Client`. Its fields and `new` are very similar to the `LambdaClient`: we load the config and add the client and region to our struct.

Listing 9.21   The S3 client

```
pub struct S3Client {
    client: Client,
    region: String,
}

impl S3Client {
    pub async fn new() -> Self {
        let config = aws_config::defaults(BehaviorVersion::latest())
            .load()
            .await;
```

```
        S3Client {
            client: Client::new(&config),
            region: "eu-west-1".to_string(),
        }
    }
}
```

Probably because S3 buckets are a more global concept than Lambdas, which are region-specific like most things in AWS, we do not pass in the region during configuration. But when we create a bucket, we do have to give a `location_constraint` to make sure the resource is placed in the right region.

Listing 9.22 `create_bucket`

```
pub async fn create_bucket(&self, bucket: &Bucket)
        -> Result<CreateBucketOutput, SdkError<CreateBucketError>> {
    let constraint = BucketLocationConstraint::from(self.region.as_str());
    let cfg = CreateBucketConfiguration::builder()
        .location_constraint(constraint)
        .build();

    self.client.create_bucket()
        .bucket(&bucket.name)
        .create_bucket_configuration(cfg)        ◁─┐  Creates the bucket in
        .send()                                      our preferred region
        .await
}              ◁── An async send asks AWS
                   to create the resource.
```

We have a bucket and a lambda, and the bucket is allowed to invoke the lambda. But we aren't doing any eventing yet! Our final method makes sure to send events when an object is created (`"s3:ObjectCreated:*"`).

Listing 9.23 `link_bucket_with_lambda`

```
pub async fn link_bucket_with_lambda(
    &self,
    bucket: &Bucket,
    lambda_arn: &str) -> Result<
            PutBucketNotificationConfigurationOutput,
            SdkError<PutBucketNotificationConfigurationError>
        > {
    self.client.put_bucket_notification_configuration()
        .bucket(&bucket.name)
        .notification_configuration(NotificationConfiguration::builder()
            .lambda_function_configurations(
                LambdaFunctionConfiguration::builder()
                    .lambda_function_arn(lambda_arn)      ◁─┐  Sends events to a Lambda
                    .events(                                  with this ARN (a.k.a.
...when an object is    ┌──▷        Event::from("s3:ObjectCreated:*")   unique identifier) ...
created in our bucket  │        )
                       │    .build()
```

```
            .expect("to create valid lambda function config")
        ).build())
    .send()
    .await
}
```

In brief, our code communicates with AWS to set up the desired resources. When we want to send events, we have to do a lot of additional work, because AWS requires consent from both parties (bucket and lambda) before allowing that.

9.7   *Errors and declarative macros*

And that's every—wait: I forgot about `errors.rs`. There's that downside of putting errors in a separate file. On the upside, I can probably get away with only showing you part of the code, because it is all pretty similar. Our custom `IacError` is an enum with one variant for each kind of error that might occur: creating a bucket or lambda might fail, and setting up the event could go awry. `IacError` implements `Error` and has the required `Display` implementation. It also has a custom method for turning into a `TokenStream`, which is what we will have to output.

Since the four functions for calling AWS in `s3` and `lambda` all throw their own error, we have four `From` trait implementations. Each implementation turns one of those AWS errors into our own, retrieving the message from the error.

Listing 9.24   Our custom `IacError`

```
#[derive(Debug)]
pub enum IacError {                      Our IacError is a combination
    BucketError(String),                 of the three kinds of things
    LambdaError(String),                 that can go wrong.
    EventError(String),
}

impl IacError {
    pub fn into_compile_error(self) -> TokenStream {     This custom method
        match self {                                     returns a sensible syn::Error
            IacError::BucketError(message) => {          for every variant.
                syn::Error::new(
                    Span::call_site(),
                    format!("bucket could not be created: {}", message)
                ).into_compile_error().into()
            },
            // similar fo the other two
        }
    }
}
                                        We implement From for the various errors
                                        thrown by AWS. When there's a useful
                                        message in the original error, we keep it.

impl From<SdkError<CreateBucketError>> for IacError {
    fn from(value: SdkError<CreateBucketError>) -> Self {
        let message = value.message()
            .map(|v| v.to_string())
            .unwrap_or_else(|| "no message".to_string());
```

```
            IacError::BucketError(message)
        }
    }
}

// similar for our three other errors
// plus simple error and display implementations
```

It seems like a waste to write boilerplate code in a book that talks so much about macros as a tool for avoiding boilerplate. And nothing is stopping us from using additional declarative or procedural macros *within* a macro—though the latter would require setting up another project. In this case, a declarative macro will do just fine. We only need to pass in two things: the variant for our error enum (expr will do, though path is also a good candidate) and the type of the AWS error (ty, as you may recall from way back).

> **NOTE**   I wrote this code and chapter while the Rust SDK was still in developer preview. In version 0.24, you could match on the error and always get back the same global types (ServiceError, for example). Now that the SDK is generally available, matching on an error returns very specific errors (like BucketAlreadyExists). More specific errors are great, but they are not good for the type of deduplication we are doing. In order to still show this example of combining procedural and declarative macros, I have gone for simply extracting the error message. This is not the best choice per se, but it works for this example.

Listing 9.25   A declarative macro for the `From` implementations

```
macro_rules! generate_from_error {
    ($mine:expr, $aws:ty) => {
        impl From<SdkError<$aws>> for IacError {
            fn from(value: SdkError<$aws>) -> Self {
                // get the message, same as before
                $mine(message)
            }
        }
    }
}

generate_from_error!(IacError::BucketError,CreateBucketError);
generate_from_error!(IacError::LambdaError,CreateFunctionError);
generate_from_error!(
    IacError::EventError,
    PutBucketNotificationConfigurationError
);
generate_from_error!(IacError::EventError,AddPermissionError);
```

If you want, you can now run the code, which should produce either an error (when you don't have credentials, or a bucket or lambda with the given name already exists, etc.) or the resources you requested. That means you have succeeded in (ab)using Rust macros to create actual cloud infrastructure. Congratulations!

NOTE The `thiserror` (https://docs.rs/thiserror/latest/thiserror/) crate is another nice way of reducing error boilerplate when you don't want to write your own errors. It's a derive macro, and by now you would probably understand most of its code.

In its current form, our macro is not very useful yet. But it offers a lot of possibilities. For example, instead of just creating a bucket, we could save its details in a struct and add methods to store things in S3. And since we'd be creating the bucket via our macro, we gain safety: at run time, a bucket with the given name *has* to be available for storing stuff or we would have seen the application fail at compile time.

9.8 The right kind of testing

When we discussed or used tests earlier in this book, we focused on unit tests. At the time, those were the right tools for the job: fast, simple, and easy to maintain. And why would we ever need more when we are just generating or transforming functions, structs, or enums?

The DSL presented in this chapter is different, though. In its current form, it is not producing any useful output. And even if it did produce something, as suggested in the previous section, would this prove that we've done what we promised to do (i.e., create resources in the cloud)? Clearly not. To verify a macro like this, we need a more complex kind of testing. End-to-end testing is one option. We could set up a project that tests our macro—and we have quite some experience with that—and use the AWS SDK to verify that the resources are created. Preferably, there would also be a cleanup step afterward. I like to test things using a combination of my continuous integration/continuous delivery pipeline and AWS Lambda. The latter provides a realistic testing environment for my code, as it is not inconceivable that my macro will be used in a lambda at some point. Plus, lambdas are also cheap and easy to spin up. Sadly, this chapter is already long enough, so implementing this type of testing in your preferred CI/CD tool is left to you.

9.9 From the real world

We have already come across several crates that present a DSL for easier creation of things. Let's recap a bit: SQLx lets us write SQL queries; with Yew we write HTML; and with Leptos we mix Rust and HTML—all within a macro. Shuttle was also mentioned in several places as an example of IaC, which takes the concept one step further. You write your code, and Shuttle takes care of the infrastructure that you need, without you explicitly defining what that is.

Take the following, run `cargo shuttle deploy`, and you have an active endpoint that returns "Hello, World":

```
async fn hello_world() -> &'static str {
    "Hello, world!"
}

#[shuttle_runtime::main]
```

```
async fn axum() -> shuttle_axum::ShuttleAxum {
    let router = Router::new().route("/hello", get(hello_world));
    Ok(router.into())
}
```

Another brief note: many projects combine the powers of declarative and procedural macros like we did here. Shuttle uses them as you would expect (i.e., to avoid duplication):

```
macro_rules! aws_engine {
    ($feature:expr, $pool_path:path, $option_path:path, $struct_ident:ident)
    => {
        paste! {
            #[cfg(feature = $feature)]
            pub struct $struct_ident{
                local_uri: Option<String>,
            }

            // struct implementations
        }
    };
}
```

And yes, `paste!` is a macro invocation *in* a declarative macro *in* a crate with procedural macros. But the other way around exists as well. Rocket has more than one declarative macro that generates procedural macros (and yes, that's a plural; we'll briefly come back to having multiple macros in one project in the next chapter):

```
macro_rules! route_attribute {
    ($name:ident => $method:expr) => (
        // ...                          ┐ Generates an
        #[proc_macro_attribute]      ◄──┘ attribute macro
        pub fn $name(args: TokenStream, input: TokenStream) -> TokenStream
        {
            emit!(attribute::route::route_attribute($method, args, input))
        }
    )
}
```

SQLx's famous `query` macro is also a declarative macro that generates a procedural macro. Note that the entry point of that procedural macro is (accidentally) quite similar to ours, in that it does only three things:

- Delegates parsing to a struct
- Makes another function handle the result of that parsing
- Returns the result or error to the user:

```
#[macro_export]
#[cfg_attr(docsrs, doc(cfg(feature = "macros")))]
macro_rules! query (
    // ...
    ($query:expr) => ({
```

```
                    $crate::sqlx_macros::expand_query!(source = $query)
            });
    );
```
Generates a function-like macro

```
    // other file //
    #[proc_macro]
    pub fn expand_query(input: TokenStream) -> TokenStream {
        let input = syn::parse_macro_input!(
          input as query::QueryMacroInput
    );
        match query::expand_input(input, FOSS_DRIVERS) {
            Ok(ts) => ts.into(),
            Err(e) => {
                if let Some(parse_err) = e.downcast_ref::<syn::Error>() {
                    parse_err.to_compile_error().into()
                } else {
                    let msg = e.to_string();
                    quote!(::std::compile_error!(#msg)).into()
                }
            }
        }
    }
```

A final note for this section: in this chapter, our macros also used quite a few printline statements to give information to users, either to show what was parsed or to tell the user that a resource is being created. How do real Rust (macro) crates handle logging? Leptos has its own macro for its logging. As the comment states, behind the scenes, plain old `println` is used when you're not in the browser:

```
/// Uses `println!()`-style formatting to log something to the console
/// (in the browser)
/// or via `println!()` (if not in the browser).
#[macro_export]
macro_rules! log {
    ($($t:tt)*) => ($crate::console_log(&format_args!($($t)*).to_string()))
}
```
Plus similar macros for warn and error

Rocket has macros to help with logging, though this one does not use `print` behind the scenes (as stated in the comment for `write_out`):

```
macro_rules! define_log_macro {
    ($name:ident: $kind:ident, $target:expr, $d:tt) => (
        #[doc(hidden)]
        #[macro_export]
        macro_rules! $name {
            ($d ($t:tt)*) => (
                $crate::log::private::$kind!(target: $target, $d ($t)*)
            )
        }
    );
    // more implementation
}

define_log_macro!(error, error_);
```
And similar for warn, info, etc.

```
// `print!` panics when stdout isn't available, but this macro doesn't.

#[cfg(not(any(debug_assertions, test, doctest)))]
macro_rules! write_out {
    ($($arg:tt)*) => ({
        use std::io::{Write, stdout, stderr};
        let _ = write!(stdout(), $($arg)*)
            .or_else(|e| write!(stderr(), "{}", e));
    })
}
```

And some projects just use good, old `println` and `eprintln` statements.

Exercises

See the appendix for solutions.

1 Try to improve the input modeling. As discussed, it should be easier for users of `IacInput` to know that we have a bucket event. Optionally, you can also rework the creation of infrastructure using the new `IacInput`.

2 Suggest the right resource (or property) when you cannot find a match. For example, when you type "buck," the error should suggest "bucket." One option is to use Levenshtein distance.

3 Currently, our code fails when the resources we add already exist. Skip creation when you detect that it is unnecessary.

4 Make it possible to add another kind of resource (from AWS or maybe from another cloud provider!) to the `iac!` macro. (Note: No solution is provided for this exercise.)

Summary

- With Infrastructure as Code (IaC), we describe the entire infrastructure of our application as text or code, which means the state of our infrastructure is documented, version controlled, and easy to create, destroy, or update.

- We can use a function-like macro to create our own IaC syntax, letting the macro create what we describe behind the scenes.

- Within struct-based parsing, there are many variations for writing code to choose from.

- The ability to create custom keywords in `syn` is very useful when you are inventing a language within your macro.

- We can use asynchronous calls within a macro to do things like creating AWS infrastructure with the Rust SDK.

- We can mix and match declarative and procedural macros any way we like, combining their powers.

10

Macros and the outside world

This chapter covers

- Using a single library to expose multiple macros
- Adding or disabling functionality with features
- Using attributes for control over what code will be generated
- Documenting and publishing a macro library
- Moving on to explore interesting macro subjects beyond this book

In previous chapters, we have often made excuses for taking shortcuts, explaining how "production-grade" macros would do things better or differently. In this, our last, chapter, we will create a macro for making available YAML config that tries to do everything right. While its functionality will be very limited, it will have proper testing, error handling, documentation, and the like, making it (almost) ready for use by other people.

And that is great because publishing a library means your macro might find use among other developers, enriching the ecosystem of the language you love. Even libraries written within a company, with a specific use case in mind, might benefit from being open source. People might discover bugs or send pull requests with fixes and improvements, helping you to improve the quality of your code, to everyone's benefit. This chapter also offers an opportunity to bring together a few miscellaneous topics, like features, which can help you make your macro as lightweight as possible.

10.1 A function-like configuration macro

Let's go over the first version of our macro, which exposes a function-like macro called `config`. Calling that macro generates a struct called `Config`, which contains a `HashMap<String,String>`. We also generate a `new` method for filling the map with configuration properties.

That means the following YAML configuration, plus a call to `new`, results in the creation of a map containing keys `user` and `password`, with the corresponding values `"admin"` and `"pass"`:

```
user: "admin"
password: "pass"
```

For simplicity's sake, we won't allow nested YAML structures—only plain keys with string values.

10.1.1 Macro project structure

We are once again going for a project with two directories (`config-macro` and `config-macro-usage`) and the optional Cargo workspace. There is also a `configuration` directory on the same level as these two directories, with an example `config.yaml` file contained within.

Listing 10.1   The example configuration

```
user: "admin"
password: "admin"
```

In our usage directory, the `trybuild` dependency has been added for compilation testing.

Listing 10.2   The `config-macro-usage` Cargo.toml dependencies

```
[dependencies]
config-macro = { path = "../config-macro", features = ["struct"] }

[dev-dependencies]
trybuild = "1.0.85"
```

The macro itself has `serde` and `serde_yaml`, used for reading the YAML.

Listing 10.3   The `config-macro` Cargo.toml

```
[dependencies]
quote = "1.0.33"
```

```
syn = { version = "2.0.39", features = ["extra-traits"]}
proc-macro2 = "1.0.69"
serde = "1.0.192"
serde_yaml = "0.9.27"
```

The workspace looks like the following listing.

Listing 10.4   The `config-macro-usage` `Cargo.toml`

```
[workspace]
resolver = "2"

members = [
    "config-macro",
    "config-macro-usage"
]
```

In `config-macro-usage`, `main.rs` contains an example of how to use the macro, as well as some happy path tests. There is also a `tests` directory with compilation failure tests, which are also left out for brevity's sake but can be found in this book's code repository (https://github.com/VanOvermeire/rust-macros-book).

Listing 10.5   Usage example and tests in `main.rs`

```
fn main() {
    config!();
    let cfg = Config::new();
    let user = cfg.0.get("user").unwrap();
    println!("{user}");
}

// some happy path tests
```

Let's turn to the implementation.

10.1.2 Code overview

The macro code contains nothing that you haven't seen before, so we will be brief. We have gone for a modular approach by already creating `input.rs` and `output.rs` files in addition to `lib.rs`.

Start with `lib.rs`, which reads the token stream input using a struct from `input.rs` and produces output via a helper function. It also contains some of the core logic of our macro: finding and reading YAML. We look for the file with the default or overridden path and pass that file to `serde_yaml` for transforming it into a `Hash-Map<String, String>`. Errors are properly handled, and panics are avoided.

Listing 10.6   `lib.rs` coordinates helper functions

```
// imports, mod input, mod output

fn find_yaml_values(input: ConfigInput)
    -> Result<HashMap<String, String>, syn::Error> {
```

```
    let file_name = input.path
        .unwrap_or_else(|| {
            "./configuration/config.yaml".to_string()
        });
```
> Uses the override, or falls back to the default, for the configuration location

```
    let file = fs::File::open(&file_name)
        .map_err(|err| {
            syn::Error::new(
                Span::call_site(),
                format!(
                    "could not read config with path {}: {}",
                    &file_name,
                    err
                )
            )
        })?;
    Ok(serde_yaml::from_reader(file)
        .map_err(|e| {
            syn::Error::new(Span::call_site(), e.to_string())
        })?)
}
```
> Opens the file, returning an informative error if that fails

> Uses serde_yaml to read the content into a HashMap

```
#[proc_macro]
pub fn config(item: TokenStream) -> TokenStream {
    let input: ConfigInput = parse_macro_input!(item);
    match find_yaml_values(input) {
        Ok(values) => generate_config_struct(values).into(),
        Err(e) => e.into_compile_error().into()
    }
}
```
> Parses the input using a custom struct

> Uses find_yaml_values to read the config and passes it along to a function that generates output

input.rs parses the incoming TokenStream. Currently, it expects one optional argument: a path for overriding the location of the configuration file, for which we created a custom keyword. Because we anticipate the possibility of other arguments in the future, we have gone for a key-value-style approach (path = "./path.yaml"), which makes it easier to add additional keys later on. We have also made sure to use proper error handling.

Listing 10.7 Parsing the input.rs

```
// syn imports

pub(crate) mod kw {
    syn::custom_keyword!(path);
}

#[derive(Debug)]
pub struct ConfigInput {
    pub path: Option<String>,
}

impl Parse for ConfigInput {
    fn parse(input: ParseStream) -> syn::Result<Self> {
```

```
        if input.is_empty() {
            return Ok(ConfigInput {
                path: None,
            });
        }

        if !input.peek(kw::path) {
            return Err(
                syn::Error::new(
                    input.span(),
                    "config macro only allows for 'path' input",
                )
            );
        }

        let _: kw::path = input.parse()
            .expect("checked that this exists");
        let _: Token![=] = input.parse()
            .map_err(|_| syn::Error::new(
                input.span(),
                "expected equals sign after path"
            ))?;
        let value: LitStr = input.parse()
            .map_err(|_| syn::Error::new(
                input.span(),
                "expected value after the equals sign"
            ))?;

        Ok(ConfigInput {
            path: Some(value.value()),
        })
    }
}
```

`output.rs` also has a very familiar feel. That, at least, is what I am hoping for, after all those earlier chapters. It takes the values from the configuration file, creating a struct and a new method.

Listing 10.8 `output.rs` **creates the right output**

```
// imports

fn generate_inserts(yaml_values: HashMap<String, String>)    ◁──┐  This function generates
    -> Vec<TokenStream> {                                        │  all the individual
    yaml_values.iter().map(|v| {                                 │  inserts into the map
        let key = v.0;                                           │  that we have to do.
        let value = v.1;
        quote!(map.insert(#key.to_string(), #value.to_string());)
    }).collect()
}

pub fn generate_config_struct(yaml_values: HashMap<String, String>)
    -> TokenStream {
    let inserts = generate_inserts(yaml_values);
```

```
quote! {
    pub struct Config(
        pub std::collections::HashMap<String,String>
    );

    impl Config {
        pub fn new() -> Self {
            let mut map = std::collections::HashMap::new();
            #(#inserts)*
            Config(map)
        }
    }
}
```

Here, we generate the struct and implementation.

With that, we can generate a struct from configuration.

10.1.3 *Using full paths*

The one thing that's new and interesting about this code is that we are using the *full path* for HashMap (e.g., struct Config(pub std::collections::HashMap<String, String>); and similar inside new). Why? There are two reasons.

First, HashMap is not included in the Rust prelude, so it will not be available by default in our user's code. So without the full path, Rust won't know where this type is coming from. This will cause our code to fail with an error and cause the compiler to suggest importing the standard HashMap:

```
error[E0412]: cannot find type `HashMap` in this scope
 --> config-macro-usage/src/main.rs:5:5
  |
5 |     config!();
  |     ^^^^^^^^^^ not found in this scope
  |
```

Think of what is happening. We are adding code to a Rust file in an application. And if we add struct Config(HashMap<String, String>);, without the path, we are referring to a type that is unfamiliar within *the user's code*, not our code. The users will have to fix the problem, probably by importing std::collections::HashMap. Maybe some of them even get lucky and there already is an import. In that case, they remain blissfully unaware of any macro compilation problems.

Still, user action is not a good outcome. Not only is it not very user friendly, but it also very directly exposes the fact that we are using a HashMap, which is an implementation detail we might like to hide if possible. With HashMap hidden, changing to a different type will be easier if that proves necessary, requiring no changes to existing application code. So by including the full path of things, we make life easier for our clients and enable the hiding of (some) implementation details.

The second reason is that users may already be using a HashMap but not the one we were expecting. Maybe they created a struct with the same name:

```
struct HashMap {}
```

If our macro did not use a full path, those users would be greeted with a confusing error caused by `std::collections::HashMap` expecting generic arguments, which the local one does not have:

```
error[E0107]: this struct takes 0 generic arguments but 2 generic
 arguments were supplied
```

This is something we have to avoid because the chance of a collision with the application code and library code grows with the size of both the project and our macro. So it's good practice to *always use full paths in generated code.* Even when it comes to things included in Rust's prelude (like `std::vec::Vec`), this may be worthwhile, because even these might not be available in certain environments or might be overridden by things declared in application code.

String or str

Throughout this book, I have often used `String` as a type and not string slices (`str`), partly because `String` is an easy and familiar type and, sometimes, because it was the only correct choice. In several other cases, strings helped avoid complexity that was not relevant to the discussion.

But just for this once, let's consider string slices, since they are a valid alternative and not that difficult to use in this particular example. After all, we are generating a `new` method that has the hardcoded values baked in. Those literals are static, meaning we can have slices with static lifetimes: `struct Config(pub std:: collections::HashMap<&'static str,&'static str>);`. Apart from that signature, only `generate_insert` has to change, as it no longer requires `to_string` calls:

```
fn generate_inserts(yaml_values: HashMap<String, String>)
    -> Vec<TokenStream> {
    yaml_values.iter().map(|v| {
        let key = v.0;
        let value = v.1;
        quote!(map.insert(#key, #value);)
    }).collect()
}


pub fn generate_config_struct(yaml_values: HashMap<String, String>)
    -> TokenStream {
    let inserts = generate_inserts(yaml_values);
    quote! {
        pub struct Config(
            pub std::collections::HashMap<&'static str,&'static str>
        );
        // unchanged new method
    }
}
```

10.2 *Adding another macro*

Currently, we are exposing a nice function-like macro. But what if our users prefer to modify an existing struct with an attribute macro, instead of generating a new struct? Well, why not offer this option as well? While a proc-macro library can only expose procedural macros (and not normal functions, structs, etc.), there is no limit to the number of macros one library can have, as seen briefly in section 9.9.

Now, let's do this ourselves. We won't show the new usage examples or tests, focusing only on what has changed in the macro directory. We reuse the `ConfigInput` struct for parsing the attribute `TokenStream`. If it contains a custom path (`(path = …)`), we can automatically handle that. To retrieve relevant details of the annotated struct, we turn to `DeriveInput`, for the same reasons as before (i.e., it is available by default and suits our use case), passing it into the output generator.

Listing 10.9 An additional macro

```
#[proc_macro_attribute]
pub fn config_struct(attr: TokenStream, item: TokenStream)
    -> TokenStream {
    let input: ConfigInput = parse_macro_input!(          Reuses ConfigInput
        attr
    );
    let ast: DeriveInput = parse_macro_input!(            Parses our attribute
        item                                             macro as a DeriveInput . . .
    );

    match find_yaml_values(input) {
        Ok(values) => generate_annotation_struct(ast, values)
            .into(),
        Err(e) => e.into_compile_error()                 . . . and gives it to our
            .into()                                      output function
    }
}
```

`input.rs` has not changed at all; it just works. But `output.rs` has to generate a different kind of output: it needs to recreate the struct, its `new` method, and field declarations.

Listing 10.10 Recreating the struct

```
// imports and earlier code

fn generate_fields(yaml_values: &HashMap<String, String>)
    -> Vec<TokenStream> {
    yaml_values.iter().map(|v| {
        let key = Ident::new(v.0, Span::call_site());
        quote! {
            pub #key: String
        }
    }).collect()
}
```

```
fn generate_inits(yaml_values: &HashMap<String, String>)
    -> Vec<TokenStream> {
    yaml_values.iter().map(|v| {
        let key = Ident::new(v.0, Span::call_site());
        let value = v.1;
        quote! {
            #key: #value.to_string()
        }
    }).collect()
}

pub fn generate_annotation_struct(
        input: DeriveInput,
        yaml_values: HashMap<String, String>
) -> TokenStream {
    let attributes = &input.attrs;
    let name = &input.ident;
    let fields = generate_fields(&yaml_values);
    let inits = generate_inits(&yaml_values);

    quote! {
        #(#attributes)*              ⟵  Make sure to keep
        pub struct #name {              the existing attributes.
            #(#fields,)*
        }

        impl #name {
            pub fn new() -> Self {
                #name {
                    #(#inits,)*
                }
            }
        }
    }
}
```

By now, all of this is child's play—except that I forgot for a moment that I had to turn the keys into identifiers, meaning I was greeted by an `expected identifier` error. Make sure to use `Ident` from `proc_macro2` as well. If your IDE selects the one from `proc_macro`, you will be warned that `the trait bound proc_macro::Ident: ToTokens is not satisfied`. `quote` expects a `ToTokens` implementation to change your code into a `TokenStream`. And that implementation is missing from the other kind of `Ident`.

With this bit of code in place, we can choose between `config!` or `#[config_struct]`—or both! But that is probably not advisable.

10.3   *Features*

One downside of having multiple macros that do the same work is that we are forcing users to pull in a lot of code that they might not need. To avoid that, we can turn to *features*. You are probably familiar with them, but just to be sure: features—sometimes also called *feature flags*—allow us to make parts of our code optional. Only if users decide they want a specific feature and activate it will that part of the library be pulled into our project.

Let's make the attribute macro optional, hiding it behind a feature called `struct` (because we need a struct to use it). First, we add it to the macro's `Cargo.toml`.

Listing 10.11 Features in `Cargo.toml`

```
[features]
struct = []
```

Next, to make things simpler, we move all the code-generating functions (`generate_fields`, `generate_inits`, `generate_annotation_struct`) for the attribute macro from `output.rs` to a separate file. Call it `struct_output.rs`.

Now we add feature configuration to our library. The entry point for our attribute macro is now annotated with `#[cfg(feature = "struct")]`, meaning it will only be included when the `struct` feature is enabled. We can do the same for the `Derive-Input` import. More importantly, our new file/module `struct_output` is only imported when the feature is active. This is why we moved those functions to a separate file: it enables hiding all three in one go. To avoid one additional import, I have used the full path for the import of `struct_output::generate_annotation_struct`.

Listing 10.12 `lib.rs` featuring a feature

```
// other imports, mod input, mod output
#[cfg(feature = "struct")]
use syn::DeriveInput;                          The imports are now only activated
#[cfg(feature = "struct")]                     when the "struct" flag is set.
mod struct_output;

// find_yaml_values
// function-like macro
                                       The same goes for
#[cfg(feature = "struct")]      ◁────  our macro entry point.
#[proc_macro_attribute]
pub fn config_struct(attr: TokenStream, item: TokenStream)
    -> TokenStream {
    let input: ConfigInput = parse_macro_input!(attr);
    let ast: DeriveInput = parse_macro_input!(item);

    match find_yaml_values(&input) {
        Ok(values) => struct_output::generate_annotation_struct(     ◁───
            ast, values, &input.exclude_from
        ).into(),                              Full path for this, or else we
        Err(e) => e.into_compile_error().into()    would need an additional
    }                                          feature-dependent import
}
```

You can verify the correctness of our code by running this code in `config-macro-usage`.

> **Listing 10.13 A usage example**

```
use config_macro::config_struct;

#[config_struct]
#[derive(Debug)]
struct ConfigStruct {}

fn main() {
    let config = ConfigStruct::new();
    println!("{config:?}");
}
```

Adds a Debug derive
to enable printing

This will fail because the attribute macro is now unknown. The function-like macro, on the other hand, would keep on working. Change the dependency on our macro library to `config-macro = { path = "../config-macro", features = ["struct"] }`, and everything works again.

This does mean that users who prefer this macro over the function-like one are unable to exclude the latter. So we could hide it behind a feature as well—maybe called `functional`. Does this mean our code would, by default, expose no macros (which is technically allowed but still pretty strange)? In that case, adding a default feature could be a good idea. That way, users can get rid of it with `config-macro = { path = "../config-macro", features = ["struct"], default-features = false }`, but we still expose at least one macro by default:

```
[features]
default = ["functional"]
struct = []
functional = []
```

That covers keeping out unneeded library code. But what about the code that we are generating? Let's suppose that the attribute macro also generated a `From` implementation for our struct, which allowed turning it into a `HashMap`, just in case someone prefers that over accessing fields:

```
let cfg = MyConfigStruct::new();
let as_map: HashMap<String, String> = cfg.into();
```

Not everyone is going to use that method, but as things stand, it is being generated nonetheless.

> **NOTE** Yes, Rust might decide to optimize your code by removing unused functions and the like. But there is no guarantee that this will happen. And it still takes time to get rid of unused code. So not having it in the first place can be worthwhile.

Maybe we can avoid that. One option would be to add an attribute to our macro that signifies we want to exclude some code generation. Let's call it `exclude`. For the moment, the only allowed value is `from`, which will make sure the `From` implementation is not generated:

```
#[config_struct(exclude = "from")]
struct ConfigStruct {}
```

To support this attribute, we need to alter our `input.rs` parsing a bit. We add the `exclude` keyword, an `exclude_from` Boolean property, and code to parse the exclude. If its string value equals `from`, we set the property to `true`. In every other case, it is `false`. The code in the following listing has the downside of only allowing a single property: either `path` or `exclude`. Take a look at the exercises if you want to fix that.

Listing 10.14   An additional property for `ConfigInput`

```
// syn imports

pub(crate) mod kw {
    syn::custom_keyword!(path);
    syn::custom_keyword!(exclude);          ◁──┐  We add the "exclude"
}                                              │  keyword.

#[derive(Debug)]
pub struct ConfigInput {
    pub path: Option<String>,
    pub exclude_from: bool,                 ◁──┐  And we need an additional property to
}                                              │  capture the exclusion information.

impl Parse for ConfigInput {
    fn parse(input: ParseStream) -> syn::Result<Self> {
        if input.is_empty() {
            // similar to earlier code; exclude is false
        } else if input.peek(kw::path) {
            // similar to earlier code; exclude is false
        } else if input.peek(kw::exclude) {
            let _: kw::exclude = input.parse()
                .expect("checked that this exists");
            let _: Token![=] = input.parse()
                .map_err(|_| syn::Error::new(
                    input.span(),
                    "expected equals sign after path"
                ))?;
            let value: LitStr = input.parse()
                .map_err(|_| syn::Error::new(
                    input.span(),
                    "expected value after the equals sign"
                ))?;
            let exclude_from = value.value() == "from";

            Ok(ConfigInput {                    If the keyword is present and
                path: None,                     matches the string "from,"
                exclude_from,           ◁────┘  sets the property to true.
            })
        }
    }
```

```
            // error case
        }
    }
```

The other changes are located in `struct_output.rs`. Two functions (`generate_inserts_for_from` and `generate_from_method`) help us generate the proper `From`. Meanwhile, `generate_annotation_struct` receives a Boolean from `lib.rs`, where we pull it from `ConfigInput`. Based on its value, we either call the new functions to generate output or generate an empty token stream. The generated code/empty stream is passed on to our final `quote`.

Listing 10.15 Additional methods and changes in `struct_output.rs`

```
// imports, generate_fields, generate_inits

fn generate_inserts_for_from(yaml_values: &HashMap<String, String>)
    -> Vec<TokenStream> {
    yaml_values.iter().map(|v| {
        let key = v.0;
        let key_as_ident = Ident::new(key, Span::call_site());
        quote!(map.insert(#key.to_string(), value.#key_as_ident);)
    }).collect()
}

fn generate_from_method(
        name: &Ident,
        yaml_values: &HashMap<String, String>
    ) -> TokenStream {
    let inserts = generate_inserts_for_from(yaml_values);
    quote! {
        impl From <#name> for std::collections::HashMap<String,String> {
            fn from(value: #name) -> Self {
                let mut map = std::collections::HashMap::new();
                #(#inserts)*
                map
            }
        }
    }
}

pub fn generate_annotation_struct(
        input: DeriveInput,
        yaml_values: HashMap<String, String>,
        exclude_from_method: &bool
    ) -> TokenStream {
    // all the other token streams
    let from = if !exclude_from_method {
        generate_from_method(name, &yaml_values)
    } else {
        quote!()
    };
    quote! {
```

Additional functions that help generate the From (annotation pointing to `generate_inserts_for_from` and `generate_from_method`)

Generates the From if the Boolean is false, or else gives back an empty stream (annotation pointing to `let from = if !exclude_from_method {`)

```
        // struct and method generation
        #from
    }
}
```

The one advantage of using this alternative is that it is extremely flexible. After all, it's handcrafted code—it could do anything. We could, say, retrieve some environment variables, compare them with a local file, and determine what to generate based on the outcome. But in many cases, including this one, you can accomplish your goals with a feature (see the exercises). And you should probably prefer built-in tooling over custom solutions unless you have a very good reason not to.

> **NOTE** In Rust, features should be additive, meaning they add functionality but never disable functionality that was already present in the crate. Cargo relies on this when resolving dependencies. Our macro obeys that rule, as its two features (struct and functional) add macros. But if, theoretically, we used a feature to exclude a `From` implementation that was present in the default set, we would be breaking this rule.

10.4 *Documenting a macro*

If you want to write a macro that other people will use, documentation is essential. No one likes exploring a crate or project that leaves you in the dark when it comes to usage. And while it is not my job to tell you what is worthwhile documenting—that depends on the situation—I can show you some of the available options.

Besides ordinary code comments (//) for internal use, we have outer documentation (///), which is used to document a single item. That is, we can add item-specific documentation to our macros. The following listing is a short example of the `config` macro.

Listing 10.16 Outer documentation for `config`

```
/// This function-like macro will generate a struct called `Config`
/// which contains a `HashMap<String,String>` with all
/// the yaml config properties.
#[proc_macro]
pub fn config(item: TokenStream) -> TokenStream {
    // implementation
}
```

If you run `cargo doc --open`, you will see that documentation was generated specifically for `config`.

We mentioned the existence of doctests in chapter 6. We can add one of them to our other macro. Because these tests are run when you do a `cargo test`, you should make sure they actually work—hence the import and the specific configuration path, since `lib.rs` is in a different location compared to my usage examples. And note the change I made to `cfg`. Without it, Rust did not generate documentation for this struct because it was hidden behind a feature. Adding the doc profile is one way to make it visible.

Listing 10.17 Outer documentation for `config_struct`

```
/// This macro allows manipulation of an existing struct
/// to serve as a 'config' struct.
/// It will replace any existing fields with those present
/// in the configuration.
///
/// ```rust
/// use config_macro::config_struct;
///
/// #[config_struct(path = "./configuration/config.yaml")]
/// struct Example {}
///
/// // Example now has a new method
/// let e = Example::new();
///
/// // e now contains a 'user' field that we can access
/// println!("{}", e.user);
/// ```
///
#[cfg(any(feature = "struct",doc))]     ⊲── The attribute is activated when
#[proc_macro_attribute]                     the struct feature is active or
pub fn config_struct(attr: TokenStream, item: TokenStream)   the doc profile is active.
    -> TokenStream {
    // implementation
}
```

Now our documentation looks like the example in figure 10.1, with more information (like the previous test) available behind the hyperlinks.

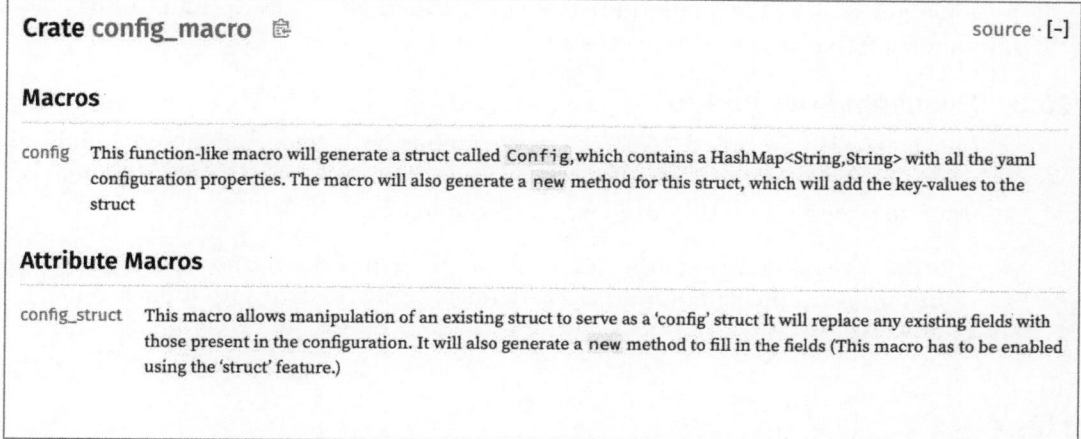

Crate config_macro   source · [–]

Macros

config   This function-like macro will generate a struct called Config, which contains a HashMap<String,String> with all the yaml configuration properties. The macro will also generate a new method for this struct, which will add the key-values to the struct

Attribute Macros

config_struct   This macro allows manipulation of an existing struct to serve as a 'config' struct It will replace any existing fields with those present in the configuration. It will also generate a new method to fill in the fields (This macro has to be enabled using the 'struct' feature.)

Figure 10.1 Outer documentation with hyperlinks to the more detailed information

Meanwhile, inner documentation (`//!`) is used to document an entire file or crate. We could add the following to `lib.rs`:

```
//! ## Documentation from lib.rs
//! Here is documentation placed directly within lib.rs...

// imports, code
```

Another neat trick is that you can import documentation from an external Markdown document. That may keep your Rust files cleaner, avoid duplicating information, and prove easier to write. The following shows an example `README.md` file located in the `config-macro` directory:

```
# Config Macro

## Overview

This crate contains macros that allow you to transform yaml config
into a struct that you can use in your application.

## Usage

Left out for brevity's sake.
```

We should now add this command to the top of our `lib.rs`:

```
#![doc = include_str!("../README.md")]

//! ## Documentation from lib.rs
//! Here is documentation placed directly within lib.rs.

// imports, code
```

The imported text will appear above the inline inner documentation. This gives us some general documentation for our crate, added above the specific (outer) documentation that we wrote earlier (see figure 10.2).

10.5 Publishing our macro

Our macro is now tested, handles errors responsibly, has documentation, and—also pretty important—does something people might find useful. Maybe it is time to publish it to crates.io with the `cargo publish` command.

> **NOTE** Please don't publish this example, though. I doubt the Rust community would appreciate hundreds of identical config macros with limited functionality.

⊟ **Config Macro**

Overview

This crate contains macros that allow you to transform yaml config into a struct that you can use in your application.

Usage

Call either the function-like `config!` macro or annotate a (preferably empty) struct with the attribute macro #
`[config_struct]`. By default, the macro looks for configuration under `configuration/config.yaml`. This can be
overwritten by using the 'path' attribute: `config!(path = "a/path/to.yaml")` or `#[config_struct(path = "a/path/to.yaml")]`.

Usage example

```
use config_macro::config;

config!(path = "../configuration/config.yaml");

// we can now call new and access the hashmap of values
let c = Config::new();
```

Feature flags

The annotation macro is hidden behind the 'struct' feature flag.

Caveats

Currently only works with YAML files, and does not support nesting. So this works:

```
user: "admin"
```

But this won't:

```
database:
    user: "admin"
```

Furthermore, we will read all properties in the config as `Strings`.

Documentation from lib.rs

Here is documentation placed directly within lib.rs...

Macros

config   This function-like macro will generate a struct called `Config`, which contains a HashMap<String,String> with all the yaml
          configuration properties. The macro will also generate a `new` method for this struct, which will add the key-values to the
          struct

Attribute Macros

config_struct   This macro allows manipulation of an existing struct to serve as a 'config' struct It will replace any existing fields with
                 those present in the configuration. It will also generate a `new` method to fill in the fields (This macro has to be enabled
                 using the 'struct' feature.)

Figure 10.2   Outer documentation

Before we do that, we should add some more information to our `Cargo.toml` file in the `config-macro` directory. In the following listing, a selection of useful fields has been added.

Listing 10.18 `config-macro` `Cargo.toml` **additions**

```
[package]
name = "config-macro"
version = "0.1.0"
edition = "2021"

description = "Macros for using config as a struct within your app"
license = "MIT"
homepage = "https://github.com/some-page"
repository = "https://github.com/some-page"
readme = "README.md"                            ◁──┐  This is actually the default, so
keywords = ["configuration", "yaml", "macro"]      │  adding it here is not required.

# dependencies, lib, features
```

In general, Rust advises not committing a `Cargo.lock` when you write a library, so it might be best to add that file to your `.gitignore` at this point. If you've already committed the file, remove it from your Git and update `.gitignore` afterward.

You may also have noticed that I've placed my documentation and publish information in the `config-macro` directory. The reason is that there is little use in publishing our `usage` or `configuration` directories. Those are for testing the library but offer no functionality, so you may want to publish the `config-macro` directory, not the entire project. Two final pointers: you will need credentials to publish to crates.io, and `cargo publish` has a `–dry-run`, which might be useful to try out first.

> **NOTE** Publishing is one reason why we have chosen a setup with two directories for this chapter, as it is currently impossible to publish crates with path dependencies. This means that the "three directories" setup we showed in earlier chapters is harder to publish because, in that case, our macro entry point is in one library, and its implementation is pulled in via a path dependency. That does not make publishing in that scenario impossible, but until—if ever—publishing with path dependencies becomes allowed, it does create complications.

Once the crate is published and becomes stable, reaching version 1, developers will expect you to use semantic versioning (also known as *semver*) when you update your library. This means that bug fixes increase the patch version (e.g., 1.1.0 => 1.1.1), functionality that is backward compatible increases the minor (e.g., 1.1.0 => 1.2.0), and backward-incompatible changes increase the major version (e.g., 1.0.0 => 2.0.0). This is especially important in Rust because Cargo allows you to specify dependencies solely by major: `trybuild = "1"`, for example. Introducing a breaking change without bumping the major version might cause projects to suddenly and unexpectedly break.

10.6 *From the real world*

Many Rust crates have excellent documentation. Go to the `lib.rs` of the libraries we discussed in this book, and you will find both inner documentation for the crate and outer documentation for the most important functionality. I will let you explore their documentation on your own.

Instead, we can briefly talk about features and multiple macros. Have you ever had this happen? You add `serde` to a project and put a `derive(Deserialize)` on a struct, and Rust does not know what to do because you forgot that the macro is hidden behind a feature. Unsurprisingly, you will find the list of `serde` features under `serde/Cargo .toml`, including one called `derive`. This also activates the `serde_derive` dependency:

```
[features]
default = ["std"]
# Provide derive(Serialize, Deserialize) macros.
derive = ["serde_derive"]
# etc.
```

In `serde/lib.rs`, you find a reexport of the two derive macros, hidden behind that feature:

```
#[cfg(feature = "serde_derive")]
#[macro_use]
extern crate serde_derive;

#[cfg(feature = "serde_derive")]
pub use serde_derive::{Deserialize, Serialize};
```

Leptos, to take one other example, has a `leptos_macro` directory where `lib.rs` exports a derive macro (`Params`), two attribute macros (`server` and `component`), and two function-like macros (`template` and `view`). It has feature flags for things like server-side rendering and tracing.

To finish this final chapter, we will explore in detail how `#[tokio::main]` works from the beginning until the end. Under the `tokio` directory of the Tokio repository, we find a list of features, including the `macros` feature. It points to the `tokio-macros` dependency.

> **Listing 10.19   Root `Cargo.toml` of Tokio**

```
[features]
macros = ["tokio-macros"]
# ...
[dependencies]
tokio-macros = { version = "1.7.0", path = "../tokio-macros",
 optional = true }
```

Head to the `tokio-macros` directory. In its `Cargo.toml`, we find that this is indeed a procedural macro library (`proc-macro = true`), with the usual dependencies (`syn`, `quote`, and `proc-macro2`). Moving on to `lib.rs`, we see it exposes several attribute macros, including #[tokio::test] and #[tokio::main]. Each macro has extensive outer documentation—about 170 lines of it, in the case of main. We can see that both the attributes and the decorated item of this attribute macro are used by the entry::main function. The workaround mentioned in listing 10.20 is an ambiguity caused by this function being called main. And, in Rust, that name serves a special purpose as an entry point.

Listing 10.20 `lib.rs` of the `tokio-macros` directory

```
/// Marks async function to be executed by the selected runtime.
/// ...
#[proc_macro_attribute]
#[cfg(not(test))] // Work around for rust-lang/rust#62127
pub fn main(args: TokenStream, item: TokenStream) -> TokenStream {
    entry::main(args, item, true)
}
```

Within entry::main, the item is first parsed into an ItemFn. In other words, Tokio expects a function, turning a syn error into a compilation error if that is not the case. Next, and only after doing a few checks, the configuration is created based on the attributes that are parsed by AttributeArgs (which, as mentioned, is no longer available in syn version 2).

  If both input and configuration are valid, parse_knobs will create an output stream.

Listing 10.21 The macro entry point in `entry.rs`

```
pub(crate) fn main(args: TokenStream, item: TokenStream, multi_thread: bool)
    -> TokenStream {
    let input: syn::ItemFn = match syn::parse(item.clone()) {      ⟵ Parses the input as
        Ok(it) => it,                                                a function or
        Err(e) => return token_stream_with_error(item, e),           returns an error
    };

    let config = if input.sig.ident == "main"
    && !input.sig.inputs.is_empty() {
        let msg = "the main function cannot accept arguments";
        Err(syn::Error::new_spanned(&input.sig.ident, msg))
    } else {
        AttributeArgs::parse_terminated        ⟵ If the function signature is
            .parse(args)                         valid, parses the attributes
            .and_then(|args| build_config(       and builds the configuration
                input.clone(),
                args,
                false,
                multi_thread))
    };

    match config {
        Ok(config) => parse_knobs(input, false, config),     ⟵ Produces output if
        Err(e) => token_stream_with_error(                     both function and
            parse_knobs(input, false, DEFAULT_ERROR_CONFIG),   config are valid
        e
```

```
        ),
    }
}
```

Listing 10.22 shows `build_config`, which we will have to show in two parts. After making sure the expected `async` keyword is present, a new, mutable configuration is created. Next, the code loops over the available arguments, adding its key-value pairs (`NameValue`) to the configuration, one by one. If an unknown identifier is found, an error is returned.

Listing 10.22 `build_config` in `entry.rs` (part 1)

```rust
fn build_config(
    input: syn::ItemFn, args: AttributeArgs,
    is_test: bool, rt_multi_thread: bool,
) -> Result<FinalConfig, syn::Error> {
    if input.sig.asyncness.is_none() {
        let msg = "the `async` keyword is missing ...";
        return Err(syn::Error::new_spanned(input.sig.fn_token, msg));
    }
    let mut config = Configuration::new(is_test, rt_multi_thread);
    let macro_name = config.macro_name();

    for arg in args {
        match arg {
            syn::NestedMeta::Meta(syn::Meta::NameValue(namevalue)) => {
                let ident = namevalue.path.get_ident()
                    .ok_or_else(|| {
                        syn::Error::new_spanned(
                            &namevalue,
                            "Must have specified ident"
                        )
                    })?
                    .to_string().to_lowercase();
                match ident.as_str() {
                    "worker_threads" => {
                        config.set_worker_threads(
                            namevalue.lit.clone(),
                            syn::spanned::Spanned::span(&namevalue.lit),
                        )?;
                    }
                    // more matching
                    name => {
                        let msg = format!(
                            "Unknown attribute {} is specified ...",
                            name,
                        );
                        return Err(syn::Error::new_spanned(namevalue, msg));
                    }
                }
            }
        }
        // ...
    }
}
```

The next code listing shows that, despite Tokio only allowing key-value pairs for attributes, the `match` does check if `path` values are present. Why? To give back a helpful error! The given path attribute is checked against known names. That way, the error can give a hint on how you should set that particular argument. For example, adding `#[tokio::main(multi_thread)]` to a function results in `error: Set the runtime flavor with #[tokio::main(flavor = "multi_thread")]`. For unknown path arguments, as well as miscellaneous unrecognized arguments, a generic "unknown attribute" error is thrown, pointing to the correct token.

Listing 10.23   build_config in entry.rs (part 2)

```
fn build_config(
    input: syn::ItemFn, args: AttributeArgs,
    is_test: bool, rt_multi_thread: bool,
) -> Result<FinalConfig, syn::Error> {
            // ...
            syn::NestedMeta::Meta(syn::Meta::Path(path)) => {
                let name = path
                    .get_ident()
                    .ok_or_else(|| syn::Error::new_spanned(
                        &path,
                        "Must have specified ident"
                    ))?
                    .to_string()
                    .to_lowercase();
                let msg = match name.as_str() {
                    "threaded_scheduler" | "multi_thread" => {
                        format!(
                            "Set the runtime flavor with ...",
                            macro_name
                        )
                    }
                    // same for other possible attributes and unknown ones
                };
                return Err(syn::Error::new_spanned(path, msg));
            }
            other => {
                return Err(syn::Error::new_spanned(
                    other,
                    "Unknown attribute inside the macro",
                ));
            }
        }
    }
    config.build()
}
```

Tokio does not accept path arguments. But, if one is present, it tries to give back a helpful error.

A generic error for unknown arguments, pointing to the faulty token (other)

`parse_knobs` is also too long to show in full, so I have left out some things that are only relevant for the `test` macro and some code for handling a rename of the `tokio` package. First, the signature of the input is modified, removing the `async`. This is because Rust does not allow its main functions to be asynchronous. So, after removing the `async`, Tokio builds a `Runtime` and blocks on the existing code (contained within `body`), removing the need for asynchronicity. Two more things to note:

- The `header` is optionally generated, depending on the incoming Boolean value, similar to what we did in this chapter with `exclude`.
- Some Clippy linting is disabled, like a warning for the use of `expect` in the building of `Runtime`. You do not want to show users a warning that they can't do anything about.

Listing 10.24 `parse_knobs` in `entry.rs`

```
fn parse_knobs(mut input: syn::ItemFn, is_test: bool, config: FinalConfig)
    -> TokenStream {
    input.sig.asyncness = None;

    let mut rt = // ...              Creates the basic
    if let Some(v) = config.worker_threads {   runtime configuration
        rt = quote! { #rt.worker_threads(#v) };   Adds some additional
    }                                              information if it is present
    // more config

    let header = if is_test {        The header is conditionally
        quote! {                     added to the generated code.
            #[::core::prelude::v1::test]
        }
    } else {
        quote! {}
    };

    let body = &input.block;
    let brace_token = input.block.brace_token;
    let body_ident = quote! { body };
    let block_expr = quote_spanned! {last_stmt_end_span=>
        #[allow(clippy::expect_used,
        [clippy::diverging_sub_expression)]]
        {
            return #rt
                .enable_all()
                .build()
                .expect("Failed building the Runtime")
                .block_on(#body_ident);   Builds the Runtime and blocks on
        }                                 the existing content of the function
    };

    input.block = syn::parse2(quote! {
        {
            #body
            #block_expr
        }
    }).expect("Parsing failure");
    input.block.brace_token = brace_token;

    let result = quote! {
        #header
        #input
```

```
    };
                              ┌ Returns after adding
    result.into()    ◁──┘ everything to result
}
```

With that, you know—in broad terms—how this quite famous macro does its work.

10.7 *Where to go from here*

Congratulations on making it to the end of this book! Together, we have explored declarative and procedural macros in a wide variety of use cases. Sometimes we added methods to structs and enums; in other cases, we changed their fields or modified function signatures and returns. Plus, you also learned about testing, error handling, and documentation and saw a lot of real-world examples.

That being said, some interesting tools and functions did not make the cut. `syn-structure` (https://docs.rs/synstructure/latest/synstructure), for example, is a tool that helps you implement derive macros. `proc-macro-crate` (https://crates.io/crates/proc-macro-crate) helps you find the name of the crate that your macro is declared in, even if it was changed in the user's application. And hidden behind `syn` feature flags are `visit` (https://docs.rs/syn/latest/syn/visit/index.html) and `fold` (https://docs.rs/syn/latest/syn/fold/index.html), two powerful helpers for stepping through nodes like an expression. You will find some information on how to use those two in the documentation. You can also check out the blog post (https://mng.bz/DdjR) I wrote about `Fold` for some inspiration or guidance. Plus, there are lots more libraries that use macros in unusual, interesting, creative ways, that are ready to be explored. If you run into trouble, you will find a lot of helpful people ready to answer macro questions on both Stack Overflow and Reddit.

Thank you for reading. I hope all of this was of some use to you. And, to end with the words of AWS's Werner Vogels: "Now go build!"

Exercises

See the appendix for solutions.

1 Make sure that we can accept both `path` and `exclude` as macro properties.
2 Instead of adding `exclude` to our attribute macro, use a feature.

Summary

- A macro library can only export procedural macros, but there is no limit on number or type.
- Features can hide optional functionality, making sure users only pull in the *library* code that they need.
- When it comes to avoiding useless *generated* code, you can use feature flags or your own custom attributes.
- A production-grade macro should have good test coverage and error handling.
- It should also have proper documentation, preferably including doctests.

appendix
Exercise solutions

Chapter 2

1 *Fill in the question marks (???), and make the following declarative macro compile.*

This is one possible solution. `ty` seems most appropriate, though `ident`—for example—would also work:

```
macro_rules! hello_world {
    ($something:ty) => {
        impl $something {
            fn hello_world(&self) {
                println!("Hello world!")
            }
        }
    };
}

struct Example {}
hello_world!(Example);

fn main() {
    let e = Example {};
    e.hello_world();
}
```

2 *In our first declarative macro example, we use* `expr` *in some of our matches. But that was not our only option. Try to replace that with* `literal`, `tt`, `ident`, *or* `ty`. *Which ones work? Which don't? Do you understand why?*

`literal` will work because we are passing in literal values (e.g., `my_vec!(1, 2, 3)`). `tt` will work as well. As we said, it accepts basically anything. `ident` will not work because we are not passing in identifiers. A valid example—that would get accepted—might be `NameOfThisStructIDeclaredInMyCode`. `ty` will not work either, because we are not passing in types. Valid examples include `String`, `i32`, etc.

3 *Allow trailing comments in the* `my_vec` *macro. You can do this by writing another matcher, but there's a simple solution with even less repetition. If you need help, take a look at the* `vec` *macro from the standard library for inspiration.*

This solution is based on the standard library code:

```
macro_rules! my_vec {
    () => {
        Vec::new()
    };
    ($($x:expr),+ $(,)?) => (
        {
            let mut v = Vec::new();
            $(
                v.push($x);
            )+
            v
        }
    );
}
```

Alternatively, you could add another rule for matching a trailing comma. In that case, you probably want to define the transcriber body only once and make one of the rules for multiple elements use the other one internally.

4 *Another thing I like for newtypes is convenient* `From` *implementations. Write a macro that generates them for our four newtypes. Alternatively, you can go for* `TryFrom` *since that is a more suitable choice when input validation is required.*

To be brief, this solution only shows the `From` implementations. It is quite similar to our earlier code for getting the underlying value:

```
macro_rules! generate_from {
    ($struct_type:ident) => {
        generate_from!($struct_type,String);
    };
    ($struct_type:ident,$return_type:ty) => {
        impl From<$struct_type> for $return_type {
            fn from(f: $struct_type) -> Self {
                f.value
            }
        }
    }
}
```

5 *Now that we have two macros, we could make our lives even easier by creating a third macro,* `generate_newtypes_methods`, *that calls our existing two macros behind the scene:*

```
macro_rules! generate_newtypes_methods {
    ($struct_type:ident) => {
        generate_get_value_string!($struct_type,String);
        generate_from!($struct_type,String);
    };
```

```
        ($struct_type:ident,$return_type:ty) => {
            generate_get_value_string!($struct_type,$return_type);
            generate_from!($struct_type,$return_type);
        }
    }
}

generate_newtypes_methods!(FirstName);
generate_newtypes_methods!(Age,i32);
```

6 *Expand our* Account *example in listings 2.12 and 2.13 with dollar and euro currencies. You can use a hardcoded exchange rate of 2 dollars to 1 euro. All existing commands will require a currency type.*

This is one of several possible solutions. We are assuming the money in our accounts is in euros:

```
// account code from DSL chapter
enum Currency {
    Euro,
    Dollar
}

impl From<&str> for Currency {
    fn from(value: &str) -> Self {
        if value.contains("euro") {
            Currency::Euro
        } else {
            // simple fallback to dollars
            Currency::Dollar
        }
    }
}

impl Currency {
    fn calculate(&self, amount: u32) -> u32 {
        match self {
            Currency::Euro => amount,
            Currency::Dollar => amount * 2
        }
    }
}

macro_rules! exchange {
    (Give $amount:literal $currency:literal to $name:ident) => {
        let curr: Currency = $currency.into();
        $name.add(curr.calculate($amount))
    }
    // others are similar to the above
}

fn main() {
        let mut the_poor = Account {
            money: 0,
        };

        exchange!(Give 10 "euros" to the_poor);
```

```
        exchange!(Give 10 "dollars" to the_poor);
        exchange!(Give 1 "euro" to the_poor);
}
```

Because we want to change a string slice to a currency, we need quotation marks around "euros" and "dollars". You could also experiment with tt and ty for alternative solutions. Or add match arms that literally match the two currencies, e.g., Give $amount:literal euros to..., Give $amount:literal dollars to..., etc.

Chapter 3

1 *Fill in the question marks (???) and make the following derive macro compile.*

Solution:

```
// imports

#[proc_macro_derive(UpperCaseName)]
pub fn uppercase(item: TokenStream) -> TokenStream {
    let ast = parse_macro_input!(item as DeriveInput);
    let name = ast.ident;
    let uppercase_name = name.to_string().to_uppercase();

    let add_uppercase = quote! {
        impl #name {
            fn uppercase(&self) {
                println!("{}", #uppercase_name);
            }
        }
    };

    add_uppercase.into()
}
```

The name of the macro can be deduced from the usage example. And we learned that macros return a TokenStream, that a DeriveInput can be used to parse input and that we can use hashtags to refer to variables.

2 *Try changing the name of the macro inside* lib.rs *and running the application. What error do you get? What do you have to do to fix things?*

If I change the name of the macro to "Helloz," I will get a very helpful error:

```
error: cannot find derive macro `Hello` in this scope
 --> src/main.rs:4:10
  |
4 | #[derive(Hello)]
  |          ^^^^^ help: a derive macro with a similar name...
  |
  |
6 | pub fn hello(item: TokenStream) -> TokenStream {
  | ---------------------------------------------- similarly named...
```

But that is only the case if I stay close to the original. If I rename it to "AnotherName," I get

```
error: cannot find derive macro `Hello` in this scope
  --> src/main.rs:4:10
   |
 4 | #[derive(Hello)]
   |          ^^^^^
```

The fix is easy. Change every derive annotation to point to the new name. For example:

```
#[derive(AnotherName)]
struct Example;
```

3 *Add a function called* testing_testing *to the output of our macro. This is an associated function, one that takes no* &self *parameter. It should write* "One two three" *to the console:*

```
use quote::quote;
use proc_macro::TokenStream;
use syn::{parse_macro_input, DeriveInput};

#[proc_macro_derive(Hello)]
pub fn hello(item: TokenStream) -> TokenStream {
    let ast = parse_macro_input!(item as DeriveInput);
    let name = ast.ident;

    let add_hello_world = quote! {
        impl #name {
            fn hello_world(&self) {
                println!("Hello world")
            }

            fn testing_testing() {
                println!("One two three")
            }
        }
    };

    add_hello_world.into()
}
```

4 *See if you can output a greeting followed by the name of the input (e.g., "Hello, Example"). Fair warning: passing* #name *to print will not be enough because that's an identifier, and you need a string. So either call* to_string *on the identifier and save the result in a variable or use the* stringify *macro to change the* #name *into a string for you.*

This is a bit more challenging, but don't worry, we will encounter these complexities in upcoming chapters as well:

```
use quote::quote;
use proc_macro::TokenStream;
use syn::{parse_macro_input, DeriveInput};

#[proc_macro_derive(Hello)]
pub fn hello(item: TokenStream) -> TokenStream {
```

```
    let ast = parse_macro_input!(item as DeriveInput);
    let name = ast.ident;

    let add_hello_world = quote! {
        impl #name {
            fn hello_world(&self) {
                println!("Hello {}", stringify!(#name))
            }
        }
    };

    add_hello_world.into()
}
```

Forget to add the `stringify`, and you will get `Example doesn't implement std::fmt ::Display`.

Chapter 4

1 *Fill in the question marks (???) and make the following macro compile.*

Solution:

```
#[proc_macro_attribute]
pub fn delete(_attr: TokenStream, _item: TokenStream) -> TokenStream {
    let public_version = quote! {};
    public_version.into()
}
```

2 *Handle structs with unnamed fields. If you use matching, your new match arm will probably look a bit like this:* `Struct(DataStruct { fields: Unnamed(FieldsUnnamed { ref unnamed, .. }), .. })`.... *Note that you will need to decide whether to output a "normal" struct or an unnamed one.*

Here are highlights of one possible solution (you can find the entire solution on GitHub):

```
use quote::{__private, quote};
// other imports and some functions

fn unnamed_fields_public(
    fields: &Punctuated<Field, Comma>,
) -> Map<Iter<Field>, fn(&Field) -> __private::TokenStream> {
    fields.iter().map(|f| {
        let ty = &f.ty;
        quote! { pub #ty }
    })
}

fn generate_unnamed_output<'a>(
    struct_name: Ident,
    builder_fields:
    Map<Iter<'a, Field>, fn(&'a Field) -> __private::TokenStream>,
) -> quote::__private::TokenStream {
```

```
        quote!(
            pub struct #struct_name(
                #(#builder_fields,)*
            );
        )
}

#[proc_macro_attribute]
pub fn public(_attr: TokenStream, item: TokenStream)
    -> TokenStream {
    let ast = parse_macro_input!(item as DeriveInput);
    let name = ast.ident;

    let basic_output = match ast.data {
        // code for named fields structs
        Struct(DataStruct {
            fields: Unnamed(FieldsUnnamed { ref unnamed, .. }),
            ..
        }) => {
            let f = unnamed_fields_public(unnamed);
            generate_unnamed_output(name, f)
        }
        _ => unimplemented!("only works for structs"),
    };

    quote!(
        #basic_output
    ).into()
}
```

Instead of making the match output the fields, we now make it generate all our code, because while we are in the match, we know exactly what kind of struct (named or unnamed) we are dealing with. That makes it easier to generate the right kind of structure. The specific retrieval and transformation logic has been moved to separate functions. This time we are using the private TokenStream from quote to avoid the additional dependency—and you can see why we said a collect could give you a nicer signature. Map<Iter<'a, Field>, fn(&'a Field) => quote::__private::TokenStream> is not great. Alternatively, you could go for an impl Iterator, which we will sometimes do in subsequent chapters.

3 *Make our macro handle enums. Two things to keep in mind: First, you do not need to add pub to the fields (only to the enum), but you do have to retrieve and re-add them (they are called* variants *under* Enum, DataEnum). *Second, your code will now also have to decide whether it has to return an enum or a struct.*

Here are highlights of one possible solution (you can find the entire solution on GitHub):

```
// imports and some functions

fn generate_enum_output(
        enum_name: Ident,
```

```
                variants: &Punctuated<Variant, Comma>
        ) -> __private::TokenStream {
        let as_iter = variants.into_iter();

        quote!(
            pub enum #enum_name {
                #(#as_iter,)*
            }
        )
}

#[proc_macro_attribute]
pub fn public(_: TokenStream, item: TokenStream) -> TokenStream {
    let ast = parse_macro_input!(item as DeriveInput);
    let name = ast.ident;

    let basic_output = match ast.data {
        // struct code
        Enum(DataEnum { ref variants, .. }) => {
            generate_enum_output(name, variants)
        },
        _ => unimplemented!("only works for structs and enums"),
    };

    quote!(
        #basic_output
    ).into()
}
```

The only things that are different are the location where we get our fields/variants and the fact that we do not need to add any visibility modifiers to those variants. Note the into_iter for the variants, since quote does not know how to handle Punctu-ated as an iterable.

4   *Keep the existing attributes of the struct instead of letting them disappear. This requires little more than getting the* attrs *(attributes) of our* item *and adding them above the struct. You might have to play around with the* quote *syntax a bit. Just remember that—unlike before— we do not need a comma to mark the end of an attribute.*

Here are highlights of one possible solution (you can find the entire solution on GitHub):

```
// imports and functions

#[proc_macro_attribute]
pub fn public(_: TokenStream, item: TokenStream) -> TokenStream {
    let ast = parse_macro_input!(item as DeriveInput);
    let name = ast.ident;
    let attributes = &ast.attrs;

    let basic_output = // create the output as before

    quote!(
        #(#attributes)*
```

```
        #basic_output
    ).into()
}
```

As you can see, this is quite easy: retrieve the `attributes` property from our AST and add it, without comma, to the output as an iterable. If you are absent-minded and add a comma to separate the attributes—for example, `#(#attributes,)*`—you will get a compile error: `expected item after attributes`.

5 *Combine all of these exercises into a single solution.*

See GitHub for the full solution. This brings everything we did earlier together in one big macro:

```
// imports and functions

#[proc_macro_attribute]
pub fn public(_: TokenStream, item: TokenStream) -> TokenStream {
    let ast = parse_macro_input!(item as DeriveInput);
    let name = ast.ident;
    let attributes = &ast.attrs;

    let basic_output = match ast.data {
        Struct(DataStruct {
            fields: Named(FieldsNamed { ref named, .. }),
            ..
        }) => {
            let f = named_fields_public(named);
            generate_named_output(name, f)
        }
        Struct(DataStruct {
            fields: Unnamed(FieldsUnnamed { ref unnamed, .. }),
            ..
        }) => {
            let f = unnamed_fields_public(unnamed);
            generate_unnamed_output(name, f)
        }
        Enum(DataEnum { ref variants, .. }) => {
            generate_enum_output(name, variants)
        },
        _ => unimplemented!("only works for structs and enums"),
    };

    quote!(
        #(#attributes)*
        #basic_output
    ).into()
}
```

6 *Using* `Punctuated::<Ident, Colon>` *is one way to parse the field, but in the case of our public fields macro, there is an even simpler solution. Just put everything in variables, as we did with* `Visibility`, *and pass the useful things to* `StructField`. *Change our* `Parse` *implementation to use this simpler parsing.*

We remove the `Punctuated` bit and simply parse field after field. We do not unwrap the colon since we do not need it, but it should always be there, so unwrapping and ignoring is a perfectly valid solution as well:

```
impl Parse for StructField {
    fn parse(input: ParseStream) -> Result<Self, syn::Error> {
        let _vis: Result<Visibility, _> = input.parse();
        let name: Ident = input.parse().unwrap();
        let _colon: Result<Colon, _> = input.parse();
        let ty: Ident = input.parse().unwrap();

        Ok(StructField {
            name,
            ty,
        })
    }
}
```

Chapter 5

1   *Write a function-like macro to generate a struct method that prints "Hello, world." It should only take the struct name as an input. Remember to declare a struct with the given name in your application code.*

Our macro code expects an identifier—the struct name—so we ask `syn` to parse that for us. Once we have the identifier, we can pass it to the output:

```
// imports

#[proc_macro]
pub fn hello(item: TokenStream) -> TokenStream {
    let ast = parse_macro_input!(item as Ident);

    quote!(
        impl #ast {
            fn hello_world(&self) {
                println!("Hello world")
            }
        }
    ).into()
}
```

We need to create the struct ourselves in the application (`main.rs`). And now we have created a method without passing in the entire struct:

```
use hello_world_only_name_exercise_macro::hello;

struct Example {
    another_value: String
}

hello!(Example);

fn main() {
```

```
    let e = Example {
        another_value: "does not disappear".to_string(),
    };
    e.hello_world();
}
```

2 *Our* private *macro creates convenience methods, but the fields can still be public and directly
accessible and our newly generated methods are not public. Change the macro so that it sets all
fields to private and generates public methods. You can ignore the complexity of re-adding the
struct attributes* and *hardcode a* new *method for your example struct.*

We need to use the field information in multiple places. So we should write a separate
method to retrieve the field name and type:

```
fn get_field_info(ast: &DeriveInput) -> Vec<(&Ident, &Type)> {
    match ast.data {
        Struct(
            DataStruct {
                fields: Named(
                    FieldsNamed {
                        ref named, ..
                    }), ..
            }
        ) => named,
        _ => unimplemented!(
            "only works for structs with named fields"
        ),
    }
        .iter()
        .map(|f| {
            let field_name = f.ident.as_ref().take().unwrap();
            let type_name = &f.ty;

            (field_name, type_name)
        })
        .collect()
}
```

Now we use this information to generate our methods. The logic is almost the same as
before, except the input is now a &Vec<(&Ident, &Type)> (a reference to the vector
makes it easier to pass the field information to multiple methods). And inside the
map, we get the field name and type from the tuple we receive:

```
fn generated_methods(
        fields: &Vec<(&Ident, &Type)>
    ) -> Vec<TokenStream2> {
    fields
        .iter()
        .map(|f| {
            let (field_name, type_name) = f;
            let method_name =
                Ident::new(
```

```
                    &format!("get_{field_name}"),
                    Span::call_site()
                );

            quote!(
                pub fn #method_name(&self) -> &#type_name {
                    &self.#field_name
                }
            )
        })
        .collect()
}
```

Making our fields private is even easier than making them public:

```
fn generate_private_fields(
        fields: &Vec<(&Ident, &Type)>
    ) -> Vec<TokenStream2> {
    fields
        .iter()
        .map(|f| {
            let (field_name, type_name) = f;

            quote!(
                #field_name: #type_name
            )
        })
        .collect()
}
```

In our `lib.rs` file, we create the struct anew in our output with the field information we generated. We also have a hardcoded `new` method for creating our `Example`. In the next chapter, we will look into generating real constructor methods:

```
// imports

#[proc_macro]
pub fn private(item: TokenStream) -> TokenStream {
    // ast and name
    let fields = get_field_info(&ast);
    let output_fields = generate_private_fields(&fields);
    let methods = generated_methods(&fields);

    quote!(
        pub struct #name {
            #(#output_fields,)*
        }

        impl #name {
            pub fn new() -> Self {
                Example {
                    string_value: "value".to_string(),
                    number_value: 2,
                }
            }
```

```
            #(#methods)*
        }
    ).into()
}
```

3 *Go look at the* Token! *source code, and see what other tokens are available. Try a different one for our composing macro, and fix the application code.*

A selection of the available tokens:

```
"&"       pub struct And/1      /// bitwise and logical AND...
"&&"      pub struct AndAnd/2   /// lazy AND, borrow, references...
// ...
"!="      pub struct Ne/2       /// not equal
"!"       pub struct Not/1      /// bitwise and logical NOT...
"|"       pub struct Or/1       /// bitwise and logical OR...
"|="      pub struct OrEq/2     /// bitwise OR assignment
// ...
```

An exclamation mark might be fun. This is what changes in lib.rs. For fun and profit, I am using the type (Not) that the Token macro will resolve to in the struct definition. In parse, we are using Token!(!) to get the Not type:

```
use proc_macro::TokenStream;
use proc_macro2::Ident;
use quote::{quote, ToTokens};
use syn::{parse_macro_input, Token};
use syn::parse::{Parse, ParseStream};
use syn::punctuated::Punctuated;
use syn::token::Not;

struct ComposeInput {
    expressions: Punctuated::<Ident, Not>,
}

impl Parse for ComposeInput {
    fn parse(input: ParseStream) -> Result<Self, syn::Error> {
        Ok(
            ComposeInput {
                expressions: Punctuated::<Ident, Token!(!)>
                    ::parse_terminated(input).unwrap(),
            }
        )
    }
}
```

The code in our application changes slightly:

```
// imports and example functions

fn main() {
    let compose = compose!(add_one ! add_one ! stringify);
    println!("{:?}", compose(5));
}
```

Chapter 6

1 *We never did write any white-box tests for structs that actually have fields, so add one that runs against the final version of our code.*

Here is a test for a struct with one field:

```
#[test]
fn builder_struct_for_one_field_struct_should_be_present_in_out() {
    let input = quote! {
        struct StructWithOneField {
            string_value: String,
        }
    };
    let expected = quote! {
        struct StructWithOneFieldBuilder {
            string_value: Option<String>,
        }

        impl StructWithOneFieldBuilder {
            pub fn string_value(mut self, input: String) -> Self {
                self.string_value = Some(input);
                self
            }

            pub fn build(self) -> StructWithOneField {
                StructWithOneField {
                    string_value: self.string_value
                      .expect(
                          concat!("field not set: " , "string_value")
                      ),
                }
            }
        }

        impl StructWithOneField {
            pub fn builder() -> StructWithOneFieldBuilder {
                StructWithOneFieldBuilder {
                    string_value: None,
                }
            }
        }
    };

    let actual = create_builder(input);

    assert_eq!(actual.to_string(), expected.to_string());
}
```

2 *We only wrote code for handling structs with named fields, not the unnamed variety, so we should cover that failure case with another* trybuild *compilation test.*

Add the following code to our tests/fails directory, next to build_enum.rs. You can pick any name you want:

```
use builder_macro::Builder;

#[derive(Builder)]
pub struct Ano(String,i32);

fn main() {}
```

As before, after running it for the first time, you should check the error you get back, which will look something like this:

```
error: proc-macro derive panicked
 --> tests/fails/build_anyonymous_struct.rs:4:10
  |
4 | #[derive(Builder)]
  |          ^^^^^^^
  |
  = help: message: not implemented: Only implemented for structs
```

If the error matches your expectations, you should add this file to your `fails` directory. The test should be green now.

3 *In Rocket, you can add headers to functions that make them into endpoints for calls. If you add* #[get("/world")] *and* #[catch(404)] *to a function called* world, *you get an error that looks like this:*

```
error[E0428]: the name `world` is defined multiple times
  --> hello/src/main.rs:23:1
   |
22 | #[get("/world")]
   | ---------------- previous definition of the type `world` here
23 | #[catch(404)]
   | ^^^^^^^^^^^^^ `world` redefined here
   |
   = note: `world` must be defined only once in the type
 namespace of this module
```

What could be causing this? Can you think of a way this problem might be avoided?

When you have two (attribute) macros and get an error regarding a duplicate definition, your first guess should be that both macros are generating custom things (functions, structs, traits) in too broad a scope, and that these definitions are colliding with each other. You can confirm your guess by expanding the code, which will in this case reveal two structs named world being created. If you remove one macro, one definition disappears. Clearly, each macro is generating a single struct. You could also go digging through the code. At the time of writing, you would end up in core/codegen/src/attribute/route/mod.rs, which has a function called codegen_route. That function is outputting this code:

```
/// Rocket code generated proxy structure.
#vis struct #handler_fn_name { }
```

Based on `handler_fn_name`, you can guess that this struct has the same name as the function that is annotated (i.e., `world`). Mystery solved!

Depending on the context, there are several ways to avoid this problem, and we have discussed most of them before. A more limited scope for the struct and other elements that you are creating (i.e., putting them between {}) is a very simple and useful solution, but it might not work depending on requirements (where will the struct be used?).

Another option is making the name more unique and less likely to collide with others. By keeping the name without uppercasing it (`world` instead of `World`, which is the standard naming convention for structs), the creators of Rocket have at the very least made collisions with structs in the user's code base very unlikely. Unfortunately, using the name as a prefix or suffix will not work in this case, because even then the two macros will generate the same name. Random suffixes would work, though in rare cases (depending on uniqueness and bad luck), you will get very weird errors (when, once in a blue moon, the supposedly unique suffixes turn out to be the same).

The most obvious solution, though, is a better error message. The macros could check whether any other Rocket macros are present on the function. If two Rocket macros for one function do not make sense, a custom error should report this to the user. For example, `#[tokio::test]` checks whether a second test (`#[test]`) attribute has been added to a function, and throws a `second test attribute is supplied` error if this is the case. But creating custom errors is the topic for the next chapter.

Chapter 7

1 *Rewrite the* `public fields` *macro to mutate the incoming* `TokenStream` *instead of creating a brand-new one.*

There are several solutions. What complicates matters a bit is that `Data`—among others—does not implement `Parse`. `FieldsNamed` does, however, so we put our public fields in curly braces. That way, we can parse them into `FieldsNamed`. And we wrap the output in the correct `Data` struct, replacing the existing `data` field of our AST (which has become mutable to make this possible). We also set the visibility to `public`. In both cases, we make good use of the `Default` trait. When that's done, we can change it into a `TokenStream`:

```
// imports

#[proc_macro_attribute]
pub fn public(_attr: TokenStream, item: TokenStream) -> TokenStream {
    let mut ast = parse_macro_input!(item as DeriveInput);

    let fields = // get fields if named, else throw panic

    let builder_fields = fields.iter().map(|f| {
        let name = &f.ident;
        let ty = &f.ty;
        quote! { pub #name: #ty }
    });
```

```
        let builder_fields_with_braces = quote!(
            {
                #(#builder_fields,)*
            }
        );

        ast.data = Data::Struct(DataStruct {
            struct_token: Default::default(),
            fields: Fields::Named(
                parse2(builder_fields_with_braces).unwrap()
            ),
            semi_token: None,
        });
        ast.vis = Visibility::Public(Default::default());

        ast.to_token_stream().into()
}
```

The resulting code is actually *longer* than the original code. But it is better at keeping existing attributes.

2 *Our function-like macro for generating methods throws* unimplemented *for non-struct inputs. Use* syn::Error *instead. You can point to the span of the name.*

Here is one possible solution. In the case of an enum, we do a bit of extra effort to help the user and point specifically to the "enum token." In other cases, we point to the name of the invalid struct or union:

```
// imports and unchanged functions

fn get_field_info(ast: &DeriveInput)
    -> Result<Vec<(&Ident, &Type)>, syn::Error> {
    Ok(match ast.data {
        Struct(
            DataStruct {
                fields: Named(
                    FieldsNamed {
                        ref named, ..
                    }), ..
            }
        ) => named,
        Enum(ref d) => return Err(
            syn::Error::new(
                d.enum_token.span(),
                "does not work for enums"
            )
        ),
        _ => return Err(
            syn::Error::new(
                ast.ident.span(),
                "only works for structs with named fields"
            )
        ),
    }
        .iter()
```

```
        .map(|f| {
            let field_name = f.ident.as_ref().take().unwrap();
            let type_name = &f.ty;

            (field_name, type_name)
        })
        .collect())
}

#[proc_macro]
pub fn private(item: TokenStream) -> TokenStream {
    let ast = parse_macro_input!(item as DeriveInput);
    let name = &ast.ident;

    let fields = match get_field_info(&ast) {
        Ok(fields) => fields,
        Err(err) => return err.to_compile_error()
            .to_token_stream().into()
    };

    // more unchanged code
}
```

3 *Now avoid the* unimplemented *with* proc_macro_error.

abort is sufficient because there is only one place our code throws an error:

```
// imports and unchanged functions

fn get_field_info(ast: &DeriveInput) -> Vec<(&Ident, &Type)> {
    match ast.data {
        Struct(
            DataStruct {
                fields: Named(
                    FieldsNamed {
                        ref named, ..
                    }), ..
            }
        ) => named,
        Enum(ref d) => abort!(
                d.enum_token, "Does not work for enums!".to_string();
                help = "This macro can only be used on structs"
        ),
        _ => abort!(
            ast.ident,
            "Only works for structs with named fields".to_string()
        ),
    }
        .iter()
        .map(|f| {
            let field_name = f.ident.as_ref().take().unwrap();
            let type_name = &f.ty;

            (field_name, type_name)
        })
```

```
            .collect()
    }

    #[proc_macro_error]
    #[proc_macro]
    pub fn private(item: TokenStream) -> TokenStream {
        // unchanged
    }
```

4 *Expand our "panic checks" to also transform panics in* while *expressions.*

This is relatively easy; just add a check for Expr::While and get the statements from body. At this point, you probably want to extract part of the map logic, which is identical to the one for Expr::If. (And IDE tools can do this refactoring for you):

```
fn handle_expression(expression: Expr, token: Option<Semi>) -> Stmt {
    match expression {
        Expr::If(mut ex_if) => {
            // same code as before
        },
        Expr::While(mut ex_while) => {
            let new_statements: Vec<Stmt> = ex_while.body.stmts
                .into_iter()
                .map(|s| match s {
                    Stmt::Macro(ref expr_macro) => {
                        let output = extract_panic_content(expr_macro);

                        if output.map(|v| v.is_empty()).unwrap_or(false) {
                            emit_error!(
                                expr_macro, "panic needs a message!"
                                    .to_string();
                                help = "try to add a message: panic!(...)";
                                note = "we will add the message to Result's
                                        Err"
                            );
                            s
                        } else {
                            extract_panic_content(expr_macro)
                                .map(|t| quote! {
                                    return Err(#t.to_string());
                                })
                                .map(parse2)
                                .map(Result::unwrap)
                                .unwrap_or(s)
                        }
                    }
                    _ => s
                })
                .collect();
            ex_while.body.stmts = new_statements;
            Stmt::Expr(Expr::While(ex_while), token)
        },
        _ => Stmt::Expr(expression, token)
    }
}
```

Here is some code to test our changes. What's important is that our while does not end with a semicolon. If it does, a panic will still be thrown, because we are specifically checking while *expressions*, not statements:

```
use panic_to_result_macro::panic_to_result;

#[derive(Debug)]
pub struct Person {
    name: String,
    age: u32,
}

#[panic_to_result]
fn create_person_while_loop(name: String, age: u32) -> Person {
    while true {
        panic!("strange failure");
    }
    Person {
        name,
        age,
    }
}

fn main() {}

#[cfg(test)]
mod tests {
    use super::*;

    #[test]
    fn should_err_on_while_loop() {
        let actual = create_person_while_loop("S".to_string(), 32);

        assert_eq!(
            actual.expect_err("This should be an err"),
            "strange failure".to_string()
        );
    }
}
```

But ideally, for these kinds of recursive code manipulations, you should turn to syn's Visit and Fold traits. See the brief note at the end of chapter 10.

Chapter 8

1 *In our rename discussion, we used a simple name for our attribute. However, some libraries specify the crate name within the attribute and have the specific command wrapped inside parentheses—for example, #[serde(rename = "name")]. Rewrite our #[rename("...")] to instead use #[builder(rename = "...")].*

By using #[builder(rename = "...")], it is much clearer that this attribute is specific to the builder macro. We start by adding attributes(builder) to our macro:

```
#[proc_macro_derive(Builder, attributes(builder))]
pub fn builder(item: TokenStream) -> TokenStream {
    create_builder(item.into()).into()
}
```

The only other change is in `builder_methods`, where we will replace our existing mapping. We use `parse_nested_meta`, check whether we have a `rename` attribute, and extract the string, while ignoring the equals sign:

```
// imports, other code

pub fn builder_methods(fields: &Punctuated<Field, Comma>)
    -> Vec<TokenStream> {
    fields.iter()
        .map(|f| {
            let (field_name, field_type) = get_name_and_type(f);
            let attr = extract_attribute_from_field(f, "builder")
                .map(|a| {
                    let mut content = None;

                    a.parse_nested_meta(|m| {
                        if m.path.is_ident("rename") {
                            let _: Token![=] = m.input.parse().unwrap();
                            let name: LitStr = m.input.parse().unwrap();
                            content = Some(
                                Ident::new(&name.value(),
                                    name.span()));
                        }
                        Ok(())
                    }).unwrap();
                    content.unwrap()
                });
            // if let... unchanged
        }).collect()
}
```

This is quite similar to `serde`, except that code is longer and uses some lower-level things like `lookahead`. We showed `from_ast` in section 8.9 of this chapter. If you follow `get_multiple_renames`, this is its implementation:

```
fn get_ser_and_de<'c, T, F, R>(
    cx: &'c Ctxt,
    attr: Symbol,
    meta: &ParseNestedMeta,
    f: F,
) -> syn::Result<(VecAttr<'c, T>, VecAttr<'c, T>)>
// where clause
{
    let mut ser_meta = VecAttr::none(cx, attr);
    let mut de_meta = VecAttr::none(cx, attr);

    let lookahead = meta.input.lookahead1();
    if lookahead.peek(Token![=]) {
        if let Some(both) = f(cx, attr, attr, meta)?.into() {
```

```
                    ser_meta.insert(&meta.path, both.clone());
                    de_meta.insert(&meta.path, both);
                }
            } else if lookahead.peek(token::Paren) {
                meta.parse_nested_meta(|meta| {
                    if meta.path == SERIALIZE {
                        if let Some(v) = f(cx, attr, SERIALIZE, &meta)?.into() {
                            ser_meta.insert(&meta.path, v);
                        }
                    }
                    // more conditionals
                    Ok(())
                })?;
            } else {
                return Err(lookahead.error());
            }
        }

        Ok((ser_meta, de_meta))
    }
```

What we did is quite similar to the first `if` branch, except we did not peek to see whether we had an equals sign. We just threw an error if the format did not match our expectations.

2 *Our default assertions generated a warning about naming conventions:* type __not-DefaultAssertion should have an upper camel case name. *Fix that warning.*

This is a minor change. We turn the `name` in `optional_default_asserts` into a string, uppercase it, and give it to `format_ident`. The change also solves another minor bug: the warning was pointing back to the offending field because we were passing its identifier (including its span) to `format_ident`. That might be confusing to users, who do not need to be aware of the existence of these additional structs:

```
pub fn optional_default_asserts(fields: &Punctuated<Field, Comma>)
    -> Vec<TokenStream> {
    fields.iter()
        .map(|f| {
            let name = &f.ident.as_ref().unwrap().to_string();
            let mut c = name.chars();
            let uppercased_name = c.next()
                    .unwrap()
                    .to_uppercase().collect::<String>() + c.as_str();

            let ty = &f.ty;
            let assertion_ident = format_ident!(
                    "__{}DefaultAssertion",
                    uppercased_name);

            quote_spanned! {ty.span()=>
                struct #assertion_ident where #ty: core::default::Default;
            }
        })
        .collect()
}
```

3 *Add an uppercase field-level attribute to our builder project, which will uppercase* String *types. As an extension, you could return an informative* (syn?) *error when the attribute is used on a field that is not a* String.

Based on our project after adding defaults, here is a test for the happy path:

```
#[test]
fn should_uppercase_the_attribute() {
    #[derive(Builder)]
    struct Gleipnir {
        #[uppercase]
        roots_of: String,
    }

    let gleipnir = Gleipnir::builder()
        .roots_of("upper".to_string())
        .build();

    assert_eq!(gleipnir.roots_of, "UPPER".to_string());
}
```

We have to add the attribute to our macro entry point:

```
#[proc_macro_derive(Builder, attributes(
builder_defaults,rename,uppercase))]]
pub fn builder(item: TokenStream) -> TokenStream {
    create_builder(item.into()).into()
}
```

To change our eventual output, we should expand original_struct_setters, where we will check for the uppercase attribute. If this attribute is present and the field is a String (we use a helper from a previous chapter to verify this), we do a to_uppercase on our optional value. If we have the attribute but the type is not a string, we return a syn::Error. In all other cases, there's nothing to do, so we return an empty stream. Finally, we have to append the uppercase mapping to our output, before the error handling. As we noted in an earlier chapter, our Vec<Result> is automatically transformed to Result<Vec>, which is convenient:

```
pub fn original_struct_setters(
        fields: &Punctuated<Field, Comma>,
        use_defaults: bool) -> Result<Vec<TokenStream>, syn::Error> {
    fields.iter().map(|f| {
        let (field_name, field_type) = get_name_and_type(f);
        let field_name_as_string = field_name
            .as_ref().unwrap().to_string();

        let uppercase_attr = extract_attribute_from_field(
            f,
            "uppercase"
        );

        let to_add = if uppercase_attr.is_some()
                && matches_type(field_type, "String") {
```

```
        quote! {
            .map(|v| v.to_uppercase())
        }
    } else if uppercase_attr.is_some() {
        return Err(
            syn::Error::new(field_name.span(),
            "can only use uppercase for String type"
        ));
    } else {
        quote!()
    };

    let handle_type = if use_defaults {
        default_fallback()
    } else {
        panic_fallback(field_name_as_string)
    };

    Ok(quote! {
        #field_name: self.#field_name #to_add.#handle_type
    })
    })
    .collect()
}
```

Now all that is left is to handle the potential Err in lib.rs:

```
let set_fields = match original_struct_setters(fields, use_defaults) {
    Ok(setters) => setters,
    Err(err) => return err.to_compile_error().to_token_stream()
};
```

The test should turn green. One alternative is to uppercase the field when it is set in the builder. You would need to check the uppercase attribute in builder_methods, uppercasing the string when the attribute is present: self.#field_name = Some (input.to_uppercase());.

Chapter 9

1 *Try to improve the input modeling. As discussed, it should be easier for users of* IacInput *to know that we have a bucket event. Optionally, you can also rework the creation of infrastructure using the new* IacInput.

All relevant changes are in input.rs, and lib.rs. input.rs is up first. The Bucket and Lambda structs are unchanged, except that we have made has_event private. While we still need that property internally, other parts of our code won't get access anymore.

IacInput has become an enum with two variants: Normal, which is a bucket, lambda, both, or nothing; and EventBucket, which is when we have a bucket linked with a lambda. In the latter situation, we know we have a bucket and lambda, so no option wrappers are required:

```
#[derive(Debug)]
pub enum IacInput {
    Normal(Option<Bucket>, Option<Lambda>),
    EventBucket(Bucket, Lambda),
}
```

has_resources has changed, in that we now use pattern matching. And its logic is now slightly simpler: if we have the EventBucket variant, we know we have resources. When we have a Normal with no properties, we do not have any resources. In every other situation, we return true. The wildcard is convenient, though not without risks: if we add another variant that might not have resources, we still return true and the compiler will not warn us:

```
impl IacInput {
    pub fn has_resources(&self) -> bool {
        match self {
            IacInput::EventBucket(_, _) => true,
            IacInput::Normal(None, None) => false,
            _ => true,
        }
    }
}
```

In Parse, we were already checking the has_event field to see if we also had a lambda. Now, when we do not throw an error, we return the EventBucket variant and unwrap the bucket and lambda. We already verified their existence, so we can use expect:

```
impl Parse for IacInput {
    fn parse(input: ParseStream) -> Result<Self, syn::Error> {
        // bucket and lambda variables
        // unchanged logic for finding the bucket and lambda

        if bucket.as_ref().map(|v| v.has_event).unwrap_or(false) {
            return if lambda.is_none() {
                Err(syn::Error::new(
                    input.span(),
                    "a lambda is required for an event ('=>')"
                ))
            } else {
                Ok(IacInput::EventBucket(
                    bucket.expect("only here when bucket exists"),
                    lambda.expect("just checked that this exists"),
                ))
            };
        }
        Ok(IacInput::Normal(bucket, lambda))
    }
}
```

Next, lib.rs and the changed create_infra method. (I have left out the println statements because they are not relevant.) The number of lines of code has not really changed, but in the EventBucket situation, things are now much simpler because we *know* we have a bucket, lambda, and event. If we have a `Normal` variant, we also have fewer situations to think about. I have kept the `if let`, but you could replace that with additional pattern matching. Plus, we managed to get rid of the mutable `output` variable that was used to store the optional lambda output:

```
async fn create_infra(iac_input: IacInput) -> Result<(), IacError> {
    let s3_client = S3Client::new().await;
    let lambda_client = LambdaClient::new().await;

    match iac_input {
        IacInput::Normal(bucket, lambda) => {
            if let Some(lambda) = lambda {
                lambda_client.create_lambda(&lambda).await?;
            }
            if let Some(bucket) = bucket {
                s3_client.create_bucket(&bucket).await?;
            }
        },
        IacInput::EventBucket(bucket, lambda) => {
            let output = lambda_client.create_lambda(&lambda).await?;
            s3_client.create_bucket(&bucket).await?;

            let lambda_arn = output.function_arn()
                .expect("creating a lambda should return its ARN");
            lambda_client.add_bucket_permission(&lambda, &bucket.name)
                .await?;
            s3_client.link_bucket_with_lambda(&bucket, &lambda_arn)
                .await?;
        }
    }
    Ok(())
}
```

Consider splitting up the `Normal` variant into a `None`, `Lambda`, `Bucket`, and `LambdaAndBucket`. It will make creating the infrastructure much simpler, though this approach will probably not scale if you add a lot of resources, since you will have an explosion of possible variants.

2 *Suggest the right resource (or property) when you cannot find a match (e.g., when you type "buck," the error should suggest "bucket"). One option is to use Levenshtein distance.*

We will use the code from before we added the AWS SDK because our solution only requires our parsing functionality. First, add this dependency to the macro:

```
edit-distance = "2.1.0"
```

All our changes are scoped to the `IacInput Parse` implementation, specifically, the `else if !input.is_empty()`, where we have something that is not a bucket or lambda.

First, we try to parse the input as an `Ident`, defaulting to the original error when we encounter problems. If the parse works, we can get the string representation of the identifier and compare its distance to the keywords. We won't return messages when the distance is very large, because it does not make sense to suggest one of our two keywords when the input has absolutely nothing in common with either.

When we do have one or more valid suggestions, we take the one with the lowest distance to the input and add that to our error message as a suggestion. We use the span of the identifier within the `Ok` branch because that is exactly what our macro is having problems with:

```rust
match input.parse::<Ident>() {
    Ok(remainder) => {
        let remainder_as_string = remainder.to_string();
        let distance_to_bucket = edit_distance(
            "bucket",
            &remainder_as_string
        );
        let distance_to_lambda = edit_distance(
            "lambda",
            &remainder_as_string
        );

        if distance_to_bucket > 10 && distance_to_lambda > 10 {
            return Err(syn::Error::new(
                remainder.span(),
                "only 'bucket' and 'lambda' resources are supported"
            ));
        }

        let suggestion = if distance_to_bucket > distance_to_lambda {
            "lambda"
        } else {
            "bucket"
        };

        return Err(syn::Error::new(
            remainder.span(),
            format!("only 'bucket' and 'lambda' resources are supported. \
                Is this a typo for {}?", suggestion
        )));
    }
    Err(_) => {
        // original error
    }
}
```

A possible improvement to this code would be to extract a helper to build the error since we now have three places where it is being used, and they are all very similar.

3 *Currently, our code fails when the resources we add already exist. Skip creation when you detect that it is unnecessary.*

We need to change `s3.rs` and `lambda.rs` to check for resource existence. The Lambda SDK has a `get_function` call, so we add it and only create the lambda if we get back an error.

We are ignoring the very real possibility that the error might be caused by a lot of things besides the function not existing. In most cases, this is fine: if there is an error, it will probably show up when we try to create the resource. One error case that can cause real bugs is the user not having the required permissions to list or read functions while still having permission to create them. In that unlikely case, the code will always try to create the resource.

When the function exists, we could (but currently do not) check the memory and time configuration, updating it if necessary with `update_function_configuration()`, which is probably the behavior a user would expect.

Finally, we are now returning a string instead of a `CreateFunctionOutput`, because we no longer have this output when the resource already exists. Instead, we return the ARN, which is what we actually need:

```
pub async fn create_lambda(&self, lambda: &Lambda)
        -> Result<String, SdkError<CreateFunctionError>> {
    match self.client.get_function()
        .function_name(&lambda.name)
        .send()
        .await {
            Err(_) => {
                let builder = self.create_lambda_builder(&lambda);
                let output = builder.send().await?;
                Ok(output.function_arn()
                    .expect("a new function to have an ARN")
                    .to_string())
            },
            Ok(output) => {
                eprintln!("function exists, skipping creation");
                Ok(output.configuration()
                    .expect("function output to have a configuration")
                    .function_arn()
                    .expect("an existing function to have an ARN")
                    .to_string())
            }
        }
}
```

For buckets, we do not have a GET call in the SDK. So, instead, we list the buckets and check whether our name is in there.

We are again ignoring a few failure cases like missing "list buckets" permissions and accounts with so many buckets that a single call won't retrieve all of them. The latter is a bit unlikely because of the (soft) AWS limit on the number of buckets (100 by default). Also, our return type has once again changed, this time to a unit type, since we don't use the output:

```
pub async fn create_bucket(&self, bucket: &Bucket)
        -> Result<(), SdkError<CreateBucketError>> {
    let bucket_output = self.client.list_buckets().send().await
        .expect("listing buckets to work");
    let buckets = bucket_output.buckets();
```

```
    let bucket_names: Vec<String> = buckets.iter()
        .map(|b| b.name().expect("bucket to have a name").to_string())
        .collect();

    if bucket_names.contains(&bucket.name) {
        eprintln!("bucket exists, skipping creation");
    } else {
        let constraint = BucketLocationConstraint::from(
            self.region.as_str()
        );
        let cfg = CreateBucketConfiguration::builder()
            .location_constraint(constraint)
            .build();

        self.client.create_bucket()
            .bucket(&bucket.name)
            .create_bucket_configuration(cfg)
            .send()
            .await?;
    };
    Ok(())
}
```

With the clients in order, `create_infra` requires a slight change because of the changed `create_lambda` return type. Instead of unwrapping the output and retrieving the function ARN, we can just unwrap the optional:

```
async fn create_infra(iac_input: IacInput) -> Result<(), IacError> {
    let s3_client = S3Client::new().await;
    let lambda_client = LambdaClient::new().await;
    let mut output = None;

    if let Some(lambda) = &iac_input.lambda {
        output = Some(lambda_client.create_lambda(lambda).await?);
    }

    if let Some(bucket) = &iac_input.bucket {
        s3_client.create_bucket(bucket).await?;

        if bucket.has_event {
            let lambda_arn = output
                .expect("when we have an event, we should have a lambda");
            let lambda = iac_input.lambda
                .expect("when we have an event, we should have a lambda");

            lambda_client.add_bucket_permission(&lambda, &bucket.name)
                .await?;
            s3_client.link_bucket_with_lambda(bucket, &lambda_arn)
                .await?;
        }
    }
    Ok(())
}
```

Two `cargo run` commands with the same macro input should now show the creation of the lambda, followed by skipping creation because it already exists. What's nice is that the event can still be created even if the bucket and lambda already exist. But running it an additional time will cause a complaint about the statement ID already existing (you may remember we hardcoded that particular ID). To fix that, you have to check the bucket configuration (`get_bucket_notification_configuration()`) to see if the configuration for our lambda ARN is already present.

4 *Make it possible to add another kind of resource (from AWS or maybe from another cloud provider) to the* `iac!` *macro. (Note: No solution is provided for this exercise.)*

What are you looking in here for? I already told you there is no solution for this exercise! But if you want something simple, try adding another AWS resource like SQS, which has very few required properties. Add any optional properties you like. (Maybe FIFO as a Boolean? Be sure to verify that the name of a FIFO queue ends in `.fifo`.)

Chapter 10

1 *Make sure that we can accept both* `path` *and* `exclude` *as macro properties.*

Our starting point is the project before we added documentation. Everything we need to change is in `input.rs`. Instead of an `if-else`, we use `while` to loop as long as the stream is not empty. We save both the `path` and `exclude_from` in mutable values, adding them to the return value once we are done looping.

We've chosen to support traits without a separator (`#[config_struct(path = "./a/config.yaml" exclude = "from")]`). If we wanted a separator, we could instead turn to `Punctuated`:

```
impl Parse for ConfigInput {
    fn parse(input: ParseStream) -> syn::Result<Self> {
        let mut path = None;
        let mut exclude_from = None;

        while !input.is_empty() {
            if input.peek(kw::path) {
                // parse the path, the equals sign, and the string
                path = Some(value.value());
            } else if input.peek(kw::exclude) {
                // parse the path, the equals sign, and the string
                exclude_from = Some(value.value() == "from");
            } else {
                // error
            }
        }

        Ok(ConfigInput {
            path,
            exclude_from: exclude_from.unwrap_or(false),
        })
    }
}
```

2 *Instead of adding* exclude *to our attribute macro, try to use a feature.*

Here too, our starting point is the code before we added documentation. Getting rid of the exclude means making some changes to lib.rs, input.rs, and struct_output.rs. Other than that, we need to change our macro's Cargo.toml to add the additional feature:

```
[features]
struct = []
from = []
```

In struct_output.rs, we add one generate_from_method that will be compiled *when the feature is active* and one that returns an empty token stream *when it is not*: #[cfg(not(feature = "from"))]. In generate_annotation_struct, we call the generate function. Depending on the situation, either a From implementation or an empty stream will be added to our output:

```
// imports and other generate functions

#[cfg(feature = "from")]
fn generate_from_method(
        name: &Ident,
        yaml_values: &HashMap<String, String>
    ) -> TokenStream {
    let inserts = generate_inserts_for_from(yaml_values);

    quote! {
        impl From <#name> for std::collections::HashMap<String,String> {
            fn from(value: #name) -> Self {
                let mut map = std::collections::HashMap::new();
                #(#inserts)*
                map
            }
        }
    }
}

#[cfg(not(feature = "from"))]
fn generate_from_method(
        _name: &Ident,
        _yaml_values: &HashMap<String, String>
    ) -> TokenStream {
    quote!()
}

pub fn generate_annotation_struct(
        input: DeriveInput,
        yaml_values: HashMap<String, String>
    ) -> TokenStream {
    let attributes = &input.attrs;
    let name = &input.ident;
    let fields = generate_fields(&yaml_values);
    let inits = generate_inits(&yaml_values);
    let from = generate_from_method(name, &yaml_values);
```

```
    quote! {
        #(#attributes)*
        pub struct #name {
            #(#fields,)*
        }

        impl #name {
            pub fn new() -> Self {
                #name {
                    #(#inits,)*
                }
            }
        }

        #from
    }
}
```

It's a slightly different way of thinking than our previous `exclude` implementation. But it is equally elegant and simple to implement, thanks to the built-in support for features.

index

A

abort_call_site 161
abort_call_site! macro 159
abort! macro 155, 157, 159, 161
additive features 248
ADTs (algebraic data types) 132
ARN (Amazon Resource Name) 224
as_ref method 118
AsRef trait 24
AsRefMut trait 24
AST (Abstract Syntax Tree) 46, 59
ast variable 62
async(keyword) 257
attr parameter 193
attribute macros 5, 60, 253–254
  making fields public with 57, 60, 67–72
    delegating tasks to custom struct 67–69
    implementing Parse trait 69–71
    using cursor 71
  public fields, setup of project 58
attribute tokens and attributes 192–197
Attribute type 168
Attribute::parse_inner 198
Attribute::parse_outer 198
AttributeArgs struct 195
attributes
  alternative naming for 170–173
  builder pattern with 179
    avoiding illegal states and type state
      pattern 180
    avoiding scattered conditionals 190
    better error messages for defaults 177–179
    sensible defaults 173–177
    with type state 182
  getting and using fields 62–66
  other kinds of 197
attributes property 192
attrs 266
  defined on struct 62
AWS (Amazon Web Services), clients 225–229
AWS CDK 205
AWS Identity Access Management (IAM) 224
AWS SAM 205

B

black-box
  tests 99
  unit tests 105
block expression 16
Box 176
braced macro 198
builder macros
  black-box unit tests 105
  improvements 116
  project setup 99
  testing 97, 116, 119, 126
    happy path test with actual property 107
    structure of setup 101–102
    types of tests 124
  unhappy path testing 122
  white-box unit tests 103–105
builder pattern
  attribute tokens and attributes 192–197
  rename attribute 164–170
    implementing attribute behavior 165–168
    parsing variations 169

builder pattern
  rename attribute *(continued)*
    testing new attribute 164
  sensible defaults 173–177
  with attributes. *See* attributes
  with type state 182

C

call_site 102
call_site() function 84, 86
cargo
  Cargo.lock file 252
  Cargo.toml file 252
  check 47
  expand 51, 60, 72, 190
  init –lib command 43
  install cargo-expand 51
  run command 288
clean code 23
Clone functionality 42
clone method 116
closure 32, 170, 172, 176
CloudFormation 205
code, expanding 21
codegen_route function 273
collect 65, 92, 152–153, 176, 195, 265
colon_token 165
composing function-like macros 89–93
concat macro 121
configuration macro 236–241
  code overview 237–240
  project structure 236
  using full paths 240–241
contract testing 125
control flow 129
CreateFunctionOutput 286
cucumber testing framework 29
curry2 function 35
cursor 71
custom_keyword macro 210
cyclomatic complexity 129

D

Data enum, defined 62
Data struct 274
DataEnum 265
dbg! macro 4
Debug functionality 42
debugging function-like macros 88
declarative macros 4, 12, 229–231
  composing 31
  currying 34

DSLs 28
  hygiene 36
  lazy_static crate 36–38
  newtypes 23
  vectors 13–19
    declaring and exporting declarative
      macros 14
    matchers 15
    nonempty matchers 15–19
    syntax basics 14
Decode trait 7
default arguments 19
Default implementation 190
Default trait 173, 274
deref method 37
#[derive] annotation 42
derive macro 5, 42, 55
  helper attributes 165
#[derive(Builder)] attribute 164
#[derive(Debug)] 67
#[derive(Deserialize)] attribute 2, 253
#[derive(Hello)] attribute 47
DeriveInput 67, 138, 174, 242, 262
  import 244
  type 62
Diagnostic 162
doc profile 249
doc, adding reference to documentation 160
doctests 125
documentation
  adding to code exercise solutions 288
  blocks 197
domain-driven design 23
Dropper struct 74
DSLs (domain-specific languages) 9, 28, 42
  creating with function-like macros 78
  hiding information with function-like
    macros 78
  infrastructure
    alternative parsing approaches 215
    using Punctuated with custom struct 215
DTOs (Data Transfer Objects) 58

E

eager evaluation 172
EC2 (Elastic Compute Cloud) 205
emit_as_item_tokens() 162
emit_call_site_error! macro 159
emit_call_site_warning! macro 159
emit_error! macro 157–159
emit_warning! macro 159
end-to-end tests 124

entry::main function 254
Enum 265
eprintln command 72
eprintln macro 234
Err 151
  type 173
  value 135
error handling 128
  alternatives to exceptions 132–134
  deciding between syn and
    proc_macro_error 159
  errors and control flow 129
  flavors 149
  overview of 155
  panics 135–136
  proc_macro_error crate for 155
  pure and impure functions 130–132
  real-world examples 159–162
  replacing panics with results 140–145
  Result type 135–136
  setup of panic project 137
  stopping panics 145–149
    changing panic into Result 145–148
    debugging observations 148
  syn error handling 150
errors 161, 229–231
eval() function 4
EventBucket variant 283
exceptions, alternatives to 132–134
exchange macro 29
exclude keyword 246
exclude property 258, 288
expand command 52
expand_no_panic 76
expect function 110, 136
expected identifier error 243
expr expression 16
expr fragments 34
expr macro 259
expr variant 144, 230
expr, defined 39
Expr::If 277
Expr::While 277
extract_panic_content helper 146–147

F

features 244–248
fields 184
  attribute macros, getting, using fields 62–66
  making public with attribute macros 57, 60,
    67, 72
    delegating tasks to custom struct 67–69

implementing Parse trait 69–71
  using cursor 71
FieldsNamed 274
Fn function 176
fn function 14, 176
Fold 258
forget call 75
format macro 52
format_args! macro 51
format_ident macro 95, 102, 280
format! macro 2, 151
fragment specifier 16
From implementation 39, 289
From macro 260
From trait 229
from_ast 279
FromIterator 153
full paths 240–241
function-like macros 6, 78
  composing 89–93
  creating mini-DSLs with 78
  debugging by writing normal code 88
  information hiding 79–88
    generating helper methods 84–88
    recreating struct 81–83
    setup of information-hiding macro 79–81
  overview 94
functional feature 245, 248
functions, pure and impure 130–132
fuzz testing 125

G

generics field 67
get call 73, 286

H

help, for checking signatures 161
hiding information with function-like
    macros 78
html macro 95
hygiene 36
  for identifiers 35–36

I

IaC (Infrastructure as Code) 204
IAM (AWS Identity Access Management) 224
IDE (integrated development environment) 10
Ident 54, 216, 285
ident 39
ident identifier 16

ident macro 259
ident_name function 52
identifier 49
if let 284
immutable returns 139
impl 176
impl block 87
impl Iterator 265
impure function 130
information hiding 79–88
    generating helper methods 84–88
    recreating struct 81–83
    setup of information-hiding macro 79–81
infrastructure DSL (domain-specific
    language) 203
    alternative parsing approaches 215
    AWS clients 225–229
    creating services 221–225
    errors and declarative macros 229–231
    implementing Parse trait for structs 209
    overview 205
    parsing input 207
    project setup and usage examples 207
    real-world example 231–234
    testing 231
    using Punctuated with custom enum and
    builder 218
inner attributes 197
integration tests 124
Into 138
Into trait 46, 81, 102
into_iter 266
is_ident method 166, 200
item parameter 59, 62
item, defined 17
ItemFn 138
ItemStruct 62
iter method 178

K

kw module 210

L

Lambda functions 205
lazy evaluation 172
lazy_static crate macro 36–38
Leptos 161
let statement 17
lib section 43
lib.rs file 43, 103, 174, 183
lifetime 17

lifetime elision rules 114
List variant 167–168
literal macro 259
literal, defined 17, 39
LitInt 211, 220
LitStr 169, 195, 211
load testing 125
location_constraint 228
log_syntax! macro 22
lookahead 279
loom 125

M

macro variable 16
macro_rules! 14, 26
macros 5, 235, 258
    adding 242
    appropriate use cases for 6–9
    attribute macros 66
        making fields public with 72
    attribute macros vs. derive macros 59
    composing 31
    configuration macro 236–241
        code overview 237–240
        project structure 236
        using full paths 240–241
    currying 34
    declarative 39
        lazy_static crate 36–38
        newtypes 23
        use cases 19
    default arguments 19
    documenting 248–250
    exercise solutions 259–262
    expanding code 21
    features 244–248
    from real world 253
    inappropriate use cases for 10
    publishing 250
    varargs 19
main functions 85, 151
main.rs file 20
@MAKE TY 37
map 65
marker trait 181
match 171, 264
matchers 12, 15–19
memcpy 122
memoization 131
meta 11, 17, 37, 167
meta enum 167
MetaList 167, 194

metaprogramming 1–2, 4–10
  appropriate use cases for macros 6–9
  defined 3
  exercises 11
  inappropriate use cases for macros 10
  macros 5
metavariable 16
methods, generating helper methods 84–88
miri interpreter 125
mixed_site() function 84
mod.rs file 20
monads 153
monomorphization 91
move, adding 177–178
mutability 139
mutation testing 125
my_vec macro 39, 260

N

name (identifier) of struct 62
NamedValue variant 167
naming conventions 201
nested property 196
new method 15, 24, 84, 96, 168, 236, 239, 241,
      269–270
newtypes 23
next_field_struct_name 188
no rules expected the token :: 14
#[no_panic] macro 76
nonempty matchers 15–19
Normal variant 282–284
Not type 271
Nothing type 76
NullPointerException 130

O

object-oriented programming 31
Ok value 135, 153
once_cell 36
one-line doc comments 197
Option 83, 173
optional_default_asserts 280
original_struct_setters 186, 281
original_struct_setters method 174
orphan rules 27
outer attributes 197
output
  field 142
  generating 48–50
  variable 284

P

panics 135–136
  replacing with results 140–145
  stopping 145–149
    changing panic into Result 145–148
    debugging observations 148
parenthesized macro 215
Parse 219, 267, 274
Parse implementation 74, 199
Parse input 91
parse method 69, 138, 210
Parse trait 73, 194
  implementing 69–71
  implementing for structs 209
parse_args method 168
parse_declaration 53
parse_macro_input 138, 193–194, 196
parse_macro_input function 49
parse_meta method 169
parse_nested_meta 196
parse_nested_meta method 169, 200
parse_number 221
parse_quote 75
parse_terminated 194
parse2 70, 76, 101, 104
PartialEq 104
partially applied function 31
paste! macro 232
pat_param, defined 17
pat, defined 17
path method 166
path property 194, 196, 258, 288
Path variant 167
path, defined 17
peek method 210
performance testing 125
PhantomData 181, 185
placeholder lifetime 114
point-free style 147
pollster crate 224
prelude 15
print macro 233
println macro 4, 51, 233–234
proc macro error 128
#[proc_macro_attribute] attribute 59
#[proc_macro_derive] attribute 59
proc_macro_error 160, 276
proc_macro_error crate, for error handling 155
proc_macro_errors 161
proc_macro2 101–102, 161, 219
proc_macro2 TokenStream 46
proc_macro2 wrapper 99

proc_macro2_diagnostics 161
proc_macro2::TokenStream 102, 151
proc-macro = true 253
proc-macro property 43
proc-macro2 219, 253
proc-macro2 package 4
procedural macros 1
    analyzing setup 45–48
    basic setup of project 42–44
    experimenting with code 50
    generating output 48–50
    Hello, World 41
    using cargo expand 51
property-based testing 125
pub keyword, indicator of public visibility 37, 66
#[public] attribute 59
public fields 57
    attribute macros vs. derive macros 59
    with attribute macros 66–67, 72
        delegating tasks to custom struct 67–69
        implementing Parse trait 69–71
        using cursor 71
public fields macro 274
public visibility, making fields public with attri-
    bute macros 60
Punctuated 70, 194–195, 218, 266–268, 288
    using with custom struct 215
pure and impure functions 130–132
pure functions 124

Q

query macro 232
query method 94
quote 59, 61, 65–66, 102, 104, 151, 176, 243,
    265–266
    + parse2 116
    declarative macro 65
    dependency 43, 58
    function 48
    library 99
    macro 46–47, 75, 81, 106, 110–111
    package 4
    spanned 177

R

README.md file 250
refactoring, enabling with testing 113
referential transparency 131
rename attribute 164–170
    implementing attribute behavior 165–168
    parsing variations 169

testing new attribute 164
require_list method 167
require_name_value method 167
require_path_only method 167
Result type 101, 135–136, 153, 173, 218, 281
return value 144
returns
    immutable 139
    mutability 139
Rocket 161
rt-multi-thread flag 224
Runtime high-level concurrency structures
    256–257
runtime overhead 28
RUST_IDE_PROC_MACRO_COMPLETION
    environment variable 222
rustc_ast 54
rustc_expand 54
rustc_span 54

S

S3 (Simple Storage Service) 205
s3:ObjectCreated 228
S3Client 227
scattered conditionals 190
SDKs (software development kits) 205
self 188
Semi variant 144
semver (semantic versioning) 252
serde package 4
serde_test 126
#[serde(rename = "name")] 201
ServiceError type 230
services, creating 221–225
Shuttle 160, 162, 203, 231–232
side effects 130
sig property 141
sig.output 142
signature 144
signature_output_as_result 151
smoke tests 124
Span 54, 84
span 161, 218
sqlx package 7
SQS (Simple Queue Service) 205
src folder 51
static ref 37
static values 36
stmt 17
stmts (statements) 76
stmts vector 143
strategy pattern 190

String pair 26
String type 281
stringify macro 55, 121, 263–264
struct feature 244, 248
struct_name 185
structs
    custom, using Punctuated with 215
    recreating 81–83
    white-box testing for 272–274
sum type 133
syn 268
    crate 24, 49
    dependency 43
    error handling 150
    errors 160, 201, 222
    feature 138
    feature flags 258
    package 4
    struct 155
    syn::Error 128, 151, 153, 162, 219, 275
    syn::Error::new 159
    syn::Error::new_spanned 159
    syn::ItemStruct construct 62

T

@TAIL 37
TDD (test-driven development) 99
template macro 253
#[test] attribute 2
test macro 199
testing
    builder macros 119, 126
        happy path test with actual property 107
    enabling refactoring 113
    happy path test 105
    infrastructure DSL 231
testing_testing function 55, 263
tests
    happy path test with actual property 107
    structure of setup 101–102
    types of tests 124
    unhappy path testing 122
    white-box unit tests 103–105
tests directory 237
tests folder 105, 126, 183
thiserror crate 231
to_string calls 241
to_string method 118
to_token_stream 138
to_tokens 104
Token macro 91, 96, 271
tokens 168

TokenStream 54, 58–59, 76, 80, 102, 104, 128,
        138, 168, 265, 274
    attribute 242
    type 45
    with the public prefix 65
TokenTree 16–17, 52
#[tokio::main] macro 73, 223
ToTokens 159
    implementation 93, 243
    trait 73, 81
transcribers 12
traverse 153
trybuild 126, 177
    crate 122
    dependency 236
TryFrom 39
TryFrom macro 260
tt (TokenTree) 16–17, 39
tt macro 259
ty (Type) 26, 39
ty macro 259
ty type 17
ty variant 230
type state 182
type state pattern 180

U

u16 213, 220
unexpected token error 199
unhappy path testing 122
unimplemented 162, 276
    arm 67
    match 67
    panic 160
    variant 136
Unions 67
unit tests, types of 123
unwrap 104
unwrap function 136
unwrap_or_default() method 175
unwrap_or_else 170, 172
update_function_configuration() function 286
usage directory 252
use one-liner 47
util/create_setup.sh script 44

V

value method 195
varargs 19
variants 265–266
Vec 176, 178, 281

vec macro 39, 260
Vec::new() method 15
Vector 196
vectors 13–19
   declaring and exporting declarative
     macros 14
   matchers 15
   nonempty matchers 15–19
   syntax basics 14
venial 53
view macro 95

vis visibility modifier 17
Visibility 267
   of struct 62

W

where clause 32
while expressions 162, 277–278
white-box testing 99
   for structs 272–274
   unit tests 103–105

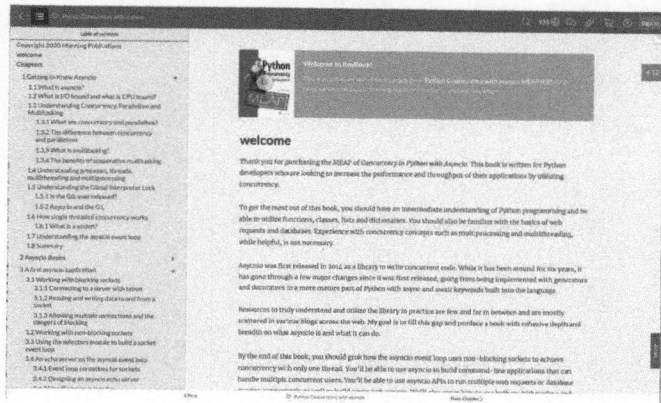

A new online reading experience

liveBook, our online reading platform, adds a new dimension to your Manning books, with features that make reading, learning, and sharing easier than ever. A liveBook version of your book is included FREE with every Manning book.

This next generation book platform is more than an online reader. It's packed with unique features to upgrade and enhance your learning experience.

- Add your own notes and bookmarks
- One-click code copy
- Learn from other readers in the discussion forum
- Audio recordings and interactive exercises
- Read all your purchased Manning content in any browser, anytime, anywhere

As an added bonus, you can search every Manning book and video in liveBook—even ones you don't yet own. Open any liveBook, and you'll be able to browse the content and read anything you like.*

Find out more at www.manning.com/livebook-program.

*Open reading is limited to 10 minutes per book daily

RELATED MANNING TITLES

Code Like a Pro in Rust
by Brenden Matthews

ISBN 9781617299643
264 pages, $59.99
February 2024

Rust Web Development
by Bastian Gruber

ISBN 9781617299001
400 pages, $49.99
December 2022

Rust Servers, Services, and Apps
by Prabhu Eshwarla

ISBN 9781617298608
328 pages, $59.99
July 2023

Rust in Action
by Tim McNamara

ISBN 9781617294556
456 pages, $59.99
July 2021

For ordering information, go to www.manning.com